The Conflicted Relationship

The Conflicted Relationship

The West and the Transformation of Asia, Africa and Latin America

THEODORE GEIGER

A volume in the series
"The Atlantic Policy Studies"

Published for the Council on Foreign Relations by

McGRAW-HILL BOOK COMPANY

New York   Toronto   London   Sydney

THE CONFLICTED RELATIONSHIP

Copyright © 1967 by Council on Foreign Relations, Inc.
All Rights Reserved.
Printed in the United States of America.
This book, or parts thereof, may not be reproduced
in any form without permission of the publishers.
Library of Congress Catalog Card Number: 67-11875
First Edition
23119

To Frances

The Atlantic Policy Studies

The Atlantic Policy Studies, a series of major works on the future of the Atlantic Community, was undertaken in 1963 by the Council on Foreign Relations with a grant from the Ford Foundation. Theodore Geiger's study of the nature of the great transition now going on throughout Asia, Africa and Latin America, and its implications for the future of relations with the Western world is the sixth of these studies to be published.

Undertaken out of a conviction that a re-examination of U.S. relations with and policies toward Western Europe was urgently needed, the Atlantic Policy Studies are an attempt to come to grips with basic questions about the future of America's Atlantic relations.

The studies are policy-oriented, seeking not only to describe and forecast but also to prescribe. Each of the ten studies is the responsibility of its author, but will consider its special problems in the light of the general aims of the program as a whole. The program is under the guidance of a Steering Committee, of which Charles M. Spofford is chairman.

The Atlantic Policy Studies are divided into four broad categories, dealing respectively with the external environment of the West; with the broad strategic problems of the Atlantic Alliance; with economic relations among the Atlantic countries and between them and less developed countries; and with Atlantic political relations.

Mr. Geiger's book is the second of two studies of the Atlantic world's external environment. The first, *Alternative to Partition,* by Zbigniew K. Brzezinski, director of the Research Institute on Communist Affairs of Columbia University when the book was written and now on leave as a member of the Policy Planning

Council of the Department of State, was published in May of 1965 by McGraw-Hill, which is also publishing all other volumes in the Atlantic Policy series.

Atlantic military problems are considered in their political context by Henry A. Kissinger, Professor of Government at Harvard University, in *The Troubled Partnership: A Reappraisal of the Atlantic Alliance,* published in April 1965.

Economic problems both within the Atlantic area and between the Atlantic nations and the rest of the world are examined in four separate studies. One by John O. Coppock, entitled *Atlantic Agricultural Unity: Is It Possible?,* was published in May 1966 in cooperation with the Food Research Institute of Stanford University, of which Mr. Coppock was a member. A second study, *Trade, Aid and Development: The Rich and Poor Nations,* by John Pincus, economist of the RAND Corporation, is appearing in January 1967. Trade arrangements and economic integration within the Atlantic Community and among the industrial countries are the subject of a third economic study, by Bela Balassa of The International Bank for Reconstruction and Development, in collaboration with a group of economists from the United States, Europe, Canada and Japan. Richard N. Cooper, Associate Professor of Economics at Yale University, will examine international financial arrangements and monetary institutions among the Atlantic nations and prescribe policies for the future in this area.

Political relations among the Atlantic nations are the subject of three studies. The future shape of political relations among the Atlantic countries is examined in my book *The Atlantic Idea and Its European Rivals,* published in November 1966. Also published in November was *European Unification in the Sixties* by Miriam Camps, Research Fellow at Chatham House and the Council on Foreign Relations. Stanley Hoffmann, Professor of Government at Harvard University, gave a series of lectures at the Council in the spring of 1965, which reviewed the principal constraints, particularly the domestic constraints, on U.S. action in Atlantic affairs. His lectures have been revised for publication as a volume in the Atlantic Policy series.

Harold van B. Cleveland
Director, Atlantic Policy Studies
Council on Foreign Relations

Preface

It may seem incongruous to call a book of this length an essay—but, at any rate, that is what it set out to be. My original intention was to write a broad impressionistic account of the main economic, political and sociocultural elements in the relationship between the countries of North America and Western Europe—the West—on the one hand, and the new nations of Asia and Africa and the older nations of Latin America, on the other hand. In keeping with the purpose of the Council on Foreign Relations' program of Atlantic Policy Studies, of which this book is a part, my aim is to reassess the nature and implications of this relationship in the light of the changes it has undergone in recent years. The effort to fulfill this assignment, however, has taken me far beyond the initial conception of this book. In seeking to understand the relationship as itself a social process reflecting and influencing the more fundamental social processes occurring within the countries at both ends of it, I have been impelled to draw on a substantially wider range of concepts and data than is customary in studying these phenomena. Nevertheless, I have tried to keep the book as much like an essay as I could.

The book is not intended primarily for experts. It is aimed, rather, at a broader audience of Americans who have some knowledge of the problems in the U.S. relationship with Asia, Africa and Latin America and who are interested in exploring different perspectives which might lead to better understanding of them. Although some technical terms are used, their meanings are clear from the context or are specifically defined. In accordance with the practice of the Atlantic Policy Studies program, footnotes have been kept to a minimum and supporting references for statements of fact and interpretation have been omitted on the assumption that they are already known to the specialist and are not of interest to the general reader. Occasionally, however, a bibliographical reference is made to indicate the source of an idea or of information drawn from outside the standard subject fields.

Not only is this book nearly devoid of scholarly references; it is also full of unscholarly generalizations. Obviously, I would not have included them unless I believed that they reflect with reasonable accuracy the common characteristics of countries and the similarities in their interests, problems and processes of social change. Moreover, I believe that generalizations are an indispensable part of the process of grasping the nature and significance of highly complex phenomena of any kind. Certainly, they oversimplify and abstract from objective reality. But the human mind has no other way of discerning patterns of order and significance either in nature or in society.

A word may be needed in explanation of the much longer historical perspective and the much greater variety of concepts and information used in this book than is customary in works on the development problems of Asia, Africa and Latin America and on the West's relationship with them. There seemed to me to be little point in repeating the approaches that others have already followed so well and that would have been likely to reach only the familiar conclusions. If the assignment to take a fresh look at fundamental assumptions and conventional ways of thinking was to be fulfilled, I concluded that it could be done only by using a broader and longer-term conceptual framework for examining the processes and problems involved. Personal observations on field-study trips in Asia, Africa and Latin America during the past decade and a half, and the insights of many scholars absorbed during years of reading in history and the social sciences have suggested such wider and different perspectives, and I have welcomed the opportunity to explore them in this book.

While certain policy implications are drawn in the final chapter, the book does not offer solutions for current difficulties between the West and Asia, Africa and Latin America, nor does it prescribe in detail the ways in which the continuing problems of the relationship should be handled. The omission of specific and detailed recommendations will be criticized by those who believe that the only purpose of analysis is to yield operational prescriptions. However, in my opinion, the primary need today is for better understanding of the nature of the social processes now going on in Asian, African and Latin American countries, of their implications for the relationship between these nations and the West, and of how—and how much—Western policies can influence the outcome in the long run. Only after it has been achieved are more effective operational prescriptions likely to be devised to fit changing situations and specific problems. Moreover, as a practical matter, because so many months are required to print and publish this book, its proposals for dealing with topical issues would probably be outdated by the time it reached the public.

This book owes much to the help and encouragement of friends and colleagues. I am deeply grateful to Harold van B. Cleveland, director of the Council's Atlantic Policy Studies, who made it possible for me to write this book and whose encouragement and critical review of the manuscript have been most helpful. The contribution of Benjamin Nelson, Professor of Sociology and History in the Graduate Faculty of The New School for Social Research, is in part indicated by the references to his own writings and, in revising the manuscript, I have benefited from his vast knowledge of history and the social process. I am most grateful for the careful reading of the manuscript by Robert E. Asher of the Brookings Institution and for his constructive suggestions for revision. John F. Miller, executive secretary of the National Planning Association, also read it with careful attention and I have very much appreciated his continuous encouragement and advice. I am much indebted to Roger D. Hansen of the National Planning Association for reading the successive drafts of the manuscript and making many helpful comments.

In accordance with its practice, the Council on Foreign Relations invited a committee of distinguished scholars and men of affairs to review the manuscript. The members of the Review Committee were John H. Adler, Frank Altschul, Robert R. Bowie, Alphonse de Rosso, William Diebold, Jr., Irving S. Friedman, Bartlett Harvey, Albert O. Hirschman, Bert F. Hoselitz, Andrew M.

Kamarck, David W. MacEachron, Karl Mathiasen, David Mayer, Nathaniel McKitterick, Manning Nash, Benjamin Nelson, Talcott Parsons, John P. Powelson and Marshall D. Shulman. I am most grateful to these busy men for the time and care they devoted to the review and for their thoughtful criticisms and helpful suggestions both during the committee meeting and in subsequent conversations and correspondence.

I should like to emphasize, however, that the analyses and interpretations in the book are entirely my own. Those to whom I am indebted for help and encouragement bear no responsibility for what I have written.

Without the interest and conscientious help of my secretary, Lilyan S. Kahn, the writing of this book would have been much more difficult. I am particularly grateful for her cheerful willingness and care in typing successive revisions. I would also like to express my thanks to Phyllis Freeman for her perceptive editing.

The debt this book owes my wife, Frances, and our children, Nancy and Tom, is beyond expression and recompense. Because the book had to be written largely during the hours at home, they had often to sacrifice their own plans to its demands, which they did with good humor and eagerness to help in every possible way. Derived from many years of editing the *Development Digest,* Frances' knowledge of the subjects treated in this book has been of inestimable assistance. Virtually every page has benefited from her thoughtful comments, and she has been both the most rigorous critic and the warmest encourager of my work. Without her help and support, this book could not have been written.

Theodore Geiger
National Planning Association
Washington, D. C.
March, 1966

Contents

The Conflicted Relationship

CHAPTER ONE

Misconceptions and Realities

In 1960, a major change in the constitution of the world political system was symbolized at the annual meeting of the United Nations General Assembly when sixteen newly independent African nations were admitted to membership and the bloc of Afro-Asian countries emerged as an active force in international affairs. Since then, an additional twenty new nations in Asia and Africa have joined the United Nations. These developments were the culmination of the great decolonization movement of the 1950s and they marked the onset of a new period in world politics.

During the preceding 150 years, world politics was centered in Europe, and the relationships among the European powers provided the initiative for and the substance of international affairs not only within Europe but also throughout the world. Other regions either played a supporting role, like the United States and the English-speaking dominions of the British Commonwealth, or were passive spectators, like Latin America, or constituted major prizes for which the European powers contended, like Asia and Africa. World War II was the final act of this European-dominated drama of world politics.

With the benefit of hindsight, it is possible to see that the first postwar decade and a half was, in effect, a brief epilogue to this drama. The two superpowers—the United States and the Soviet Union—were themselves parts of Western society, the westernmost and easternmost extensions of European civilization. Their conflict seemed to perpetuate the familiar pattern of world politics since their initiatives and reactions dominated relationships throughout

the world. But in the late 1950s and early 1960s, the epilogue itself was brought to an end by four major developments: the nuclear stalemate; the economic and political renaissance of Western
Europe and the growing restlessness of the East European satel-
lites, which had the effect of loosening the control of the two
superpowers over their respective allies; the emergence of China as
a revolutionary rival of the Soviet Union and an implacable op-
ponent of the United States; and the assumption by the countries
of Asia and Africa—and to some extent even by those of Latin
America—of active and independent roles in world politics.

The dominant characteristic of this new period is the fact that,
for the first time in human history, world politics is truly global,
planet-wide. While the superpowers play leading roles because of
their wealth, size and power, and while the conflicts among them
continue to be major themes of the new drama, the rest of mankind is no longer the passive prize for which the leading actors
contend nor is it the unimportant supporting cast or merely the
audience. Today, every continent plays an active role. Any nation
can initiate a major crisis. World peace depends as much upon decisions in Hanoi and Havana, Cairo and Léopoldville, Accra and
Djakarta, as on those in Moscow, Peking and Washington. For
these reasons, the new period in world politics is termed "multi-
polar" or "polycentric."

The concern of this book is with one aspect of this highly
complex and uncertain new period—the relationships between the
nations of North America and Western Europe, on the one hand,
and those of Asia, Africa and Latin America, on the other. I shall
designate the first group of countries "the West" although, as we
shall see later in this chapter, they do not constitute the whole of
Western society in the broadest sense of the term. Also, I shall
have in mind mainly the United States because it has been the active leader of the group of nations constituting the West and, as
such, it has to a significant extent impressed upon the others its
own assumptions and expectations regarding the nature and probable outcome of international problems. Recently, however, West
Europeans have been becoming somewhat skeptical of certain of
these assumptions and expectations, as have some Americans.

Looking back over the past fifteen years, we can identify several major conceptions that have dominated Western thinking and policy regarding relations with Asia, Africa and Latin America.

An initial major assumption was that, in consequence of the cold war, the international political system was fundamentally divided into two groups of countries. On the one side was the "Free World" of peace-loving, democratically inclined nations, observing the rule of law, respecting one another's sovereign independence, and dedicated to the protection of human rights and the advancement of human welfare. On the other side was the "Communist Bloc" of totalitarian states under the rigid control of the Soviet Union and fanatically committed to bringing about, by any means, Communist revolutions in all parts of the world. Both the United States and the Soviet Union—each in its own terms—accepted this description of world politics, as did the latter's revolutionary rival, China. For the Communist states, Marxist-Leninist doctrine dictated the inevitability of this world division into two contending camps, with that of "the revolution" destined by the laws of history to prevail in the final conflict. To the West, it seemed obvious that the overshadowing threat to the independence of any country —particularly of the new Asian and African nations—was revolutionary communism, owing to its unremitting efforts to fulfill its "historical destiny." The West assumed that Asian and African countries would naturally and quickly range themselves under the banner of the Free World not only in self-protection but also because of their commitment to the democratic and humanitarian values that characterize it.

The Latin American countries accepted this conception of the world political system and, with varying degrees of enthusiasm, expanded their defensive alliance with the United States to take account of it. Also, in the early 1950s, some of the newly independent Asian nations felt sufficiently threatened by the Soviet Union and China to enter into defensive military alliances (Southeast Asia Treaty Organization and Central Treaty Organization) with the United States and other leading Western states. But, the much more common reactions in Asia and Africa were declarations of "nonalignment" and the growth of "positive neutralism." Even the Asian countries that joined in defensive pacts with the West had reservations about being considered members of the Free

World, and they did not regard the United States as their leader in a world-wide contest between freedom and slavery. Except for the few that have been under armed Communist attack, virtually all Asian and African countries have sooner or later thought of themselves as committed to neither side.

Western recognition that Asia and Africa did not accept the assumption that they would immediately join the Free World soon led to a revision of this concept. Now the West grudgingly accepted the fact that they were uncommitted, but it assumed that they could not long remain in that situation. As the possibility of nuclear conflict between the Soviet Union and the United States receded, the cold war was more and more viewed as a contest for the "souls" of the uncommitted. It was assumed that each side was engaged in proving the superiority of its socioeconomic system and had to reinforce the merits of its case by the lavishness of its subsidies, ostensibly given from altruistic concern for the good of the recipients. Asian and African countries gladly accepted these subsidies and, indeed, some became adept at playing off one donor against another for purposes of their own. Nevertheless, the great majority of recipients have continued to hope that they would not be compelled to choose sides among the superpowers.[1]

The refusal of virtually all Asian and African countries to consider themselves members of a U.S.-led Free World has also expressed their feeling that cultural and racial differences between them and the West could not be ignored. Conversely, the willingness of Latin American countries to commit themselves to the Western side has reflected the fact that the cultural and social differences between them and North America and Western Europe are minor compared with those between Asia and Africa and the West. Asians and Africans have not accepted the Western view that such differences are unimportant in the face of the common danger of Soviet or Chinese communism. They have regarded this threat as being far less serious than the Western nations, particu-

---

[1] Some of the largest and most influential nations—e.g., Algeria, Egypt, Ghana, India, Indonesia—have tried to constitute themselves a unified "third force" in world politics, and have endeavored to develop agreement on a common active policy largely through a series of international conferences and state visits. However, the results have fallen far short of their expectations for reasons that later chapters will make clear.

larly the United States, believe it to be. Moreover, they have felt protected by the apparently unconditional Western—in recent years, primarily American—policy of containing Communist expansion everywhere.

They have tended also to consider the West's ambivalent attitude regarding cultural and racial differences either naïveté or hypocrisy. On the one hand, they have long been exposed to the West's racial prejudice and cultural condescension toward them. On the other hand, they are aware that Westerners tend to ignore the role of cultural factors in diagnosing and prescribing for the problems of Asian and African countries and, in part for this reason, to assume that Asian and African societies aspire to be and will soon become replicas of Western society. Asians and Africans are not ambivalent about the significance of racial and cultural differences and attach great importance to them, as we shall see in later chapters. However much they may desire to obtain many of the benefits of Western science and technology, they do not feel that their countries are—or are likely to become—parts of Western society.

Westerners, particularly Americans, have often been bewildered, exasperated or alarmed at the failure of Asian and African countries to conform to the West's expectations regarding their behavior in international affairs. Not only have these countries refused to commit themselves to the West and continue to insist they have no intention of doing so in the future, but they have also not acted in other respects in accordance with the West's conception of their rational interests. Asian and African countries have strong reasons of self-interest for friendly cooperation with the West. Western Europe and North America are by far the largest markets for their exports and their main source of imported goods and investment capital. While their trade with the Communist states could be increased, it could not substitute for their trade with the West, even if the Soviet Union and China were willing, owing to Communist economic limitations. Hence, the West assumed that the interests of Asian and African countries would compel them not only to cooperate in economic relationships but also to support Western political and defense policies vis-à-vis the Soviet Union and China.

There has, of course, been very extensive economic cooperation between the West and Asia and Africa in consequence of their
mutual economic interests. But, Asian and African countries have
tended increasingly to stress the differences between their own
economic interests as primarily raw material producers and those
of the industrialized Western nations. Asian and African expectations for composing these differences have been expressed in terms
with which the West has been unwilling to agree—a divergence
that was manifested at the United Nations Conference on Trade
and Development in 1964 and has continued in subsequent activities. More significantly, however, the interests of Asian and African
countries in satisfactory economic relationships with the West—
large and important as they are recognized to be—have not
prevented more and more of these nations from opposing Western,
especially American, policies and initiatives in international political affairs. The question of China's admission to the United
Nations and the American role in Vietnam have been the most
conspicuous issues among recent evidences of this tendency.

Such behavior has seemed all the more perverse to the United
States because of its assumptions regarding the role and importance of the financial aid and technical assistance it has been providing to Asia and Africa. Over and above the interests of these
countries in normal commercial and investment relationships with
the West, the United States assumed that the needs of a "revolution of rising expectations" would compel them to seek massive financial resources and large-scale technical assistance from the
Western nations. Asian and African dependence on aid would give
the West—especially the United States as the largest donor—
powerful "leverage" for influencing their policies and actions.

By the "revolution of rising expectations," Westerners mean
that the major social groups in Asian and African countries are
intent upon achieving higher living standards and greater social
justice and are concentrating their attention and energies on
realizing these objectives. But, very few Asian and African countries conform to this Western notion of their goals and priorities.
As we shall see in later chapters, the great mass of their people still
passively accept the lot to which they were born. Even their modern educated elites are generally unwilling to decide upon and un-

able to implement effectively the measures necessary to increase economic growth rates significantly and to accomplish major social reforms. Nonetheless, Western statesmen, officials and opinion leaders have continued to warn against the dire consequences likely to occur unless substantial progress is quickly made toward satisfying these supposed revolutions of rising expectations. The consequences envisaged have been either that Asian and African countries would voluntarily join the "Communist Bloc" in order to satisfy their rising consumption expectations (as though any Communist nation has met or is likely soon to meet its own expectations, much less theirs!) or, with greater sophistication, that the frustration of their aspirations would lead to increasing popular unrest, social collapse and Communist take-over.

On the basis of these assumptions, many Westerners—particularly Americans—have regarded the aid provided to these countries as the most important aspect of their relationship with the West. Although their trade with the West is several times larger than the amount of aid they receive, the latter is believed to be much more significant—a judgment that is supported by a variety of rationales. Foreign aid is assumed to be the "missing catalyst" required to speed up the processes of economic development and social change. Or, it is the "marginal increment of resources" that makes the difference between success or failure in achieving an adequate rate of economic growth and the freedom of action for social reform. Another version of this assumption is that the reduction or cessation of aid would lead to economic collapse, which would in turn open the way for Communist take-overs. In other words, foreign aid is assumed to be the crucial element in the present existence and future prospects of Asian and African countries. Their recognition of their critical dependence on it is expected to make them support Western policies.

While most Asian and African countries have been happy to receive aid and eager to obtain more, they have not regarded it as so essential to their existence that they have felt compelled to accept Western leadership in international affairs. True, a few Asian and African countries have for various reasons been substantially dependent on Western economic aid—e.g., Laos, South Korea and South Vietnam in consequence of past or present Com-

munist attacks; Jordan and some of the interior African states because they are unable to generate sufficient revenues to support national independence; the Congo and the Dominican Republic
owing to civil wars; and Algeria, Egypt, India and Pakistan in consequence of their inability to produce sufficient food or to earn
enough foreign exchange to import it along with the capital goods
necessary for economic growth. Yet, not all of these nations have
been conspicuous or consistent supporters of Western policies.
Moreover, the Soviet Union and China have also been willing to
provide aid—although not nearly so much as the West—based on
assumptions of their own as to how the Communist revolution
would thereby be fostered. This competitive situation has enabled
some Asian and African countries to obtain aid from both sides
and thereby to lessen their dependence on one or the other. Although this tactic is not available to more than a few nations
simultaneously because the Communist states can afford to provide only restricted amounts of aid, it has nevertheless limited the
"leverage" that the West can exercise on the foreign policies of
Asian and African countries through the granting or withholding
of aid.

The disappointment of the West's expectations regarding the
behavior of Asian and African countries and the limitations of its
influence over them are paralleled by—and, indeed, as we have in-
timated, largely spring from—certain misconceptions regarding the
nature of the social processes occurring within these nations and
the extent to which they could be influenced by Western actions.
Had these assumptions about internal conditions conformed to
realities, Western expectations regarding the external behavior of
Asian and African countries might have had much greater validity.
Conversely, the failure of these countries to act in the world political system in accordance with Western expectations should have
raised doubts about the assumptions regarding their internal conditions that formed the basis for these expectations. This is an
anomalous situation, particularly for Americans, who consider
themselves to be—and often are—a highly pragmatic people. Why
is it that, even today, misconceptions continue to be prominent not
only in the reasoning and conclusions of opinion makers generally,
including some university scholars, but also in the assumptions and

policies of responsible government officials? Why have Americans been so slow and so reluctant to recognize how far their assumptions and expectations diverge from reality?

The divergence certainly cannot be blamed on the technical inadequacy of the social sciences. Although our information about and understanding of the complex, multidimensional character of the social process are still in the early stages of development, nevertheless economics, sociology, political science, social psychology and anthropology could already provide concepts and analytical techniques useful for advancing our knowledge of the nature and probable evolution of the societies of Asia and Africa. Furthermore, the West has the strong motivation of self-interest in seeking to understand better the realities of Asia and Africa in order to deal more effectively with the countries of these regions. While there has been a tendency to exaggerate the importance of Asia and Africa to Western security and welfare, the West certainly has a major interest in maintaining and improving its economic relations with these countries and in carrying on political relationships with them that are conducive to world peace and order.

If neither intellectual deficiencies nor insufficient self-interest can account for the persistence of such misconceptions, what other factors are involved? An answer to this question is proposed in Chapter 2, which examines the cultural and historical roots of contemporary Western ways of thinking about Asia and Africa and the West's relationship with them. But, it is not sufficient to know why the West has generated and clung to misconceptions and unrealistic expectations. If the West is to make its assumptions and policies conform better to realities, it must also have a more accurate understanding of the highly complex social processes now occurring in Asia and Africa and of their probable outcome. Accordingly, these subjects are explored in Chapters 3, 4 and 5. In Chapters 6 and 7, attention is focused on Latin America to explain why it should not be grouped in the same category as Asia and Africa and to discuss the nature and prospects of its current transformation. Finally in Chapter 8, the implications of the analysis are drawn in general terms for Western, and particularly American, policies regarding Asia, Africa and Latin America.

Before turning to these subjects, however, it would be useful to clarify the approach used in this book. The reader may already have noticed that the nations of Asia, Africa and Latin America have not been designated by any of the adjectives formed from the verb "to develop." Over the past fifteen years, Asian, African and Latin American countries have been successively called "underdeveloped," "less developed" and "developing." This increasingly euphemistic sequence of terms has in part reflected the sensitivities of these nations and the solicitude of the West to avoid offending them. But, in part also, the use of these terms has been indicative of a way of thinking about Asia, Africa and Latin America that has much greater significance. This is the notion that the different countries of these regions can be lumped together in a single category because they are all presumed to have a common characteristic of overriding importance. All are believed to be engaged in a process of "development" which, when completed, will transform them into "developed" countries. In consequence, the profound differences among Asian, African and Latin American countries and between them and the West in culture, social structure and historical background and the implications of these differences for the future can be disregarded as principles of classification significant for analysis and policy making.

In my view, however, the term "development" is misleading for precisely this reason. It diverts attention from the much more meaningful ways of characterizing and classifying countries on the basis of their common cultural, social and historical elements—all of which have major implications for the nature of their societies in the future. Since one of the main purposes of this book is to explore such implications, we shall be concerned with the similarities and differences among Asian, African and Latin American countries with respect to social, cultural and historical characteristics. Hence, except occasionally to avoid excessive repetition of geographical terms, and in Chapters 5, 7 and 8 in a limited and specifically defined sense, the term "development" will be used in its ordinary dictionary meaning of "evolution."

The term "development" is misleading not only as a principle for classifying countries but also as a designation for the complex process of social change occurring within them. In recent years, the original notion that the development process was solely or mainly economic in nature has been recognized as much too limited. Present terminological fashion dictates that more varied and specific adjectives—e.g., "agricultural," "industrial," "political," "social," "educational," "managerial," etc.—be used to distinguish among different kinds of development. However necessary such distinctions are for analytical purposes, they have promoted a tendency to regard each of these aspects as autonomous and, therefore, as involving primarily technical problems—that is, problems that can be met by devising the most efficient means for increasing resources and skills and for improving their use. But there are important relationships not only within but also among these and the many other aspects of the social process as a whole, and the significant difficulties are not primarily technical but consist of the pressures, constraints and conflicts involved in these interrelationships and interactions.[2] Hence, I shall endeavor to focus upon the social process as a whole so as to illuminate the complex relationships among its major aspects.

Next, I should like to delimit my own classifications and define some terms. I regard "Western civilization"—the broadest of the designations of the West—as embracing four great subcultures: Western Europe, Eastern Europe including the Soviet Union, North America, and Latin America.[3] The terms "the West" and "Western society" are used to refer collectively to Western Europe and North America—the former usually in a world political context and the latter in a sociocultural sense. The category of Asian

[2] There are two additional related objections to the current use of the term "development." First, it contains a normative element—a value judgment— which tends to be misleading particularly when this is not recognized, as is often the case. Implicit in the practice of designating Asia, Africa and Latin America as "developing" and the Western nations as "developed" is the notion that Western institutions, values and norms are "better." Second, the term "development" is misleading in implying a movement from the simple to the complex. Such a movement is certainly taking place in Africa where, by any standard, the traditional societies were simpler and less articulated than those now evolving in the region. But, in Asia, it would be difficult to formulate a valid standard in terms of which the traditional society of India, for example, could be considered simple and monodimensional as compared either with the contemporary Indian society or with that of the West.

[3] Australia and New Zealand are probably in process of evolving a subculture of their own.

and African countries also includes many great subcultures—e.g., the Arab-Moslem societies of the Maghreb and the Near East; the non-Arab Moslem societies of Afghanistan, Iran and Turkey; the Hindu societies of India, Ceylon and the Himalayan states; the numerous societies of Southeast Asia with their different mixtures of Indian, Chinese, Islamic and indigenous elements; and the new nations of Africa south of the Sahara with their common background of tribal societies. Despite the many important differences among and within these major subcultures, I believe that it is legitimate for the specific purposes of this book to group them in a single category as explained in Chapter 3. Although geographically and culturally part of Asia, China, Mongolia, North Korea, North Vietnam and Siberia are not included in the category of Asian and African countries because their relationship with the West is today dominated by the fact that they are Communist states and not by the kinds of considerations discussed in this book. Israel and Japan are also excluded from the category of Asian and African countries for other reasons: the former because its culture is predominantly Western and the latter because it has already completed the transitional process described in Chapter 4.

The terms "culture" and "society" are used in this book with the meanings agreed upon by the anthropologist A. L. Kroeber and the sociologist Talcott Parsons.[4] Culture refers to "transmitted and created content and patterns of values, ideas, and other symbolic-meaningful systems as factors in the shaping of human behavior, and the artifacts produced through behavior." Society refers to "the specifically relational system of interaction among individuals and collectives." Thus, ideas and values and material products and techniques of all kinds comprise the culture, while interpersonal and group relationships constitute the society. Specific patterns of relationships among individuals and groups (collectives) form the different institutions and institutional systems within the society—e.g., the family, the church, the school, the government department; the economic system, the political system, the educational system, etc.

In addition to the contemporary characteristics of societies and

[4] A. L. Kroeber and Talcott Parsons, "The Concepts of Culture and of Social System," *American Sociological Review*, V. 23, no. 5, October 1958, pp. 582–583.

cultures, we shall be much concerned in this book with their past histories. Although, as Chapter 2 will explain, Western society has by nature been time conscious, its preoccupation in recent centuries with progress has oriented it more toward the future than the past. This is particularly true today of policy makers and prescriptive analysts who must perforce focus on the formulation of future goals and the development of means for achieving them. Particularly in the United States, with its activist attitudes, those concerned with policy making for and analysis of American relations with Asia, Africa and Latin America have tended to ignore the histories of these regions.

Yet, the past experiences of these societies are among the most important factors determining their future evolution. For this reason, we shall pay explicit attention to the historical dimension of the phenomena under discussion. For example, Chapter 2 traces back rather far the sociocultural roots of contemporary Western —especially American—attitudes and expectations regarding Asia, Africa and Latin America. My purpose is not only to illuminate their origins but also to convey some notion of the continued compulsion exerted by ways of thinking that are so deeply imbedded in the past experiences of Western society. Similarly, Chapter 6 sketches the history of Latin America since the sixteenth century, again not simply because so many North Americans know so little about it but, more importantly, because an understanding of the heritage of the past four and a half centuries largely explains why that region has not enjoyed the same kind of development as have other parts of Western civilization. True, history rarely repeats itself. But—to elaborate Santayana's aphorism—those who know nothing about it are prone to repeat the mistakes of the past. And, neither prescriptive analysis nor policy making is likely to be realistic and, therefore, effective in dealing with the future unless it has taken specifically into account the power of the past.

CHAPTER TWO

Western Attitudes
and Expectations

In examining the nature of their relationships with Asia, Africa and Latin America, Westerners tend to focus primarily upon the political, defense and economic interests involved. For the West, these countries are regarded as trading partners of potentially increasing value; and, more fundamentally, the West has an interest in ensuring that neither the problems nor the initiatives of these nations impair the effective functioning of the international economic system or undermine Western security in a precarious world political system. However, such rational interests alone cannot account for the fervor and persistence with which the United States has been conducting its relationships with Asia, Africa and Latin America and has been pressing its European allies to increase their contributions to the security and economic advancement of these regions. If the specific defense, political and economic interests of the United States were the only factors involved in American motivation, the misconceptions and unrealistic expectations outlined in Chapter 1 would have been recognized and corrected within a year or two, as is usually the case in the pragmatic American society. The fact that many of them still persist indicates that other factors complement, distort and in part offset considerations of rational interest in the determination of Western, and particularly American, attitudes and expectations. This chapter examines the nature and historical sources of these other considerations and the ways in which they affect the pursuit of rational interest.

These other factors are of two kinds. The first are cultural: the concepts and perspectives in terms of which people tend to see and deal with nature and society, and the values and behavioral norms in terms of which people understand what they should strive to do and what they should avoid thinking about and doing. The second are social: the institutions and relationships within which people live and work, and through which they acquire their ways of perceiving, believing, aspiring and doing. These two sets of factors, operating both consciously and unconsciously, continuously interact with rational considerations.

Moreover, because they are rooted in the subconscious levels of the personality, these factors are usually the means whereby "affective," or emotional, processes also color rational analysis and often charge it with strong feeling. Since human beings are always the formulators and communicators of concepts, values and expectations, the influence of psychological processes and the element of subjectivity can never be eliminated no matter how impersonal the purpose or disinterested the individual involved. For example, logical analysis and empirical verification can and usually do eliminate inconsistencies and factual errors in scientific investigation and even in rhetorical argumentation. But, the choice of subjects on which to work, the ways in which these subjects are approached, the intensity and significance of the convictions regarding them, and even the willingness to revise ideas about them in the light of logical analysis and empirical evidence—all reflect certain cultural biases, social constraints and psychological feelings of which people are seldom conscious. Hence, even persons engaged in the scientific study or in the official conduct of Western relations with Asia, Africa and Latin America can never be exempt from the effects of cultural, social and psychological factors on their attitudes, judgments and actions concerning the rational interests involved.

Among the most important cultural factors entering into the formation of Western attitudes and expectations regarding Asia, Africa and Latin America are the elements comprising Western society's conception of its own nature and destiny. Historically, this conception has been formed within the religious tradition of the West. All societies have implicitly or explicitly expressed their conceptions of their nature and purposes and their sense of the fitness of things in their religious traditions. Even when, as in Western society during recent centuries, such conceptions are secularized and lose their transcendental dimensions and sanctions, they nevertheless tend to preserve their original content and significance in their new forms. In consequence, we shall be concerned in this and subsequent chapters with the religious origins and current religious or secularized expressions of the values and expectations of the societies with which we will deal.

In Western society, the specific concepts and values important for this study are of two types. The older are religious in origin, expressing the redemptive character of the Judaeo-Christian tradition, and are usually designated as the senses of Western mission and guilt. Although their specifically religious formulations continue to be significant, their influence is felt today mainly in various secularized versions evolved during the past three centuries. The more recent—although also largely religious in origin—are more directly related to Western philosophical and scientific concepts of man's capacity to understand and transform his natural and social environments. They have been powerfully reinforced by the successful exercise of the Western will to knowledge and action since the late Middle Ages. These and other values, motivations and expectations interact with one another and with the conceptions of Western political and economic interests to form the attitudes of the West toward Asia, Africa and Latin America.

However, attitudes vary significantly in content and intensity among the different countries comprising Western society. The will to action, the senses of mission and guilt, and the expectation that social problems can readily be solved are most highly developed and most strongly felt in the predominantly Protestant, democratic and technologically oriented countries of North America and central and northern Europe. These elements are weaker and more diffuse in the predominantly Catholic, more authoritarian and less technologically advanced countries of southern Europe. We shall consider first the three major elements entering into Western attitudes and then the variety of ways in which they interact with and neutralize one another in the conceptions and expectations of Americans.

The Will to Action and the Sense of Superiority

In Chapter 3, the major characteristics of Western society will be outlined in order to contrast them with those of Asian and African societies. Here, we need to be concerned only with those aspects important for understanding Western attitudes toward Asia and Africa. They are Western society's dynamism and restlessness, its orientation toward achievement in this world, its increasing aspiration in recent centuries to master nature and human destiny, and its growing faith in reason and the scientific method as the instruments of human knowledge and power. Since the late Middle Ages, these characteristics have been self-reinforcing. The attitudes inculcated by one generation have impelled the next generation to actions whose success has in turn strengthened the self-confidence and will to action of the succeeding generation.

The working out of this process has been the dominant motif of the history of Western society during the past five hundred years. With the beginning of the age of discovery in the fifteenth century, the West embarked upon a period of geopolitical expansion and conquest that culminated in the world empires of the nineteenth and early twentieth centuries and the planetary hegemony they signified. Paralleling and reinforcing this geopolitical expansion—today directed toward the exploration of outer space —was a process of economic development resulting from the invention and spread of the industrial type of economy characterized by mechanization and the rational organization of large-scale production. This development has transformed the nature of Western production and distribution, penetrated the societies of virtually all regions of the planet, and for the first time in human history made it possible for large numbers of people to attain material abundance. Finally, scientific knowledge of natural processes and the ability to control them have also grown at a cumulative rate, particularly in physics, chemistry, biology and their applied technologies. Thus, in most of the major dimensions of human experience, Western society has in recent centuries burst through the physical, economic and intellectual boundaries that previously circumscribed its concepts and actions.

The unprecedented dynamism and expansionism of Western society in modern times may be characterized as its "will to action." The term is metaphoric and, therefore, should be understood as descriptive only, and not as explanatory. Nonetheless, it is a useful figure of speech since it serves to highlight one of Western society's most important characteristics, and one that is particularly significant for understanding Western attitudes toward Asia and Africa.

The fact that European countries were convinced in the nineteenth century that their political and economic interests would be served by domination over Asia and Africa was not in itself sufficient to ensure that they would actually establish colonial empires. In addition, they needed both the means of power and the will to use them. The first was provided by the technological and economic achievements of Western society; the second by the self-confidence and the sense of superiority inherent in the Western value system and continuously reinforced by Western successes. In combination, these means and motives provided the will to take action to realize the Western interests believed to be served by colonial rule.

For more than a hundred years, the European imperial nations expressed their will to action and sense of power in part through domination over the peoples of Asia and Africa, and in part directly in conflicts and wars among themselves. However, by the mid-twentieth century, the determining factors in this relationship had changed significantly. In consequence of the West's own impact upon Asia and Africa, the cost of maintaining Western rule came gradually to exceed the benefits believed to be involved for Western political and economic interests. Two world wars of unprecedented scale and destructiveness sapped Europe's power at the same time as the maintenance of imperial rule grew increasingly difficult in the face of rising colonial demands for independence. More profoundly, political, economic and intellectual changes in Western Europe and in its relationships with the United States and the Soviet Union impaired the self-confidence and will to action of the former imperial nations. Hence, with varying degrees of resistance and acquiescence after World War II, they acceded to Asian and African demands for independence.

Thereafter, particularly on the Continent, European attention turned inward. Lacking the means and the freedom of action to play independent roles alongside the two superpowers and concerned with the restoration of their war-shattered economies, the continental countries embarked upon a process of economic growth and integration that has made possible an unparalleled rise in living standards, no longer only for European elites but for the great mass of the people as well. Thus, protected by the American nuclear deterrent and relieved of the responsibility for the maintenance of world order by American power and will to action, continental Western Europe has been able to focus its energies upon its internal unification and increasing welfare.

True, France has continued to exercise a large measure of influence over the affairs of its former African colonies, and President de Gaulle has aspired to play, with the support of his Common Market partners, an active and independent role in world politics. However, there has been little willingness on the part of the other continental countries to accept French leadership toward such an objective and to devote resources to achieving it on a scale sufficient to provide President de Gaulle with the necessary military and economic power. Without their support, France lacks the resources to play a leading role in the world.

What remains today of the will to action of the continental West European countries in their relations with Asia and Africa is largely their sense of superiority. This is derived from the West's unchallenged success in the fields of activity accorded the highest values by Western society: science and technology, economic productivity, political effectiveness, military prowess, and artistic and intellectual innovation. It is heightened by the evident disparities between the West's own achievements in these respects and those of Asian and African countries since their independence was obtained. Moreover, the self-inflicted wounds to continental Europe's self-confidence entailed by the defeats and occupations of two world wars are to some extent assuaged by its feeling of superiority over other societies on the planet.

The effects of the passing of empire and of the loss of great power status on British attitudes toward Asia and Africa have been more complex and have been compounded by other factors of greater importance in Britain than on the Continent. Sustained by its achievements in World War II, the British will to action still plays a role of some significance in British motivation. Although no longer the center of a globe-encircling empire—to which it gave independence much more readily and constructively than did the other colonial powers—the United Kingdom still feels impelled to find active roles for itself in world politics. However, it has in the postwar period been unable to discover roles that are both desired and practicable. Those that Britain has wished to play have been beyond either its own resources or the limits of what the other nations concerned have been prepared to do; and, until recently, it had little interest in the realistic alternatives.

Britain could have taken the lead in the postwar unification of Western Europe but was unwilling to make the sacrifice of sovereignty thereby entailed. Instead, it sought sometimes simultaneously and at other times successively—although with equal futility —to preserve its wartime relationship as a major partner of the United States in the leadership of the Western coalition, and to convert the prewar culturally homogeneous, all-white Commonwealth into a culturally diverse, multi-ethnic association of nations united by their willingness to accept British leadership presumably because they had all once been its colonies. The first of these roles required resources far beyond Britain's capabilities. The second role has turned out to be largely ceremonial and sentimental, because the interests and attitudes of the newer Asian and African members have been too divergent from those of the older Western members. Thus, Britain's efforts to express its continuing will to action in the postwar period have been frustrated by its own limitations and by its unwillingness to meet the real opportunities and needs in the contemporary world.

Despite this frustration of the British will to action, the sense of superiority is still deeply ingrained in the British national character, although its effects are mitigated and diffused by the senses of mission and guilt. Both conservatively and liberally oriented Britons are at one, although for different reasons, in the desire to exercise a significant influence over Asian and African countries. The conservative motivation has been to maintain the great power status to which the assumed superiority of British institutions entitles the United Kingdom. The liberal motivation—particularly in the left wing of the Labour party—has been the notion that Asian and African countries would accept British leadership in world affairs once the moral superiority and disinterestedness of British foreign policy were clearly demonstrated to them. Both groups have sought to achieve their objectives by providing aid to these countries, although British resources available for this purpose have been severely limited for most of the postwar period by balance-of-payments considerations. In addition, both groups have been moved by and, to the extent that resources were available, have acted upon a sense of responsibility for the security of those countries formerly under British rule, as in the cases of the 1964 army mutinies in East Africa and the Indonesian "confrontation" with Malaysia. However, it is unlikely that the United Kingdom will be willing and able to carry out such responsibilities much longer.

Today, the security of Western society rests predominantly upon the power and will to action of the United States. They play a major—but by no means exclusive—role in American attitudes toward Asia and Africa, although with special characteristics and inhibitions reflecting America's distinctive history. Until the end of the nineteenth century, American dynamism and expansionism were expressed in the conquest and development of its own western territories. When, at the turn of the century, the United States emerged as a world power, the division of Asia and Africa among the European nations was practically completed. Thus, except for the Philippines, the United States has not ruled nor tried to dominate any part of Asia or Africa. Its desire to make its power actively felt in those regions has generally taken two forms. For its own economic interest, it has sought equal access for its citizens to trade and invest in Asian and African countries, a classic example of which was the "open-door" policy toward China at the beginning of the twentieth century. Politically—despite its rule over the Philippines—the United States has been anti-colonial, using its moral influence to support political independence for Asian and African countries during the colonial period, and subsequently using its military power and economic resources to help them maintain their independence.

Today, American power and will to action do not manifest themselves in the desire for direct rule over Asia and Africa; they take other forms. One is a sense of obligation to defend Asian and African countries against Communist subversion and aggression. Another is the expectation that these countries will follow American leadership and advice in their participation in world politics and in the management of their internal political and economic affairs. These motives are buttressed by the other major elements that enter into American attitudes toward Asia and Africa—the positivistic conviction of human mastery over nature and society, and the Western senses of mission and guilt.

The Conviction of Mastery over Nature and Society

The active, assertive and directive characteristics of Western society have been expressed not only in promoting its political and economic interests but also in investigating natural and social processes. Since the late Middle Ages, Western society has been characterized by increasing faith in the efficacy of reason and the scientific method as means for understanding nature and society, and by growing capacity to use empirical and experimental techniques in dealing with physical and social problems. These efforts have gone from success to success in advancing knowledge of the natural world and enhancing the ability to manipulate and control it. In consequence, during recent centuries, both a general popular attitude and a formal philosophical approach have developed which together constitute a major strand in the dramatic design of Western culture. They embrace the set of concepts and expectations generally characterized as the rationalistic, materialistic, pragmatic and positivistic elements in Western culture. On the one hand, they have been the essential factors in the scientific, technological and social reform achievements of Western society; on the other hand, they have continually generated utopian expectations and contributed to the moral ambiguities in the use of power.

The ideas and expectations expressing the rationalistic and manipulative strands in Western society are associated with a number of diverse trends in Western thought and attitudes from the sixteenth century on. Among the most influential men and movements have been Bacon, Descartes, Newton, Hume, the French *philosophes*, Kant, English utilitarianism, German idealism of the right and left, the different varieties of socialism, Darwinism and the founding of the modern social sciences. Regardless of their different origins, divergent orientations and complex interrelationships, these philosophers and intellectual movements shared certain ideas and attitudes. They all affirmed the capacity of human reason to discover, understand and control man's natural and social environments. They maintained that conscious, rationally determined actions could progressively improve the material and social conditions of life, and they tended to look to the future rather than to the past not only for the realization but also for the model of a perfected society. With varying degrees of singlemindedness, they insisted that institutions and behavioral norms had to justify themselves by their contemporary contribution to human welfare and not by their preservation of tradition.

Another manifestation of Western rationalistic activism has been the idea of the inevitability of progress and of the eventual perfection of society as science liberates human reason from ignorance and superstition. These convictions were expressed in their most sophisticated forms during the nineteenth and early decades of the twentieth centuries, generally in opposition to the older theological conceptions of the Creation, Fall, Last Judgment and Redemption of mankind. However, there was an evolutionary connection between medieval and early modern religious ideas of the working of Providence in history toward the millennium—the thousand-year reign of Christ over the perfected earthly kingdom —and nineteenth- and twentieth-century secular concepts of the progress of society in accordance with natural laws toward an eventual utopian state.[1] Reinforced by Pelagian notions about the essential goodness of human nature and encouraged by the demonstrable achievements of science, explicit and implicit utopian expectations have played a major role in the development of the Western conviction of mastery over nature and society.

I shall refer to this rationalistic, manipulative and perfectionis-

[1] This transformation has been traced in detail in Ernest Lee Tuveson, *Millennium and Utopia, a Study of the Background of the Idea of Progress* (Berkeley and Los Angeles: University of California Press, 1949).

tic conviction as the distinctive "positivism" of Western culture. This term is used here in a much more general sense than in the nineteenth-century philosophy formulated by Saint-Simon and Auguste Comte; their doctrines were specific varieties of the general Western positivism. As elaborated in Comtean and many other versions by philosophers and social scientists, Western positivism insists that industrial technology and the social sciences can together solve the problems of society and rapidly usher in an era of equality and abundance for all. The key role in this process of social transformation is played by a scientifically trained elite of administrators, managers, sociologists, economists and engineers who are above class and partisan interests and are capable of acting objectively in the name and for the good of society as a whole. Springing from similar philosophical and social backgrounds, Marxism propounds a similar set of relationships, although in different terms. Dialectical materialism replaces the social sciences as the instrument of human knowledge, and the Communist party—"the vanguard of the proletariat"—replaces the technocrats as the active agents of social change. Like Marxism, positivism is conducive to authoritarian elitism except where, as in the countries of North America and northern Europe, there is a strong democratic tradition to offset it.

Positivism has been more highly developed and has played more important roles in the United States and Latin America than in Western Europe in consequence of certain factors indigenous to this hemisphere. The special characteristics and significance of Latin American positivism are discussed in Chapter 6. Here we are concerned with the two versions important in the United States which I shall call respectively "common-sense popular positivism," having no European or Latin American counterpart; and "technocratic elite-group positivism," generally similar to the European and Latin American types but with certain distinctive North American emphases.

Common-sense popular positivism is the product of the blending of two sets of unique North American experiences: the settlement of the wilderness, largely by the seventeenth- and eighteenth-century English colonists and their descendants, through movement of the frontier westward to the Pacific; and the process of urbanization in considerable part as a result of nineteenth- and early twentieth-century immigration. The conquest of the wilderness took the form predominantly of the development of family farms and small rural towns through an interaction between the potentialities and limitations of the natural environment and the institutions and values adapted by the settlers from their English heritage.

Except in the slave-owning South, this rural society tended to be democratic and egalitarian, generally suspicious of a distant central government, and usually inclined to rely upon individual initiative and local cooperation to solve immediate physical and social problems. These attitudes provided the energy, initiative and organizational ability necessary to make the wilderness productive and to sustain a dynamic and satisfying rural society—a result which, in turn, reinforced the values and expectations that made it possible. Moderate and steady success in these efforts, the continuous availability of new fertile land west of the existing settlements, and the high degree of social and geographical mobility contributed to making this rural American society open, optimistic, self-reliant and activistic.

These characteristics were reinforced and supplemented by those developed in the course of the nineteenth- and early twentieth-century urbanization to which the immigrants from Ireland and continental Europe made so large a contribution. In the main, this later immigration, like the earlier, consisted of individuals and families with the initiative, energy and courage to leave their familiar European environment to make a new beginning in America. Escaping from the confines of the still essentially authoritarian societies in the European countries of their birth, these immigrant groups were thrown on their own resources in the New World, and joined together for self-protection and mutual help in ethnic societies, church groups, trade-unions, cultural and sports clubs, and other types of organizations. Readily adapting themselves to the democratic environment, the newer immigrants took advantage of the openness and fluidity of American society to achieve economic and social advancement through their own efforts and with the help of the government, which—in part because of their more paternalistic and authoritarian Catholic backgrounds—they regarded with much less suspicion than did their established rural Protestant compatriots. Their experiences and the influence of the dominant Protestant culture also tended to make the newer immigrants optimistic and activistic. In turn, their own cultural heritage helped to mitigate the Puritan rigors of the dominant culture and to bring a warmer and more expressive attitude toward interpersonal relations and a propensity for sentimentality in dealing with the problems of society.

Thus, both the earlier and the later immigrant experiences combined to foster reliance upon individual initiative and group cooperation in the solution of practical problems. The knowledge required for these efforts was derived from ordinary everyday experience and did not demand specialized training and highly technical skills. The kinds of problems with which people were most immediately concerned were susceptible to analysis and prescription on the basis of common sense—that is, of generally shared ideas about nature and society which seemed plausible in the light of ordinary observation and which, when acted upon, appeared to be pragmatically effective. This set of attitudes and convictions comprising common-sense popular positivism is today one of the most extensive and deeply rooted characteristics of American society, and is unique within the West.

During the same period, a more sophisticated version of positivism evolved in the United States which is one of the two most extreme forms of the West's faith in its mastery over nature and society.[2] This technocratic elite-group positivism may be defined as the conviction—not only among American elite groups but also, in much less articulated fashion, among the population as a whole —that every physical obstacle and social difficulty can sooner or later be overcome by the appropriate group of experts equipped with the latest scientific techniques and sufficient funds. American faith in this prescription is continuously maintained and strengthened because, in a great many instances, it does in fact yield the expected results.

Technocratic positivism is to some extent inconsistent with common-sense positivism, even though both sets of convictions may be held simultaneously by the same individuals and groups. Technocratic positivism postulates professionals trained in highly

[a] The other is Latin America, as explained in Chapter 6.

technical skills, using specialized scientific knowledge, and preferably working in teams whose members are selected in accordance with the specific requirements of each assignment. Common-sense positivism relies upon ordinary men and women with practical experience but no special training or scientific knowledge, using generally accepted ideas and explanations that have a reasonable degree of pragmatic validity, and organized on an *ad-hoc* basis from among those who are willing to participate of their own accord or can be persuaded to do so. Thus, the agents and the types of knowledge and methods of the two kinds of American positivism are different, a situation that often contributes to divergent explanations of and prescriptions for dealing with particular physical and social problems.

Another difference between the two forms of American positivism is the authoritarian elitist tendency inherent in the technocratic approach. However, owing to the preponderant American commitment to democratic and egalitarian values, this authoritarianism is largely potential and, when expressed, is generally concealed in euphemisms. Nonetheless, there have always been elitist tendencies in American society. The Puritans considered themselves an elite predestined to serve by precept and example as a moral paradigm for the rest of mankind; the southern slave-owning aristocracy was convinced that its social superiority entitled it to political power; and, from the Civil War until the great depression of the 1930s, the business elite assumed that its entrepreneurial success *ipso facto* qualified it to make national policy on all of the major problems confronting the country.

Today, in contrast, the most characteristic form of American elitism is technocratic.[3] In all of the major institutional systems of American society—the government, the economy, the military, the church, the schools, the press, the scientific research community —technically trained administrators, managers, analysts and operators are increasingly becoming the major decision makers. Their power depends upon their technical qualifications and expe-

---

[3] Under the influence of Thorstein Veblen, Harold Scott and others in the early decades of the twentieth century, the technocratic elite was assumed to consist of engineers. Today, the term is used much more broadly; indeed, the technocrats par excellence are the social scientists and professionally trained administrators and managers rather than the engineers.

rience, as well as upon the relevant personality factors, and less
and less upon individual ownership or control of economic assets
or upon inherited status. Even in politics, there appears to be a
trend toward greater educational and technical qualifications on
the part of younger candidates for public office, although in this
field at least the traditional American egalitarian view that "anyone can be President" is still strong.

The rise of the technocratic elite in the United States has, of
course, been the result of social and intellectual developments of
the mid-twentieth century beyond the scope of our inquiry. But, it
both reflects and fosters the distinctive American form of technocratic positivism. This conviction is continuously reinforced by its
own pragmatic effectiveness, which encourages utopian expectations with respect to further efforts to control and reform society
and thereby strengthens the motivation to undertake them.[4] But
when, as is often the case, rational interests and nonrational re-
sistances nullify or pervert these efforts, the frustration of utopian
expectations often leads to disillusionment and to a lowering of
morale among the technocratic elite groups. This reaction is particularly noticeable with respect to U.S. foreign-policy initiatives.
Although the capacity to influence developments beyond a country's borders is always inherently much more restricted than in its
own domestic affairs, positivistic expectations often blind Americans to this limitation.

As we have seen, Western policy can no longer realistically
consider the possibility of reasserting direct political rule over
Asian and African countries. Hence, the Western will to action
with respect to these nations has to be expressed today in other
forms—primarily through efforts to influence their foreign policies and their current social transformations. But, for the West
to undertake such efforts, it must not only perceive that its self-
interest is affected. It must also believe that its actions can
in fact exercise control over the "development" of Asian and
African countries and their participation in world affairs. Without
this positivistic conviction, the expression of Western activism

---

[4] Current manifestations of this tendency are analyzed in Robert Boguslaw,
The New Utopians: A Study of System Design and Social Change (Englewood
Cliffs, New Jersey: Prentice-Hall, Inc., 1965).

toward these countries would in contemporary circumstances appear to Westerners—and particularly to Americans—to be futile.

The Senses of Mission and Guilt

Among the systems of culture evolved on this planet, Western society is surely the most time conscious, self-aware and reflective. It is conscious of and continually engaged in examining its own nature and destiny and the motivations and values that enter into its behavior. It is aware that it has had a past and will have a future, both significantly different from its present. The consciousness of history—of continuous change in the course of time—contrasts with the predominantly ahistorical and static world views prevalent in other cultures.

Both the sense of history and the tendency to reflectiveness help to account for the fact that, since antiquity, Western culture has been redemptive—a quality expressed in the fusion of Hebraic and Hellenistic religious elements usually designated today as the Judaeo-Christian tradition. The Hellenistic neoplatonic and gnostic strand in Christianity, with its expectation of redemption *from* this world, was generally paramount until the Renaissance. But, the Judaic prophetic strand has from time to time been asserted in programs for redemption *in* this world, as in certain of the popular medieval heresies, in the millenarian Protestant sects during the sixteenth and seventeenth centuries, and in the social gospel movement in recent liberal Protestantism. Today, the inspiration of the prophetic tradition provides the moral dimension and validation for activistic secular rationalism, particularly in the more extreme positivistic versions of it that have developed in American society.

In both its this-worldly and its other-worldly forms, the Christian gospel—the good news of redemption—was meant for all, regardless of race, culture or social position, by virtue of their common humanity. Thus, Western redemptivism has always included a missionary obligation, although it has not been actively expressed at every period in Western history. Nonetheless, this sense of mission has been an essential element in Western society, particularly as it has affected Western attitudes toward the other cultures with which it has come into contact. Today, the Western sense of mission expresses itself in three main forms which shade into one another and contain many variants and combinations.

The first is the continuation of traditional Christian missionary activity, both Catholic and Protestant. Explicitly religious in nature, it aims to bring to the non-Christian inhabitants of the planet knowledge of the specifically Christian roads to redemption so as to convert them to the distinctive pattern of belief and behavior prescribed by Christian theology, ritual and morality. In addition, since the mid-nineteenth century, Christian missionary activity has consisted not simply of preaching the gospel and organizing congregations of converts, but also of efforts to improve their health, occupational skills and living standards through medical and educational programs. Thus, as will be explained in Chapter 3, through the inculcation of Christian attitudes and behavior and through social-reform efforts, Christian missionary activity —particularly by the Protestant sects—has been endeavoring to disseminate a Westernized way of life within Asian and African countries. This traditional missionary obligation to bring the gospel to all mankind constitutes both the historical source and a major form of expression of the contemporary Western sense of mission to transform all other cultures on the planet into replicas of Western society.

A second major contemporary form of the Western sense of mission is a secularized and humanistic development of the religious missionary obligation. Prophetic expectations of redemption in this world were secularized by eighteenth-century rationalism and faith in social progress, and given scientific formulation in nineteenth-century utilitarianism, social Darwinism, positivism, socialism and related intellectual movements. With respect to Asia and Africa, one important expression of this secularized sense of the Western mission was the concept of the "white man's burden" —the obligation to bring honest and efficient government to the colonial areas under European control and to eliminate the cruelties and injustices of traditional social, political and religious customs. In the twentieth century, such justifications have developed into the more positive and activistic conviction that the adoption of the Western way of life is the only means by which other societies could expect to achieve living standards and political liberties comparable to those of the West. This secularized humanistic form of the Western sense of mission is reinforced by various historical and sociological theories that assume or purport to demonstrate the inevitable Westernization of the entire planet through the processes of industrialization and urbanization.

The third contemporary form of the Western sense of mission is Marxism-Leninism. Although it originated within and shares the secularized character of nineteenth-century rationalism, it is more focused and intense than the other varieties, and its organizational discipline and faith in historical inevitability invest it with quasi-religious characteristics. Marxism-Leninism prophesies the inevitability of world-wide Communist revolution in consequence of the weakening of "capitalist imperialism" through recurrent deepening crises and its overthrow in a final struggle. It promises redemption in this world through the establishment of a new order of society in which inequality and injustice will be eliminated; all will share equitably in economic abundance; and man will no longer be alienated from the fruits of his labor, from his fellow men, and from his own "true" nature. The duty of those who are "on the side of history" is to serve the revolution with unselfish devotion under the unquestioned leadership of the Communist party, the destined instrument of revolutionary fulfillment. Thus, the Marxist-Leninist sense of mission is eschatological, messianic and utopian, and it is a major influence on the attitudes and expectations of the Soviet and Chinese ruling elites with respect to Asia and Africa. Within the West, however, it is today of comparatively minor importance in directly influencing attitudes toward Asia and Africa, although indirectly it has helped to foster internationalism and utopianism in the European labor movement and among left-wing intellectuals on both sides of the Atlantic.

Secular humanistic forms of the Western sense of mission have predominated in the formation of Western attitudes toward Asia and Africa, particularly since decolonization began after World War II. Even during the colonial period, there was a general expectation in Europe that, in consequence of Western influence and assistance in modernization, the countries of Asia and Africa would eventually develop the political and economic capabilities necessary for independence in the course of evolving into Western-

type democratic and industrialized societies. However, the decolonization process began much sooner than the European ruling
powers had anticipated, and their gradualistic programs for fostering the capacity for self-government and economic growth were
only in the early stages when independence was obtained by most
Asian and African countries. In consequence, the Western sense of
mission remained unfulfilled. In the post-independence period, this
unfulfilled sense of mission has become a motive for Western willingness to provide financial aid and technical assistance to Asian
and African countries. As observed earlier, such Western programs of assistance are, in contemporary circumstances, the major
means by which the sense of mission to spread the Western way of
life to all parts of the planet can be effectively expressed.

Closely related to this sense of mission is the Western sense of
guilt. As long as its mission in Asia and Africa remains unfulfilled,
the West feels a sense of guilt because it obviously possesses the
resources and the skills which it believes are the major means for
carrying out its self-imposed obligation to Westernize the planet.
But, this sense of guilt also reflects other characteristics of the
Western system of values and attitudes.

One concept of central importance in the Western religious
tradition that contributes to it is the ambiguity of human nature,
which is today expressed in both religious and secular forms. The
doctrine of the fall of man is the essential element justifying the
need for redemption, and imposing the related obligations of self-
improvement and of promoting the welfare of others. Regardless
of whether redemption is obtained through faith or through good
works, there is an obvious gap between what man is and what he
should and could be. The disparity reflects the deficiencies of
human nature, whether resulting from God's will or from man's
perversity. Thus, a deep sense of guilt is inherent in Western society by reason of the nature of Western religious doctrine. Secularized forms of the Christian sense of guilt may be seen, for
example, in contemporary existentialism—in which the gap between "essence" and "existence" corresponds to the difference
between what man could be and what he is—as well as in modern
depth psychology.

Another major factor in the Western sense of guilt is the aspiring and achieving character of Western society, reflecting its dynamism and fluidity, and its positivistic conviction that purposeful human action can master nature and transform society. Goals and objectives are continually being set that go beyond existing capabilities and accomplishments. Individuals, groups and entire nations strive to extend their knowledge, expand their power, and improve their conditions of life. Delay or inability to accomplish these goals generates anxiety in the form of a sense of guilt, because the typical Western explanation is not that objectives have been unrealistic but that efforts have been inadequate. So marked is this characteristic that some social anthropologists have described the West as a "guilt society," in contrast to primitive and traditional societies, which are regarded as "shame societies" because their most typical form of anxiety is the sense of shame over actual or apparent loss of status and prestige.

The Western sense of guilt toward Asia and Africa reflects both a failure to attain ethical standards of intention and action in interpersonal relations with the people of these countries, and a failure to achieve anticipated results in assisting their political and economic advancement. As noted above, the Western sense of mission has in part been a justification of colonialism, which was regarded as a necessary means for spreading the Western way of life to other societies. But, while it helped to satisfy the sense of mission, colonialism also heightened the sense of guilt. It violated Western ethical standards since it entailed the imposition of Western rule against the wishes of the subject peoples and denied them their natural right to work out their own destinies. Western efforts to prepare Asian and African countries for political independence and economic growth manifestly fell far short of their objectives and, in the post-colonial period, Western aid programs have similarly failed to make the expected decisive contribution to accelerating Asian and African "development."

In addition, the Western sense of guilt has been intensified by the racial differences between the colonial rulers and the subject peoples. Notions about the racial superiority of white Westerners conflict with Western values regarding the equality and dignity of all men. A related source of guilt has been the sense of cultural superiority fostered by the preeminence of Western society in science and technology and in political and economic effectiveness. Western satisfaction in these achievements augments the Western sense of guilt over the disparities between its own performance in these respects and that of Asian and African societies. Again, this results from a deep conflict between the Western values involved. On the one hand, Western cultural achievements are regarded as a justifiable reward for the West's superior capabilities. On the other hand, the continued more rapid progress of the West only widens the gap between its own accomplishments and those of other societies. By increasing the distance Asia and Africa must cover, faster Western progress magnifies their difficulties, thereby violating Western standards of equality and fairness.

Within Western society, there are important variations in the intensity and content of the senses of mission and guilt. As in the case of the will to action, they are much weaker and more diffuse on the Continent than in Britain and the United States.

Since the end of the colonial period, the continental European sense of mission has been largely cultural. The European sense of superiority and, to a lesser extent, the European predilection for concepts of historical inevitability foster the conviction that Asians and Africans must naturally aspire to imitate European culture, whose unparalleled excellence must be apparent to any non-European who becomes acquainted with it. All that is needed is to provide opportunities for Asians and Africans to experience European culture through education and exposure to a European environment either in Europe or in their own countries. What is important for them to acquire, and what they will naturally and inevitably adopt, are European attitudes—ways of thinking and feeling—and hence a European manner or style of life. Thus, the content of the continental sense of mission has been and is today primarily cultural. This emphasis was reflected during the colonial period (and still is in Portuguese and Spanish colonial policy) in the concept of the *évolué*—the Asian or African who is entitled to the same political and economic treatment as a European because he has adopted European attitudes and style of life. The development by the people of these countries of Western political and economic institutions, and their acquisition of the techniques and skills for operating them effectively have been and still are considered much less important by continental Europeans, and efforts to foster them were comparatively neglected during the colonial period.

In contrast, the British sense of mission toward Asia and Africa has been predominantly institutional rather than cultural. British political and social institutions—the Parliament, the cabinet, political parties, the judiciary, the universities, the public schools, the established and independent churches, the civilian-dominated army and navy, etc.—have been and still are thought to be naturally superior to those of other nations and societies, and naturally to be imitated by them. However, the attitudes and life style of a British gentleman could rarely be transmitted across cultural boundaries, and few Asians and Africans have achieved a sufficient approximation of them to be accepted on more than a basis of politeness in the West End, the home counties, or at Oxford and Cambridge. British policy stressed the development—albeit slow—in the Asian and African colonies of political, judicial, educational and other institutions on the British model, and confidently expected them to endure without essential change after independence was granted. Since the disappointment of this expectation early in the post-independence period, the British sense of mission to provide an institutional model to which every "self respecting" nation would inevitably aspire survives mainly among the generations whose basic attitude formation and education took place prior to World War II.

It is, however, in the United States that the Western senses of mission and guilt are today most completely and powerfully expressed. One of the most widely held convictions in the United States is that American society is a unique creation significant not only for the American people but also for all mankind. This conviction is compounded of two main elements which have fused in the twentieth century and have been strongly reinforced—in a sense validated—by the world leadership role which the United States has been willing and able to play by virtue of its will to action and its economic resources and military power. The first is derived from the Puritan conception that America's mission was to serve as a moral paradigm for the rest of the world; the second is the vocational expression of the belief that the political, eco-

nomic and technological successes of American society have made
it a model that others naturally aspire to imitate.

The idea that America must serve as a moral example to the
rest of mankind was expressed in the Puritan certitude that their
settlement in the New World constituted, in the words of John
Winthrop, "a city upon a hill'—a shining demonstration that the
elect of God were creating in the wilderness a society embodying
the Christian virtues. Although this moral paradigm has been
secularized and permeated with utopian expectations over the intervening centuries, as H. Richard Niebuhr has explained, it has
never lost its moralistic content, which today constitutes a major
dimension of America's sense of mission.[5] Americans generally
believe that their society is inherently more virtuous than any
other, even within the West, and therefore merits both admiration
and emulation on moral grounds. This conviction extends also to
America's relations with other countries. Indeed, so strong is this
belief that, even when the national interest requires an exercise of
power that cannot readily be described in moralistic euphemisms,
Americans are often themselves more shocked and dismayed than
are their foreign critics. Americans' conviction of the virtue of
their own motivations and actions is not hypocritical and, in consequence, constitutes a major self-restraint upon the exercise of
American power. But, it also generates a sense on the part of the
American people that they are misunderstood by other nations
more inclined to see U.S. actions as the expression of power and
self-interest rather than of virtuous altruism.

The second element in the contemporary American sense of
mission reflects the political, economic and technological achievements of American society over the past two centuries. Although
today other nations may not know or remember, Americans have
not forgotten that it was their revolution in the eighteenth century
that "fired the shot heard round the world" and thereby ushered in
the modern era of democratic revolutions and wars of independence. Since then, Americans have built a stable and functioning
democratic political system embracing a larger number of people
of different cultural and racial backgrounds than any other nation

[5] H. Richard Niebuhr, *The Kingdom of God in America* (New York: Harper
and Brothers, 1937).

on the planet. They have developed an economic system with higher productivity and living standards, and broader scope for individual choice and initiative than any other. American technology generally leads the world, particularly in the areas of greatest importance for the future security, health and welfare of mankind. Americans are aware of these unprecedented political, economic and technological achievements both from direct experience of their own conditions of life and by comparison with the conditions in other countries. Thus, Americans tend to feel that their society is a model for other nations to imitate not only morally but also with respect to political and economic systems and the application of science and technology to improving the conditions of life.

The sense of America's mission to serve as both a moral and a social paradigm for the rest of mankind is expressed actively and not passively in consequence of the strength of the American will to action and of its positivistic conviction. Americans believe that they have a vocation to play an active role in helping other countries to achieve the "American way of life" which is assumed to be their aspiration. This vocation is expressed collectively in the national policy of providing financial aid and technical assistance to other countries—largely at American initiative and by the active participation of American officials in the planning and implementation of the programs of the recipient nations. It is expressed individually by tens of thousands of Americans who have chosen to live abroad and work in government-aid programs and in religious missions, educational institutions, business firms and other private organizations operating in all parts of Asia, Africa and Latin America. Regardless of whether the collective and individual motivations involved are altruistic or self-interested, all of these activities in greater or lesser degree are manifestations of the American desire to serve both as a moral and social model for other societies and as an active agent helping those countries trying to emulate the United States.

This activistic character of the American sense of mission also helps to generate a sense of guilt. For, many Americans feel that the lack of progress made by Asia, Africa and Latin America in achieving the American way of life results more from the inadequacy of their own vocational activities than from insufficient efforts by the countries concerned. The great and growing disparity between American living standards and those of other countries is also a source of guilt for Americans, particularly within the elite groups, who are influenced both by traditional Christian norms regarding the obligations of the rich and by modern secular concepts of equal rights.

In sum, the senses of mission and guilt, working in somewhat contradictory ways, are responsible for Western—and especially for American—willingness to play a paradigmatic role vis-à-vis the newly independent countries of Asia and Africa.[6] Mission and guilt help both to define the functions performed in that role by the West and to motivate its willingness to perform them. They are major reasons why Western nations provide financial aid and technical assistance to Asian, African and Latin American countries. In effect, the senses of mission and guilt constitute the moral dimension—always an essential element in the motivation for collective action in Western society—which justifies the exercise of the Western will to action and validates the expression of Western positivism. Without the senses of mission and guilt, these other two major components of Western attitudes toward Asia and Africa would be felt to be intolerably cynical and self-interested.

Ambiguities and Conflicts in American Attitudes

The concepts, values and expectations sketched in the foregoing pages are sometimes expressed separately and in their pure forms in the explicit motivations and rationales of individuals, groups and nations within the West. More often, however, they are combined in many different ways, not only mutually reinforcing but also contradicting, distorting and nullifying one another. The results are the many variations and the deep ambiguities and conflicts that characterize Western—and particularly American—attitudes toward Asia and Africa.

Recognition of their complex and ambivalent nature is crucial

[6] As Chapter 4 will explain, Asian and African countries have for their part cast the West in a paradigmatic role of a highly ambivalent kind. These reciprocal attitudes constitute the quintessential element in the relationship between the West and Asia and Africa.

to an understanding of these Western attitudes and of their influence on relationships between the two groups of countries. For, the ambiguities and conflicts in Western attitudes are as pronounced and significant as are those in Asian and African attitudes toward the West, discussed in Chapter 4. Although different in content, they are counterparts and to some extent stimulate and support one another.

Because Americans have a greater will to action, stronger positivistic convictions, and deeper senses of mission and guilt than other Westerners, the United States has been the most energetic and optimistic participant in the affairs of the newly independent nations of Asia and Africa and of the older countries of Latin America. The United States has felt the strongest obligation to defend them against external aggression and internal subversion, and in recent years has been providing them with 50 per cent more financial aid and technical assistance than all of the other Western nations combined. It has sought to make its own performance an example to persuade the other Western nations to increase their involvement in the affairs of these regions. At the same time, the perceptual and conceptual biases of American culture and the influence of America's own historical experiences help to account for American reluctance to recognize the social realities of contemporary Asia, Africa and Latin America, and for the ambiguities and conflicts that are evident in American attitudes toward them. Since the motivational influence of cultural and social factors and the resulting misconceptions and ambiguities are most evident in the American attitude toward foreign aid, a brief discussion of it may help to clarify their operation and interaction.[7]

In addition to the three major elements already described, another related cultural component particularly relevant to attitudes on foreign aid must be mentioned—the American concept of charity as derived from the Judaeo-Christian tradition. This needs to be further defined, for there is a significant difference between Catholic and Protestant concepts. Catholic doctrine focuses mainly

[7] This analysis is based on a fuller account in Theodore Geiger and Roger D. Hansen, "Decision Making on Foreign Aid," in Raymond A Bauer, editor, *The Study of the Policy Process* (New York: The Free Press, forthcoming.) For this monograph, Benjamin Nelson directed our attention to the differing Catholic and Protestant views on charity (discussed here) and on implicit and explicit faith (discussed in Chapter 3).

on the implications of charity for the donor who, by making an individual act of sacrifice to relieve the distress of the poor and unfortunate, is engaging in an "imitation of Christ." Calvin, Knox, Wesley and other Protestant reformers rejected this conception of charity as sentimental, capricious and self-serving. Instead, they insisted that charity is justified mainly by its effects on the recipient. According to this Protestant concept of "efficient good works," charity has to be organized specifically to help the recipient help himself, and charitable acts that do not conform to this standard are to be regarded as wasteful and, hence, immoral. Moreover, recipients have to demonstrate their worthiness to receive charity, that is, to qualify as "deserving poor" by following advice and by being hard working, respectful and grateful.

The Protestant concept of charity has dominated the theory and practice of American philanthropy, as expressed in Andrew Carnegie's notion of the "trusteeship of wealth" and in the large-scale, systematic organization and efficient operation of the innumerable philanthropic foundations and charitable trusts that exist in the United States. It guides the government's social-welfare activities and has even heavily influenced the American Catholic approach to charity. Along with the senses of mission and guilt, it provides the moral dimension for U.S. foreign-aid activities. Combined with American positivism, it is reflected in the expectation that Asian and African countries should be willing and able to accomplish major social reforms and economic innovations as a demonstration of their capacity to help themselves and, therefore, of their worthiness to receive aid. Combined with the American will to action, this concept leads to the expectation that Asian and African countries will gratefully follow American advice in conducting their domestic and international affairs.

The importance of these cultural elements in American attitudes toward foreign aid may be seen in the reasons given by Americans generally for supporting economic assistance to Asian, African and Latin American countries. Over the past fifteen years, public-opinion polls have indicated that the percentage of Americans responding favorably to such questions as "Are you for or against foreign aid?" and "Do you feel that we should help underdeveloped countries whether they pay us back or not?" has varied from seventy in the earlier years to about fifty in the later. Within these totals, the reasons most often cited for favoring foreign aid have consistently been various humanitarian and charitable expressions of the senses of mission and guilt. Reasons reflecting the American will to action and national interests—e.g., preventing disorder and communism in the recipient countries, income and employment benefits to the American economy, etc.—have constituted a much smaller percentage of the total. In the official domestic rationales of the U.S. government—both the Executive Branch and the Congress—the relative importance of these two kinds of motives has usually been reversed, reflecting obvious national interest responsibilities and the rationalized character of the governmental institutions concerned. However, in the U.S. government's pronouncements directed toward the recipient countries, the relative importance of the two types of motivation is again reversed, with altruistic concern for their economic and social advancement predominating. While the reasons for these differences in rationales are obvious, they nevertheless do reflect a conflict embarrassing to many Americans—that between self-interest and altruism.

An important ambiguity arises from the failure of the U.S. aid program to achieve the expectations regarding it. Asian, African and Latin American countries frequently behave toward the United States in ways that seem ungrateful to Americans; they often disregard American advice; and they appear to be unwilling to institute the drastic social reforms and economic innovations that Americans believe they should be able to accomplish easily and quickly in consequence of the aid they receive from the United States. Because of such frustrated expectations, many Americans —including many who favor foreign aid—express in public-opinion polls such exasperated reactions as "Our aid is wasted," "We're only throwing money down the drain," "Those people aren't helping themselves," "Why should we give them anything when they're not grateful?"

These and other conflicting reactions also reflect the influence of America's unique historical experiences, which have helped to engender a widespread conviction that emulation of America's achievements should not be very difficult for other nations. The

Civil War in the nineteenth century and the Great Depression in the twentieth century have probably been the most traumatic experiences the American nation has undergone since achieving its independence. But, difficult and painful as these experiences were, they were successfully endured, and the American people have otherwise enjoyed almost unbroken success in their efforts to settle their country and develop its political and economic institutions. Thus, it is difficult for Americans to appreciate the nature and implications of the much less happy histories of most other countries. Moreover, America did not have to meet the challenge of political and economic advancement weighed down by the values and institutions of a traditional society and the inhibitions and loss of self-confidence resulting from conquest and alien rule. For this reason, Americans often fail to grasp the magnitude of the difficulties faced by Asian and African countries in attempting to accelerate their transformations, and they soon lose patience with the slowness of Latin Americans to abandon inherited values and norms, particularly when they directly and conspicuously interfere with the modernization process.

Not only has the history of the United States imbued its people with optimism; it has also fostered an overly rationalistic and voluntaristic view of the nature of social change. Individual and local group initiative and cooperation have played so large a role in the achievements of American society that they have encouraged the belief that these modes of behavior can be readily adopted and applied in any society once their merits have been rationally explained. Similarly, the unique ethnic and interest-group pluralism of American society and the absence in recent decades of deeply divisive clashes of interest have fostered the view that there are no irreconcilable social conflicts. If only men of good will could be persuaded to sit around the same table, compromises would be found among the most divergent objectives, and disagreements over methods for achieving them could be settled on the basis of relative efficiency—that is, on their technical merits. The fact that rational decision making of this kind plays so prominent a part in American society encourages the view that it must naturally do so in all other societies. Thus, Americans tend to believe that Asian, African and Latin American countries are merely perverse when they fail to reach a consensus on realistic national objectives and to pursue them efficiently and conscientiously.

The conviction that other countries could easily and rapidly emulate the American example if only they made a rational decision to do so is strongly reinforced by both forms of positivism prevalent in American society. Common-sense positivism, itself fostered by the diverse ethnic and cultural origins of the American people, makes them prone to discount the strength of cultural differences as obstacles to their cooperation with Asians, Africans and Latin Americans. Americans have a personalistic faith in their capacity to overcome cultural barriers and conflicts of interest by sheer good will and sincerity—a conviction that plays an important role in the U.S. foreign-aid program with its large missions of officials and technicians stationed in the recipient countries. Similarly, confidence in technocratic positivism also encourages a disregard of the social and cultural obstacles to political and economic development in Asia, Africa and Latin America. In this form of American positivism, the problems involved are regarded as primarily technical in nature—that is, requiring largely an assessment of means in terms of their relevance to objectives and of their relative efficiency in achieving them—and, therefore, as capable of being solved by specialists and civil servants on the basis of rational considerations alone.

These attitudes and expectations not only conflict with reality; they also lead to important exaggerations and ambiguities in feelings and beliefs. Because they fail to appreciate the magnitude of the difficulties faced by Asian, African and Latin American countries, Americans cannot understand why the pace of social change in those countries is so slow. On the one hand, as we have seen, the senses of mission and guilt lead to the explanation most frequently given that American aid has been too small. On the other hand, the lag is sometimes attributed to deficiencies of understanding and of will on the part of Asians, Africans and Latin Americans; and, in consequence, there is a tendency to dismiss them as morally deficient and incompetent and hence not likely to accomplish very much. The unfounded belief that these deficiencies exist and prevent significant "development" progress contradicts the equally unrealistic expectation that social change could be readily and swiftly accomplished if only American aid were large enough. The attribution of the slowness of progress to the supposed innate inadequacies of Asians, Africans and Latin Americans also plays a role in American attitudes toward foreign aid. On the one hand, the strong American senses of mission and guilt impel the giving of aid to these countries. On the other hand, their failure to imitate America's example and their inability to realize American expectations of what aid should enable them to do generate a feeling that Asians, Africans and Latin Americans are unworthy recipients and, therefore, that it is immoral to waste resources on them. Consequently, the American attitude oscillates between the desire to provide aid as an expression of America's moral obligation and the belief that it should be withheld as an expression of America's moral condemnation.

Among elite groups with a strong faith in technocratic positivism, a parallel conflict exists. They tend to believe that accelerating the process of social change in Asia, Africa and Latin America depends upon finding technical panaceas—some new administrative arrangement or program technique—that can overcome the evident inability of the U.S. foreign-aid program and of the recipient countries to produce the substantial progress expected within the time envisaged. But, when the new fashions in organization and programming also fail to produce the results anticipated, they do not question the validity of their positivistic assumptions but rather conclude that Asians, Africans and Latin Americans have not understood the importance of the new techniques and have not applied them with sufficient vigor.

A final example of the effects of cultural and social factors on American attitudes may be seen in the rhetorical character of many of the rationales used in the United States to support and justify the foreign-aid activity. On the one hand, considerations of national interest combine with the will to action, positivistic convictions and the senses of mission and guilt to motivate strong support for it, particularly among the elite groups. On the other hand, the frustration of expectations of rapid progress in Asia, Africa and Latin America and the frequent absence of grateful support of American policies on their part lead to disillusionment and exasperation and increase opposition to the program. The strength of their own complex motivations has impelled many proponents of aid, particularly among the elite groups, to focus with such intensity upon maintaining and, if possible, increasing the size of the aid program that they shun critical analysis of its assumptions, methods and accomplishments and become uneasy and defensive when others, who also favor the program, call attention to its shortcomings.

Indeed, much of what purports to be scientific analysis of aid requirements, objectives and methods is really rhetoric for expressing and stimulating American motivation to provide aid. The American Indians used to engage in war dances designed to relieve the braves' anxieties and whip up their enthusiasm to the point where they were eager to attack the enemy. The rhetoric of foreign aid fulfills the same purpose but, unlike its Indian counterpart, the emotions expressed in the preparatory dance seem to be mistaken for the realities of the actual combat. However successful this rhetoric may be in articulating elite-group feelings and in whipping up popular enthusiasm for foreign aid, the rationales asserted —e.g., preventing collapse and communism in the recipient countries, satisfying their "revolution of rising expectations," narrowing the gap between rich and poor nations, providing the decisive increment of resources to accelerate economic growth and accomplish social reforms—bear too little relationship to what is actually happening in Asia, Africa and Latin America and to the influence that the West could have upon the fundamental, complex and uncertain processes of social change in those regions.[8]

[8] The pseudo-diagnostic character of these rhetorical arguments will be clarified by subsequent chapters. A word may, however, be said about the "gap-closing" rationale, a favorite of newspaper columnists, editorial writers and other opinion leaders. A glance at comparative population and economic growth rates makes it clear that, even on the most optimistic assumptions regarding the magnitude of future capital transfers to Asian and African countries, the disparity in per-capita income between most of them and the West is not likely to narrow substantially during the remainder of this century, and probably will widen. From 1960 through 1966, North America and Western Europe enjoyed an average real per-capita growth of GNP of 3.3 per cent a year, a rate they are likely to be able to sustain in the future granted the emphasis on growth in official policy, the elimination of substantial recessions during the business cycle, and the increasing co-ordination of national economic policies among the Western countries. Only a few Asian and African nations have been or are likely to be able to achieve and, more important, to sustain real per-capita rates of GNP growth sufficiently in excess of 3.3 per cent a year to narrow the gap significantly.

Despite the ambiguities in American attitudes toward foreign aid, the cultural values and historical experiences expressed in them consitute essential elements in American motivation to assist the countries of Asia, Africa and Latin America. Foreign aid does serve the national interest, but its benefits in this respect are neither sufficiently direct nor substantial enough to maintain public and congressional support over the long period during which it should be provided. Hence, the continuation of this activity depends upon the fact that it expresses the values and self-conceptions of American society. The danger in motivation of this kind is that its intensity and affective basis—the very elements that make it effective—obscure the perception of reality and thereby lead to mistaken policies, unproductive actions and frustrated expectations. For this reason, continuous efforts need to be made to recognize such misconceptions and unrealistic expectations and to minimize their adverse effects not only on analysis and policy making but also on public and congressional understanding.

CHAPTER THREE

From the Traditional
to the Transitional Society:
The Encounter of the West
with Asia and Africa

It is difficult for many Westerners to grasp the nature and implications of the impact of their own society upon the traditional societies of Asia and Africa. Born and educated within social institutions and a system of values essentially different from those of Asia and Africa, Westerners have little basis in their own experience for understanding the distinctive characteristics of these historical cultures. In consequence, there is a natural tendency for Westerners to think that traditional societies are separated from their own only by a difference in the level of technology or, more broadly, in the particular stage of development each has reached along a course of evolution that is assumed to be identical for all societies.

To correct this fundamental misapprehension, this chapter first surveys the essential features and distinctive evolution of the traditional societies of Asia and Africa; next, it describes the nature and assesses the impact upon them of their encounter with the West during recent centuries; and, finally, it outlines the main characteristics of the transitional societies that have emerged from this relationship.

The Traditional Society

Although they differ widely in complexity of social and political organization, level of technology, and artistic and intellectual achievements, the indigenous societies that have evolved historically in Asia and Africa have had certain significant characteristics in common. I shall define these features in broad outline, rather than describe any particular Asian or African society, past or present, although illustrations will be drawn from one or another of them. In effect, this is an application of Max Weber's method of distinguishing the characteristics of the general, or "ideal," type of the traditional society amid the many specific varieties of it that exist and have existed in Asia, the Middle East and Africa. The aspects selected for discussion are those believed to be determinative of this class of societies as a whole; that is, they are essential, and not derivative or accidental, characteristics.

The traditional society is agrarian: the great bulk of the population lives in the countryside; the products of field, pasture and forest constitute the main output of the economy; and control over the use of land and the distribution of agricultural production is the chief form of wealth as well as a major support for political power. Rural families and villages have a high degree of self-sufficiency. The individual family households meet most of their consumption needs from their own production or by exchanging portions of it for the handicrafts and specialized services of potters, millers, weavers and other craftsmen in the village. Other portions of the village's output of agricultural products, and sometimes of handicrafts, are exchanged for essential commodities not available locally—e.g., salt, metals, vegetable oils, fabricated articles needed for ceremonial and religious purposes, etc.—in many cases through the agency of ethnically distinct outsiders specializing in long-distance trade. However, by far the largest portion of the village's output not consumed locally is extracted from it by the ruling political and religious elites in the forms of tribute, taxes, tithes, quasi-feudal dues, sharecropping arrangements and a myriad of other specific fixed obligations. In addition, unpaid labor services (*corvées*) of many kinds are generally required of the rural population for work on roads, irrigation and canal systems, fortifications, temples, tombs and other large-scale construction projects.

This pattern of largely self-sufficient rural households and villages constitutes the universal and most enduring characteristic of the traditional society. In Asia and Africa, it has existed along with agricultural techniques that differ very widely in sophistication and productivity. At one extreme has been the shifting cultivation generally prevalent throughout tropical Africa and the mountain and jungle areas of South and Southeast Asia. This low-productivity technique consists of clearing small plots in the rain forest or savannah, planting food and other crops for a year or two until output falls drastically, and then allowing the soil to regenerate under natural vegetation for a long period. At the other extreme have been the very much more productive systems of irrigated cultivation first developed for paddy rice in the river plains of India and China and for wheat and other cereals in the Middle Eastern river plains.

Similarly, a wide range of political organizations has evolved from, or has been imposed upon, the basic rural institutions of traditional Asian and African societies. Where agricultural productivity was sufficiently high to produce substantial "surpluses" above the subsistence needs of the rural society, as in the river plains of the Middle East, North China and North India, or where long-distance trade monopolies yielded comparatively large incomes, as along the upper Niger River in sub-Saharan Africa, the military and religious elites created ethnic kingdoms and eventually large multi-ethnic empires, with fairly elaborate administrative machinery. But, changes in these political institutions and the replacement of one ruling elite by another always left the rural society essentially intact. As Karl Marx observed, until the establishment of British colonial rule in India, the successive imperial conquerors in Asia and Africa merely substituted one group of tax collectors for another.

The cities that arose in the economically more productive kingdoms and empires were in the main centers for administration, religious observance, trade and the handicraft production of war matériel and luxury goods for the ruling elites and for export. No

Asian or African urban center ever evolved of its own accord into a self-governing city like the ancient Greek *polis* or the medieval European commune. Urban merchants and craftsmen were adjuncts of the ruler's court or of the temple and did not themselves develop dynamic economic and political institutions capable of helping to transform the traditional society from within, as happened during several strategic periods in the evolution of Western society.

The traditional society has embraced many different types of social units, of which the various forms of the extended or joint family have been the most important and universal. The biologically and psychologically basic nuclear family of father, mother and child is firmly embedded within the extended family, which generally comprises three generations and numerous degrees of collateral relatives living together in one or several rural homesteads or villages, and to a lesser extent in urban households.

Throughout tropical Africa and in parts of Asia where multi-ethnic empires have not developed, extended families are generally combined into clans, often living in the same or neighboring villages, and these in turn are the constituent units of tribes tracing their descent from a common mythological ancestor or migrating group. In the politically more developed parts of Asia and the Middle East, more elaborate patterns of social organization evolved, although everywhere and at every social level, including the ruling elites, the extended family has continued to be the primary social unit. Perhaps the best known of these more specialized patterns—although by no means the most typical—is the Hindu caste system. Each caste consists of families restricted to the same occupation or group of related occupations; and the economic and social relationships among the hierarchy of castes are rigidly defined and enforced by religious sanctions. Other important forms of social affiliation prevalent in India, the Middle East and parts of Southeast Asia are sects, monastic orders and brotherhoods within the major indigenous religions, and craftsmen's and merchants' guilds.

The social roles played by individuals and their relationships with one another are determined by "ascription"—that is, by inherited status and immemorial custom. The rearing and education of

children; marriage arrangements; the exercise of authority within
the family, village and tribe; the assignment of economic and social tasks; the distribution of goods and services; the settlement of
disputes of all kinds; the religious practices; and virtually every
aspect of social roles and relationships are regulated by traditional
norms handed down from one generation to another and generally
buttressed by strong religious sanctions. In the more primitive societies of tropical Africa and the mountainous and jungle regions
of Asia, these roles and relationships primarily express kinship
arrangements and obligations. While kinship continues to be important in the more complex societies, their roles and relationships
also reflect customary obligations among non-related social
groups, such as between the elites and the peasants, and between
higher and lower Hindu castes.

Thus, the life career of each individual depends very largely
upon the status into which he is born and only very exceptionally
upon his personal achievement. Indeed, people in the traditional
society neither think of themselves nor function as isolated and self-
responsible individuals. All of the institutions, concepts and values
of the traditional society foster the identification of the individual
with the social units in which he participates. He both thinks of
himself and acts primarily as a member of the family, village and
tribe in accordance with the inherited status that determines his
roles and the immemorial customs that regulate his relationships
with others.

This process of identification of the individual with the social
group is not diffused by competing loyalties or weakened by expectations of upward social mobility. In the traditional society, individuals do not participate in rival or divergently oriented social
groups and institutions, as they do in Western society. In the latter,
home and school, church and business, trade-union and political
party, social club and scientific society, and a multitude of other
affiliations vie for the loyalty and concern of the individual and
present him with values and goals that are often inconsistent. Such
"differentiation," to use the sociological term, is rudimentary in
the traditional society. Even in India, the multiplicity of castes and
the antagonism among religious sects do not significantly weaken
the identification process. Indeed, it is strengthened by the fact that

no one can belong to two castes at the same time or pass from a lower to a higher caste except by deception.

Attitudes and values, philosophy and religion, folklore and the arts reflect and reinforce the homogeneity and stability of the social institutions and relationships of the traditional society. Unlike Christianity and its Near Eastern predecessors and offshoots, Asian and African religions do not promise redemption of the individual in or from this world through his faith or his good works. Instead, many of the higher religions of these regions, particularly those evolved in or derived from India, stress the illusory character of the material world and envisage, as the reward for human merit, the eventual loss of individual identity through absorption by the absolute. Moreover, merit is acquired not through passionate striving and virtuous activity, as in Christianity, but by withdrawal, indifference and contemplation. Hence, there is no indigenous ethic—religious or secular—of social progress and individual improvement.[1] Even in the doctrine of the transmigration of souls —widespread in Eastern Asia after the diffusion of Hinduism and Buddhism—proper conduct and right thinking would ensure a person's reincarnation at a higher social level but not rewards within his present lifetime, and Nirvana, the loss of personal identity, is still the final goal.

In contrast to the religions of Indian origin, Chinese Confucianism did not reject the world as illusory and valueless. However, despite its concern with good government and proper social relationships, Confucianism does not envisage social perfectibility but only social rectification—a return to the divinely ordained norms and conditions believed to have existed in the past.

Thus, neither religious millennia nor secular utopias have been promised by or developed from the indigenous Asian and African religions. Social institutions and relationships are generally regarded as immutable, and there is no concept of the renovation and transformation of society either by divine or human agencies. Instead, value systems stress acceptance of one's status and roles,

[1] Certain Buddhist sects in China and Japan promised translation to a paradise after death—for example, the "Pure Land" sect—but none envisaged salvation in this world. However, the Zen sect developed attitudes and norms affecting behavior in this world that played a significant role in the modernization of Japan (see Chapter 4).

conscientious performance of the functions and ceremonies pertinent to them, and unquestioning obedience to elders and to religious and secular authorities.[2]

In these and other ways, all aspects of the traditional society combine to stabilize its institutions, relationships, values and behavioral norms. Left to itself, the traditional society only elaborates, refines or makes more sophisticated the elements of which it is composed; it never changes their essential character. Tribes and empires have conquered and imposed their own particular forms of political institutions on others. Ruling elites have extracted greater or smaller "surpluses" from the agrarian economy by a wide range of different methods. Great religious movements have swept through large parts of Asia and Africa. But none of these developments has ever altered essentially the basic institutions and values of the traditional society. The inception of fundamental changes in the traditional society has come only from outside—from the encounter with the West.

The Dynamic Characteristics of Western Society

In order to illuminate the nature and significance of the impact of the West upon the traditional societies of Asia and Africa, it will be helpful to review briefly certain distinctive characteristics of Western society. Again, for the sake of clarity and contrast, I shall use the Weberian method of defining an "ideal" type rather than attempting to describe the intricate historical development and complex existing varieties of Western society.

While the economic system of the traditional society consists predominantly of agrarian units oriented largely toward self-sufficient production, the farms and factories of the West produce almost completely for sale to other producing, distributing and consuming units. The increasingly specialized division of labor and the growing degree of rationalization, mechanization and automation of production processes both in industry and in agriculture

---

[2] See Max Weber, *The Religion of China* (Glencoe, Illinois: The Free Press, 1951); *The Religion of India* (Glencoe, Illinois: The Free Press, 1958); and also Max Weber, "Religious Rejections of the World and Their Directions" in H. H. Gerth and C. Wright Mills, translators and editors, *From Max Weber: Essays in Sociology* (New York: Oxford University Press, 1958).

have resulted in high and rising productivity and living standards. Production and consumption and saving and investment take place within a complex market mechanism comprised of innumerable monetary transactions among buyers and sellers and borrowers and lenders; characterized by different kinds and degrees of competition and monopoly; and signaling its trends by changes in objective quantitative indicators (prices, wages, interest rates, profits, etc.). Scientific and technological research provide a continuous stream of more diversified and improved materials, products and processes. Initiative, innovation, moderate risk taking, and the ability in making economic decisions to take into account varied and changing economic and political factors, both existing and prospective, play major roles in the success or failure of all types of economic enterprises in Western society.

The political and social institutions of the West are equally differentiated and complex. Governments carry on a growing range of functions of all kinds necessary for ensuring national defense, maintaining and improving the effective functioning of the economic system, meeting desirable standards of social welfare, protecting public health, providing educational and training facilities, supporting scientific and technological research and development, and regulating private behavior so as to minimize injustice and exploitation and equalize the conditions of competition and opportunity. A host of mutually supporting, overlapping and sometimes contending social organizations and institutions serve a wide variety of purposes. Individuals and social groups compete for political power and social prestige and to retain and increase their shares of income and wealth.

In such a differentiated and competitive society, people think of themselves and act primarily as separate, self-instigating and self-responsible individuals. In place of the unchanging extended family, with which the individual primarily identifies himself for life in the traditional society, Westerners know only the small transitory nuclear family of husband, wife and children. The individual is born and spends his childhood in one nuclear family, which he leaves upon maturity to found another. Although family loyalty is certainly strong in Western society, the process of maturation in it consists essentially of the development of self-

identity and of personal independence by each successive generation, and of participation in more and more roles and relationships
that have nothing to do with kinship arrangements and obligations.
Even during childhood, and especially after becoming an adult,
the individual participates in many other social institutions beside
the family—all of which divide and compete for his attention and
loyalty.

Thus, the process of social identification is weakened and
diffused by the multiplicity of social institutions and groups in
which the Westerner participates simultaneously and at different
periods during his life. At the same time, his sense of self-identity
is greatly strengthened by the nature of his participation in the
political and economic systems. As a voter, taxpayer and direct
recipient of many social-welfare benefits and services, he functions
vis-à-vis the government as an individual and personally takes the
consequences of violating the law. Similarly, as a worker or man-
ager, professional or civil servant, the Westerner earns his own
income as an individual and is held personally responsible for the
performance of his assigned tasks. Social mobility is high, and the
individual's life career is very significantly influenced by his own
aspirations and efforts. Self-esteem and social recognition depend
largely upon personal achievement and advancement in economic,
political, intellectual and artistic activities rather than upon inherited status.

As in the traditional society, values and ideas both foster and
express the determinative characteristics of Western society. It is
neither possible here nor necessary for our analysis to discuss the
sources and development of Western values and ideas. However, it
is relevant to give some sense of the rich diversity and often contradictory complexity of Western religious and secular thought. To
do so we need only list its origins in Hebraic redemptive activism
and social reformism, Hellenic philosophy and science, Hellenistic
messianism and syncretism, Stoic humanism, and Roman political
and legal universalism; and its even more complex differentiations,
recombinations and further transformations in medieval Christianity, the Renaissance, the Protestant Reformation and Catholic
Counter Reformation, the rise of modern science and the Enlightenment, the American and French Revolutions, nineteenth-century

romanticism, liberalism, popular democracy, nationalism and socialism, and twentieth-century totalitarianism and existentialism. Various as this historical catalogue may be, it does not adequately convey the incessant dynamic tensions within and among these great movements of Western thought: between Platonic and Aristotelian approaches in religion and philosophy, between empirical and theoretical orientations in the natural and social sciences, between expressionism and formalism in literature and art, between authoritarianism and voluntarism in social and political concepts —and between tradition and innovation in all of them. Nor does it indicate the equally complex interactions between Western thought and the commercial, industrial and technological revolutions that have occurred since the eleventh century. Suffice it to say, during the two thousand years of its development, Western society has passed through a series of fundamental social, economic and intellectual transformations largely generated from within, although often accelerated and colored by external encounters, as during the Crusades and the Age of Discovery.

These developments and experiences have made Western society individualistic, differentiated, competitive, ambivalent and restless. As explained in Chapter 2, it is strongly oriented toward the advancement of human knowledge and mastery of the natural environment, toward economic progress and rising living standards, and toward social reform and individual improvement. Its essentially dynamic character during the past thousand years is exemplified by the use of the term "revolution" to denote so many different periods since the eleventh century of rapid and fundamental change in its political, economic and intellectual systems. In contrast, between the Neolithic revolution—which introduced settled agriculture many thousands of years ago—and the encounter with the West, historians have identified no revolutions in the traditional societies of Asia and Africa.

One aspect of the development of Western society that needs particular stress is the crucial integrating role played in modern times by certain concepts and institutions: the national state and the sense of national identity, the rule of law and the impartial administration of justice, the idea of the general or public interest transcending—but not suppressing or superseding—the interests and loyalties of particular social groups and institutions, the obligation of social responsibility and social service constraining the pursuit of individual and group goals, and the concepts of mutual toleration and of distributive justice. As Western society has become increasingly differentiated, complex and competitive, the effective expressions of these values and concepts in law and morality, in attitudes and behavioral norms have been major factors in holding the society together and giving it a sense of direction and purpose despite its disparate elements and the confusing rapidity and novelty of the changes it has experienced. Nonetheless, such a dynamic and heterogeneous society continually runs the risk of social disintegration. These disintegrative tendencies generate in individuals feelings of atomization and *anomie,* seriously weaken the socializing functions of the family, the church and other institutions, and have even paralyzed democratic forms of government. The reaction to such excessive differentiation may be excessive integration, as exemplified by totalitarianism, enforced conformism, and loss of individual freedom and self-responsibility.

The Impact of the West on the Traditional Society

For the traditional societies of Asia and Africa, their encounter with this dynamic and expansionary Western society during the past hundred years has been a unique and decisive experience. Throughout their long histories, Asian and African societies have known many conquerors, and most have absorbed important cultural borrowings from their neighbors. But, particularly in the major societies, such as India and China, the previous conquerors were sooner or later assimilated into the indigenous culture. Elsewhere, the conquerors sometimes replaced the indigenous institutions with their own particular form of traditional society, as happened in parts of Southeast Asia and the Middle East. Cultural borrowings—whether diffused by conquest, migration, trade or Buddhist and Moslem missionary activity—were always from one form of traditional society to another. Because such cultural borrowings were not essentially alien, they were consistent with indigenous institutions, values and attitudes, involving in many cases further developments, refinements or additions to them.

In contrast to this mutual interaction among the particular historical forms of the traditional society in Asia and Africa, their encounter with Western society has been of a fundamentally different character. It has wrenched these societies from the course in which they have been fixed since their Neolithic revolutions several thousand years ago. They have been started upon radically new developments in the ways in which their people live and work together; in the modes in which they perceive themselves, their relationships with one another and the world around them; and in the individual and social goals to which they aspire. The encounter with the West has introduced into the traditional society novel influences that are not simply inconsistent with, but have been actively eroding and disintegrating, its immemorial institutions, attitudes and behavioral norms.

Limitations of space do not permit a detailed account to be given of the impact of the West upon Asia and Africa. However, a brief characterization would be useful of the essential common features of this encounter as they have been expressed in the many varieties of it that have occurred in Asia and Africa since the consolidation of British rule in India a century and a half ago.

A major aspect, fraught with dangerous possibilities for the future, has been the population explosion in parts of Asia and Africa, although as yet it appears to be approaching critical proportions only in Egypt, India, Indonesia and Pakistan. The establishment of Western rule eliminated or greatly reduced the biblical calamities of pestilence, war and famine, and the Malthusian deterrent to human fecundity resulting from bare subsistence incomes, which previously kept population growth under control in the traditional society. Colonial rulers maintained peace, introduced Western practices of public health and preventive and curative medicine, and mitigated the periodic food shortages through increased production, improved transportation and distribution, and emergency imports. In these circumstances, while infant mortality declined and life expectancy increased, birth rates also tended to rise with incomes. Historians have estimated, for example, that the Indian peninsula had a stable population of about 100 million for many centuries prior to the establishment of British rule; in the past 100 years, the population of India and Pakistan has risen more than fivefold.

The population explosion was facilitated by another major aspect of the impact of the West. This was the introduction of the market economy—of production solely for sale—into the economic system of the traditional society which, as we have seen, was predominantly engaged in subsistence activities. The market economy was introduced into Asia and Africa in many different forms, at different times in various parts of these two continents, and has had different consequences in different places. Four widely prevalent developments may be distinguished.

The first was the investment of Western capital in the production of agricultural commodities (sugar, tobacco, coffee, cocoa, cotton, and other fibers, vegetable oils, citrus fruits and bananas, rubber, and other tree and ground crops), in mining (copper and other nonferrous metals, iron ore, gold and diamonds) and, more recently, in petroleum production. These plantations, mines and other extractive activities have generally been large-scale operations, using advanced Western production and managerial techniques, and employing comparatively large numbers of workers on a wage basis, although often supplemented by the provision of food, clothing and housing. The output of these operations was almost wholly for export to the industrialized nations of the West.

A second form of the introduction of the market economy was the spread to the local people of production for export of these and other agricultural products—and even in a few cases of mineral extraction (e.g., locally owned tin operations in Malaya)—either through voluntary imitation or by deliberate encouragement or pressure of the ruling colonial authorities. This spread of commercial agriculture beyond the foreign-owned plantations was particularly important in India and parts of Southeast Asia, West Africa and the Middle East. In other places, of which Indonesia under Dutch rule was probably the leading example, the colonial authorities tried to restrict the spread of export agriculture among the local people, thereby confining Western-type economic activities to an "enclave economy."

A third form was the introduction of Western industrial products and methods of manufacture. During the nineteenth century and the early decades of the twentieth century, the import of low-cost factory-made Western consumer goods—particularly textiles and household commodities—severely restricted, and in many places completely destroyed, the traditional handicraft industries in both town and countryside. More recently, as factories to manufacture these products have been established in Asian and African countries, their output has been superseding imports from the West of manufactured consumer goods, building materials, processed foods and beverages, etc. In a few countries, production costs have been low enough to permit the export to Western countries of textiles, clothing, toys, and other labor-intensive or comparatively simple manufactured goods. The factory system spread within Asian and African countries mainly at the initiative and with the financial, technical and managerial resources of Western investors, but indigenous entrepreneurs also participated in this process, especially in India. The factory system resulted not only in increasing employment for wage labor but also in a growing demand for raw materials, parts and components, containers, operating supplies, and ancillary services. More recently, domestic sources have begun to supply these supporting goods and services in India and in a few of the other large Asian and African countries.

Finally, the establishment of Western forms of governmental administration by the ruling colonial powers also accelerated the spread of the market economy both directly and through stimulation of the three foregoing processes. The financing of a modern administration required substantial money revenues, and the "surplus" in kind of the traditional subsistence economy was neither large enough nor in the appropriate form to meet this need. Accordingly, money taxes of various types were imposed directly upon individuals, and duties were levied upon both imports and exports. The obligation to pay money taxes, where it could be enforced, compelled Asians and Africans to supplement—and sometimes to abandon—their subsistence activities by working part time or wholly for wages and by raising some commercial agricultural products either for export or for sale to the populations of local plantations, mines, towns and cities.

In addition to fostering the spread of the market economy, the introduction of Western forms of government and administration constituted in itself another major aspect of the impact of the West. In many parts of Asia and Africa, the traditional political elites were superseded and, where they were permitted to exercise political authority and administrative responsibilities—as in the Indian native states, and the regions of "indirect rule" in British Africa—their prestige was gradually undermined and their administrative activities were closely supervised by Western advisers, agents and local commissioners. Thus, under both direct and indirect types of Western rule, traditional systems of administration were more or less rapidly eroded.

While governmental activities in the traditional society were always limited largely to waging war, collecting taxes and tribute, constructing and maintaining public works, and dispensing customary justice, the advent of colonial rule witnessed the addition of many new ideas and standards. One important innovation was the introduction of Western legal concepts and codes: the impartial and disinterested administration of justice, the idea of private property, the law of contracts and of corporate entities, administrative law and accountability, and new forms of criminal law. At first, these and other legal innovations existed side by side with traditional customs and procedures; but, as the great legal sociologist Sir Henry Sumner Maine observed in British India a hundred years ago, the new gradually superseded the traditional forms as more and more people found them better suited to the growing market economy and for dealing effectively with the colonial rulers.[3] These developments fostered the legal profession, particularly in India and the Middle East, and the admission of local people to the lower ranks of the expanding administrative service. They also expressed and helped to stimulate the emergence of impersonal relationships based on negotiated agreements and statutory rights and obligations among individuals and between them and administrative authorities, which Maine characterized in a famous phrase as the movement "from status to contract." [4]

[3] Henry Sumner Maine, *Village-Communities in the East and West* (London: John Murray, 1871), pp. 71–73. Based on firsthand knowledge of India in the middle of the last century, this book contains many rewarding insights for those interested today in the transitional process.

[4] Henry Sumner Maine, *Ancient Law* (London: J. Murray, 1861).

The transformation of governmental institutions and legal concepts and practices was soon followed by the introduction of Western political institutions, particularly representative assemblies and political parties. Representative assemblies, especially at the local level, were often instituted by the colonial power as a means of enlisting the support of traditional elites—tribal chiefs, landowners, sheiks and other notables—for the maintenance of European rule. At first, the functions of these representative bodies were largely informational and ceremonial. However, as independence movements took root and spread among the newer elites of lawyers, businessmen and people with secondary and university educations, these bodies became the instruments by which the beginnings of self-government were instituted. Their membership included more and more representatives of the modern elites; their functions were broadened to encompass legislation of various kinds; and regional and national assemblies were superimposed upon the local bodies.

These developments were accelerated by, and in turn stimulated, the founding and growth of political parties—another major innovation in the traditional society. The introduction of political parties involved highly significant changes. A new type of political leader came into being whose authority and prestige did not depend upon inherited status, military power, or customary control over the land and its products. The new politician relied upon his personal ability to generate and manipulate popular opinion as expressed either through the ballot box or by mass demonstrations, strikes and riots. The notion that the people should have a voice in determining their own destiny; the emergence of politics as a profession; and the institutions of representative government were among the most revolutionary innovations in the traditional society generated by the impact of the West.

Equally important changes were initiated in social relationships and institutions. One of the most fundamental took place in the countryside, first in India and then in other parts of southern Asia and the Middle East. It is generally thought that landlordism was an intrinsic and ancient feature of the traditional agrarian society. But, except in China, this was not the case. The various forms of landlordism, which today constitute a major aspect of the agrarian problem in many Asian and Middle Eastern countries, are largely the consequence of changes in rural institutions and relationships that have occurred since the establishment of Western rule or hegemony and the introduction and spread of the money economy. In a sense, the process was analogous to, though not identical with, that which occurred in Europe during the Middle Ages, when the peasants' obligations to manorial lords were commuted from produce and labor services into money payments.

For example, in the early years of British rule in India, the need to ensure a large and reliable money revenue hastened the disintegration of communal village tenures and of the traditional system of collecting taxes in kind. On about 40 per cent of India's arable land, money revenue obligations were assumed by the former local tax collectors—the *zamindars*—in return for which they were recognized as landlords and their legal right to collect rents from the peasants was enforced. In other parts of India, the dissolution of communal tenures enabled the peasants themselves —the *ryots*—to become landowners in return for assuming tax obligations. During the nineteenth and early twentieth centuries, landlordism spread even to those Asian countries not under European rule, notably Iran and the then Turkish provinces in western Asia and North Africa.

Thus, landlordism resulted from the conversion of the many different forms of communal tenures and of the various methods of elite-group sharing of the "surplus" into the equivalent of private property in land. This innovation opened the way for other developments of major importance in rural society: the gradual differentiation of the peasantry into rich, poor and landless; moneylending and the growth of an inextricable burden of debt on more and more peasants; and the erection of new barriers to technological improvement in agriculture, which reinforced the conservatism of traditional peasant attitudes. In turn, these developments were inevitably attended by social conflict in the countryside and growing migration of landless or discontented peasants to the cities.

Because of their contemporary importance, certain aspects of these developments need to be discussed in greater detail. The new landlords and wealthy peasants tended gradually to become moneylenders, purchasers of local crops for transport to the cities and seaports, and often retail distributors of such imported manufactured goods as the peasants could afford to buy. However, although they became increasingly widespread throughout Asia and the Middle East, these rural entrepreneurs were not on the whole a dynamic element in the agrarian economy. Initially, the establishment of a system of distribution, transportation and credit made an important contribution to monetizing the rural economy and raising its productivity. But after this contribution had been made, the new system was capable only of spreading over wider and wider areas and not of further qualitative change. The rural entrepreneurs usually reinvested their profits in further credit extensions to the peasantry, in the acquisition of additional land, in personal consumption and the hoarding of precious metals, rather than in raising agricultural productivity or in initiating manufacturing. Indeed, the nature of the new agrarian system virtually precluded further evolution toward more productive forms. With a growing burden of debt, the peasants had few, if any, resources beyond their own labor for improving the productivity of their lands, and no incentive for improving those that they cultivated as tenants or hired hands of the landlords. With so much of their capital invested in continually renewed and expanded credits to the peasants, the landlords and rural entrepreneurs often could not mobilize sufficient liquid funds to finance agricultural improvements, nor did they generally wish to introduce ideas and techniques that might eventually provide the peasants with the means for overcoming their economic dependence. Thus, throughout Asia and the Middle East, the new rural economy tended to stagnate at the first and least productive stage in the development of commercial agriculture.

The growth of commercial agriculture for export and the spread of the market economy, however, provided opportunities for Asians and Africans in the cities to engage in wholesaling and retailing, moneylending and banking, exporting and importing, the service trades and eventually modern forms of industry. Often these new urban entrepreneurs were members of certain ethnic groups and religious sects that had inferior or disadvantaged status in the traditional society or were migrants from other Asian and African countries. Most of them remained small retailers, but the few who eventually accumulated sufficient capital and experience to establish manufacturing activities were able to make a much greater contribution to economic growth and change than were the rural entrepreneurs. Even so, their willingness and ability to invest in increasingly productive activities, to adopt improved management methods, and to broaden their economic and social outlook were in most cases significantly inhibited by inadequate education and training, insufficient capital, and the persistence of traditional attitudes and loyalties.

Another major aspect of the impact of the West on Asia and Africa was the introduction of secular and modern forms of education. In the more complex traditional societies, formal education was customarily provided by the organized religious sects within Islam, Buddhism and Hinduism, and was oriented toward the perpetuation of the doctrines, codes and practices governing both religious and secular affairs. The simpler traditional societies, such as those of tropical Africa and the mountainous and jungle regions of Southeast Asia, lacked formal schooling of any kind, except for the training of religious elites.

With the establishment of colonial rule, a beginning was made in providing Western-type education, at first largely through the efforts of Catholic and Protestant missionaries, and hence under Christian religious auspices and orientation. However, even in the nineteenth century, small numbers of English- and French-speaking graduates of mission secondary schools were admitted to universities in Western Europe. In the twentieth century, secular primary, secondary and university education was gradually established in Asian countries, under governmental or private auspices; in Africa, it was much slower at all levels and did not get under way until after World War II.

Although even today only a small fraction of the population of most Asian and African countries has had any primary schooling, nevertheless such facilities for modern secular education as have become available either in these countries or abroad have had a profound effect on attitudes, expectations and skills. Not only have vast areas of substantive knowledge and techniques been opened up that were hitherto unknown, but education has also served as a major channel for introducing Western ideas regarding man's mastery over nature, ability to change and improve society, popular sovereignty, national independence and individual freedom. In many instances, these ideas were introduced, and have been continuously reinforced, by Western missionaries, Catholic and Protestant, whose proselytizing efforts in Asia and Africa often long preceded the establishment of European colonial rule. Except in the Philippines, Christianity has nowhere superseded the traditional Asian religions, but in some countries groups of converts have been made, particularly in India and the former French dominions in Southeast Asia. Although in sub-Saharan Africa Christianity met less resistance from the traditional animistic religions, it has nevertheless been spreading slowly, especially in the countryside. In contrast, Islam has had far greater acceptance in Africa south of the Sahara owing in part to the much less alien demands it makes with respect both to belief and to behavior.

Nevertheless, despite its limited acceptance in both Asia and Africa and its uncertain prospects for the future in those regions, Christianity has had a very significant effect on attitudes and ideas. One of its most important influences in Asia and Africa has been its role in the generation of dynamic redemptive expectations and movements, both religious and secular, which will be explained in the next chapter. In addition, the missionaries have disseminated related Christian concepts of the worth of the individual and of the moral obligations of rulers and subjects, as well as contributed substantially to the spread of literacy and modern skills through their educational activities. Moreover, freed by the adoption of Christianity from traditional caste and status limitations, many Asian and African converts and their descendants have been willing and able to engage in modern occupations, such as government service, politics, the legal and teaching professions, business enterprise, and the skilled and service trades.

Naturally, the converts to Christianity have been most strongly affected by Western norms of behavior—Protestants more markedly than Catholics. Owing to its commitment to the classical concept of natural law, Catholicism holds that all people have a natural capacity for faith and for distinguishing between good and evil; therefore, those who lived before Christ or to whom the gospel has not yet been brought can implicitly have elements of religious truth and morality in their beliefs and behavior. Because of this concept of "implicit faith," Catholic missionaries have been inclined to a considerable measure of tolerance of indigenous customs and practices and have generally not required converts to change completely their traditional modes of living and working together. In contrast, Protestants—particularly the evangelical Calvinist sects— have rejected implicit faith, holding that there can be no salvation without Christ. They have in consequence insisted that their Asian and African converts demonstrate their "explicit faith" by "living like Christians"—that is, by adopting as fully as possible Western modes of dress and ways of living and working. These differences help to explain both the wider acceptance of Catholicism in Asia and Africa and the more profound influence of Protestantism on its converts.

The effects of the spread of secular education and of Christian teachings have been strongly reinforced in the mid-twentieth century by the proliferation in Asia and Africa of Western forms of mass media—newspapers and other publications, radio, films and even television. All of these channels for cross-cultural communication opened glimpses of a way of life, conceptions of the individual, and attitudes toward nature and society quite different from those of the traditional Asian and African cultures.

Moreover, these new attitudes tended inevitably to be expressed in typical Western concepts, notably nationalism and socialism, although—as we shall see in the next chapter—their content in Asia and Africa differs significantly from Western expressions of them. Nationalism met the need to conceptualize the strivings for independence, even in tropical Africa and in parts of Southeast Asia where neither the indigenous societies nor the political boundaries negotiated among the ruling colonial powers provided a historical or cultural basis for the formation of reasonably homogeneous nation-states. Marxian and other forms of socialism also found wide acceptance among the new elites in Asian and African countries. During the colonial period, the facets of Marxism that appealed most strongly to Asians and Africans were the plausible and self-absolving explanation it provided of the causes and implications of their colonial status and the inevitable victory and retribution it promised them. In contrast, evolutionary forms of socialism are felt to be more relevant to aspirations in the post-independence period by appearing to provide a way in which the communalism of the traditional society could be adapted to the requirements of economic growth and the achievement of social justice.

These new attitudes and ideas were strengthened by, and in turn helped to foster, the new economic and political institutions and activities introduced by colonial rulers. Together, these two forms of the encounter with the West have injected elements of instability and change into Asian and African societies which they had never known before, and by now these new factors have made it impossible for most of these societies—should they so desire— to return to their own particular variants of the traditional society.

Three Major Aspects of the Encounter

The encounter between the traditional societies of Asia and Africa and Western society over the past hundred years has had three major aspects that play a central role in the current transition through which these countries are passing.

The first is the *failure of the traditional society*. With only four exceptions—Iran, Thailand and Turkey in Asia, and Liberia in Africa—no traditional society or country was able to prevent political conquest by a Western nation at some time during the past century and a half. Even these four exceptions came under strong Western political influence, and were able to preserve their independence largely because of rivalries among the colonial powers or a special relationship with a Western nation, as in the case of Liberia. Nowhere—not even in these four countries—have the traditional forms of economic, social and political organization remained intact under the impact of Western economic and cultural penetration. No matter how notable their past artistic and intellectual achievements, no matter how extensive their former empires, no matter how great the wealth or how unquestioned the power of their ruling elites, none of the traditional Asian and African societies has been able to maintain its cultural integrity. Wherever a traditional economic, political or social institution has been forced *directly* to compete with a Western institution, it has sooner or later suffered a fundamental impairment and has either disappeared or entered upon a process of adaptation and transformation.

This general failure of the traditional society—a unique experience in its long history—has had major psychological consequences for Asians and Africans that are difficult for Westerners to appreciate. Since the late Middle Ages, Western society as a whole has not experienced any remotely comparable external encounter, nor have the military defeats suffered by particular Western nations in recent historical times—e.g., Czarist Russia, France, Germany—produced a comparable sociocultural shock. In consequence, Westerners generally fail to appreciate the debilitating influence of this experience upon the self-confidence and sense of identity of Asians and Africans, whose personalities have been formed since birth in the consciousness that their own historical achievements—regardless of how early or glorious they may have been—have been unable to withstand competition from those of another society with a different culture.

The second aspect—the converse of the first—is the enormous *inertia* [5] *of the traditional society,* that is, the tendency of its institutions, relationships, values and norms to preserve their character and to continue to operate more or less as they always have done. Even in countries such as Egypt, India, Indonesia, Malaya and the Philippines, which have been exposed for the longest period to Western influences, there are still vast portions of the society and culture in which traditional institutions, attitudes and norms have not as yet been in direct competition with Western institutions and activities, or in which the confrontation by external forces has affected only their peripheral or superficial elements. And, throughout most of the Middle East, tropical Africa and parts of Southeast Asia, the encounter with the West began much more recently than in the countries noted above.

Thus, despite the fact that the impact of the West has fundamentally disorganized and partly swept away the attitudinal, institutional and intellectual frameworks of the traditional society, most of its characteristic institutions, attitudes and practices have

[5] By analogy with their meanings in physics, I shall use the term "inertia" to refer to the capacity of the traditional society to resist change, and the term "momentum" to refer to its capacity to continue to operate in its characteristic fashion.

not yet disappeared or been transformed, and they will persist certainly for decades and probably for generations. This continued momentum of the traditional society cannot be explained solely by the fact that large areas of it have not yet been in direct competition with Western institutions and activities. Among other causes are the vast numbers of people who still live wholly or partly within the traditional society, and the long millennia for which it has endured without essential change. But, to a much more important degree, its continued momentum results from its organic and homogeneous character. Its basic social units fit naturally into one another with little, if any, mutual strain and inconsistency. Its attitudes, values and concepts express and reinforce its homogeneity and stability. This is why, despite its failure to prevent conquest by the West and its increasing dislocation and dissolution, the traditional society is still functional, and its inertia constitutes a most powerful, though passive and largely unconscious, resistance to rapid or easy social change.

The third significant aspect—the corollary of the first—is the *alien character of the forces for change.* The new institutions, activities and concepts—the active forces for change in Asia and Africa—are of external origin and development. So, too, are the standards by which individual performance and national progress in every aspect of their current transition are judged. In the economy, the new activities—commercial agriculture, industrial production, commerce and banking—and the new institutions—private and state enterprises and producers and consumers' cooperatives of various kinds—are derived from the West. The same is true in government and politics, in defense, in education and science, and in mass communication.

In the West, the people who carry on these activities and staff these institutions are trained for such work through an increasingly lengthy and complex educational process. More important, they are familiar throughout their lives with a culture that has an inherent capacity to change and develop. In contrast, Asians and Africans are not habituated since birth to the new institutions and activities of their societies. Their mastery of modern skills is inhibited by the unfamiliarity and complexity of modern economic and political activities, and the inadequacy of the available facilities for obtaining the requisite education and training. Nevertheless, the standard by which Asian and African performance is judged in the new activities and institutions is not adjusted to take account of such sociocultural limitations, but is of necessity fixed by the purposes and functions of these activities and institutions.

Just as the failure of the traditional society has affected the self-conceptions and the self-confidence of Asians and Africans, so, too, have their sense of identity and their estimate of their own capabilities been lessened by the fact that their performance of alien activities has inevitably been judged by the standards applied to Westerners, despite the latter's advantages of being born and educated amid the values and norms most conducive to successful performance of these activities. The application of such alien standards is undeniably harsh and unfair, but it is nevertheless a fact of life that cannot be conjured away by the justifiable resentment of Asians and Africans or the well-meaning indulgence of Westerners.

These three major aspects of the impact of the West on Asia and Africa provide the cultural and psychological setting—the *mise en scène*—within which individuals and social groups now and for the foreseeable future will operate in these countries. They condition the development of individual personality; they are major determinants of the roles and interrelationships of new and old social groups; and they lie at the root of the problems of the contemporary transitional societies of Asia and Africa.

The Characteristics of the Transitional Society

In consequence of their encounter with the West, the countries of these regions may be regarded as constituting today particular variants of the transitional society.[6] The term "transitional" avoids the misleading connotations of "developing" noted in Chapter 1; and its implication of process and change without indication of substantive content is also an advantage since the outcome of the transition in Asia and Africa cannot now be foreseen. (Again,

[6] Use of terms based on "transition" was suggested in the pioneering essays of Bert F. Hoselitz written a decade or more ago and collected in his *Sociological Aspects of Economic Growth* (Glencoe, Illinois: The Free Press, 1960).

I am using the Weberian method of describing "ideal" types.)

The beginning of any existing variant of the transitional society may be dated from the establishment of Western colonial rule or, in the four countries never conquered by a European power, from their penetration by strong Western political, economic and intellectual influences. In India and other parts of southern Asia, this process began in the early nineteenth century; in the Middle East and North Africa, in the mid-nineteenth century; and throughout tropical Africa, in the late nineteenth century. However, this method of dating is somewhat arbitrary, since it is generally impossible to point to a specific year or short span of years in which a traditional society can be said to have started its transition. Rather, the movement from the traditional to the transitional society is a process that occurs by degrees. Even today, in all parts of Asia and Africa, a large majority—in some places (e.g., the interior countries of Africa and the mountainous inland regions of southern Asia) virtually all of the population—still lives wholly or predominantly in the traditional society. Their participation in the modern market economy is intermittent or is at most only supplementary to their primary subsistence activities, and their contacts with modern political and governmental institutions are minimal. Conversely, in Japan, the transitional process probably began before continuous and extensive contact with the West was established largely in consequence of indigenous factors, which will be discussed in Chapter 4.

Clearly then, in Asia and Africa, the transitional process has been under way in greater or lesser degree for a considerable period. However, the length of time that the transition has been in process is not necessarily an indication of the extent of the transformation. The transitional process is slow, difficult and uncertain, involving complex changes and interactions within and among all levels and dimensions of the society—psychological, social, economic, political and intellectual. The analogous development in Western society began in the eleventh century in Italy, France and the Low Countries and was not completed until the nineteenth century in these countries and until the twentieth century in Russia and Eastern Europe. Asia and Africa are unlikely to need so long a period, owing to the conscious efforts being made in these regions to accelerate the process, and to the example and help of the West. Even so, countries can stagnate, or make only barely perceptible progress, for considerable periods in the course of the transitional process. Hence, in many—probably in most—Asian and African countries, it will require several generations before the character of the new societies that may emerge from the transitional process will be discernible and before substantial and sustained progress toward that eventual outcome will be assured. The transitional process and its probable outcome are analyzed in Chapter 4; here, our concern is to grasp the essential characteristics of the existing transitional societies.

Among their major characteristics are the differentiation and heterogeneity that distinguish them from the organic, homogeneous traditional society. In the latter, as we have seen, the constituent social units—families, villages, clans, tribes, castes, sects— fitted naturally within one another or, as in the more complex Asian and Middle Eastern empires, were usually able to live side by side in reasonable harmony. Stabilized over the centuries by status and custom, their respective interests and interrelations were largely noncompetitive; indeed, they were usually mutually supporting. Within and among the constituent social units of the tribe or kingdom, conflicts of interest were generally handled by elaborate procedures of adjudication sanctioned by custom and enforced by a potent communal disapproval and, when necessary, by the authoritarian ruler. Open conflicts of interest within these traditional societies were not endemic; they were usually family feuds and the result of efforts by the ruling elites to exact greater taxes and tithes from the peasants, who generally responded by passive resistance and, only when driven to extremities, engaged in sporadic revolts, brigandage and flights from the land. Sustained and open conflicts most often occurred between tribes and between kingdoms, rather than within them, and were fought over land, cattle, slaves, tribute and trade.

In the transitional society, as the result of the encounter with the West, the organic bonds among the traditional social units have been dissolving and their customary procedures and constraints have become more and more inappropriate to the emerging problems. The greatly increased social mobility; the penetration of the largely self-sufficient subsistence economy by market forces; the introduction of new forms of economic activity and of wealth and income; the establishment of pervasive and impersonal governmental institutions and legal systems; the spread of urbanization; the new intellectual concepts and perspectives—these and many other consequences of the encounter with the West have been fostering a conscious sense of their separate identities among the traditional social units and groups that survive in the transitional society. Although the identification of individuals with their families, tribes, sects and castes tends to become less complete and absorbing than it was in the homogeneous traditional society, the need for a sense of identity becomes correspondingly greater in the increasingly differentiated transitional society. Hence, people become more conscious of themselves as members of social units and groups and more aware of cultural and racial differences and of actual or imagined conflicts of interest. Each group increasingly conceives of itself as an independent social unit with interests, loyalties and aspirations of its own that are of paramount priority. Societies composed of such independent and single-minded social units are "particularistic," to use a term of Talcott Parsons.

The particularism of Asian and African countries consists not simply of traditional social units and groups now released from the organic bonds of the traditional society. It has been further complicated by the development of new, modern-type institutions, associations and groups within and alongside the surviving traditional social units. These include private and state enterprises; political parties, factions and cliques; religious congregations and associations; trade-unions, youth organizations; social clubs; professional societies; and many other kinds of modern affiliations, whose forms are generally borrowed from Western society. Also, people become more conscious of themselves as individuals, with interests of their own, which may differ significantly from those of both the traditional and the modern social units and groups in which they participate.

This increasingly differentiated particularism of the transitional society was both fostered and held in check by the policies of the European powers during the period of colonial rule. On the one hand, the artificial political boundaries resulting from the nineteenth-century imperial competition endowed many Asian and African countries with their existing ethnic diversity; and the Europeans' policy of "divide and rule" within their colonies often initiated and always intensified ethnic, religious, political and economic rivalries and suspicions. On the other hand, the European powers were generally able to maintain civil order within their colonies and to insist that conflicts be adjudicated peacefully through traditional procedures or modern legal systems and, toward the end of the period, through parliamentary processes of compromise and consensus. For their part, Asians and Africans were able to restrain their mutual rivalries and to cooperate in the common cause of achieving national independence.

With the passing of colonial rule, however, these constraints have been seriously weakened in several ways. To the new ruling elites, the maintenance of civil order, the achievement of compromise and consensus, and the impartial administration of justice are not paramount considerations, as they were to the former Western rulers, for whom they constituted both major interests and important expressions of Western values. The administrative capacity of the new governments to realize these social values is also substantially less than that of the former colonial rulers. In addition, the current concern within Asian and African countries with the alleged "neoimperialism" and "neocolonialism" of the West—while a significant unifying factor, as we shall see—is by no means so effective a constraint upon particularistic conflicts and suspicions as was the earlier common opposition to colonial rulers.

Moreover, in the post-independence transitional society, the diverse social units, groups, institutions and individuals have not only greater freedom but also greater opportunity to pursue their divergent and conflicting interests. The new accessibility and uses of political power; the new forms of property, investment and division of income; and the new availability and prestige of education provide greater and more frequent opportunities for the expression and promotion of group and individual interests. As these new opportunities arise, the restraining bonds of the organic traditional society are dissolving. In consequence, particularistic interests stand out more clearly in their own right and become more sharply differentiated from one another, and are felt to be more compelling, than during the colonial period. For example, since it provides major opportunities for acquiring power and wealth, the possession of political office is bitterly contested not only by the new parties, factions and cliques but also by the traditional tribes, sects and castes. Or, in contrast to subsistence economic activities, production and consumption through market processes mean that the survival and prosperity of the new commercial farmers, industrial entrepreneurs, wholesalers and retailers—whether organized in private or state enterprises—are dependent either upon their competitive efficiency vis-à-vis one another or upon their competitive ability to obtain monopolistic privileges or government subsidies.

This intensity, or "life-or-death" character, of particularistic interests in the transitional society may be most clearly seen in ethnic struggles. Throughout the countries of Asia and Africa, majority ethnic groups and religious sects try to impose their traditional languages and cultures upon the linguistic and religious minorities within their rather arbitrary national boundaries, while the minorities struggle even more fanatically to preserve their linguistic and cultural autonomy, and often to obtain political independence as well. In India, the avowedly nonsectarian and noncommunalist Congress party has had to make important political concessions to linguistic particularism and religious sectarianism. Despite the good intentions of the government, discrimination against lower-caste Hindus continues, and the laws against "untouchability" have proved extremely difficult to enforce in the face of the age-old debasement of a sixth of India's vast population. These Indian ethnic conflicts express both traditional socioreligious differences and modern disagreements over national economic policies and the distribution of their benefits. They have had greater scope to express themselves in the post-independence period and have done so with greater intensity.

In tropical Africa, ethnic conflicts are even more pronounced because of the great linguistic diversity of the region, the absence in recent centuries of large enduring territorial kingdoms and empires, and the arbitrary character of many national boundaries. The recurrent threats to political unity and effective central government in Nigeria reflect the precarious balance between the power of particularistic ethnic loyalties, on the one hand, and the desire to preserve the large national entity as an essential precondition for fostering economic growth and playing a significant role in world and African affairs, on the other hand.

Thus, at all levels and in all dimensions of the transitional society, there has been differentiation and fragmentation into a multitude of particular groups and individuals, some traditional and some modern, all with greater freedom to pursue conflicting interests and goals which each feels are more compelling than in the traditional society. This "life-or-death" particularism characteristic of the transitional society has three closely related consequences of major significance for the problems and prospects of Asian and African countries.

First, particularism is the principal factor inhibiting the development of the new sense of national identity needed to replace the traditional sense of cultural identity shattered by the impact of the West. Westerners are so accustomed to characterizing these countries as highly nationalistic that we often fail to make some important distinctions regarding the nature and extent of their nationalism. In their external relationships, particularly with the West but also with one another, these countries are unquestionably nationalistic; as we shall see, this external nationalism plays an essential role in the search for a new identity. However, it is not yet based upon a widespread and strong national consciousness in their *internal* activities and relationships. For example, in their dealings with one another, the inhabitants of India generally feel that they are Hindus, Moslems or Sikhs; Maharashtrans, Punjabis or Madrasis; Brahmans, Sudras or Harijans, rather than Indians. Similarly, in their relations with their fellow citizens, Africans are Yorubas, Ibos, Hausas, Ashantis, Bakongos, Kikuyus and Mugandas, and not Nigerians, Ghanaians, Congolese, Kenyans and Ugandans. Such particularistic, or parochial, identifications are much deeper and more compelling than the limited and occasional sense of nationality. In the ethnically less heterogeneous countries of the Middle East and Southeast Asia, there is a somewhat stronger sense of national identity in domestic affairs; nonetheless, family, village, tribe, guild, sect, and partisan and factional identifications and loyalties still continue to be powerful.

The second consequence of Asian and African particularism is the absence of a consensus regarding national objectives, and of a concept of the national interest or common good as transcending particular interests and orienting them toward national goals. The conventional Western picture of an Asian or African country is that of a nation single-mindedly devoted to achieving "national development"—rising productivity, higher living standards, social reforms, greater political effectiveness, etc.—and held back only by shortages of the necessary financial resources and technical and administrative skills. Yet, when examined from within, no Asian or African country conforms to this picture—indeed, if any did, its problem of "development" would be only technical and hence readily solved. However, this consequence of particularism, owing to its importance for the problems and prospects of Asia and Africa, will receive fuller treatment in Chapter 5.

Of course, there are—and will increasingly be—dedicated members of the new elites in most countries with an overriding sense of national interest and purpose. But, even in the few countries where they are politically predominant, they have been able to make only modest headway against the strong crosscurrents of particularistic interests and parochial loyalties. In the majority of Asian and African countries, even the new elites are unable or unwilling to forgo the easy opportunities to advance their own group and individual interests, with little regard for national consequences. Only when particularistic and national interests coincide or support one another—as does happen with some frequency—is the latter pursued with the same fervor as the former. South Vietnam in Asia and the Congo in Africa are the most striking examples in their respective regions of countries whose ruling elites and major ethnic groups have been unable to subordinate their particularistic interests to the common good even for the sake of national survival. In one form or another, Algeria, Burma, Ceylon, Indonesia, Iraq, Lebanon, Morocco, Nigeria, the Sudan and other countries have been confronted in recent years with internal dissensions whose consequences might have been similarly tragic—and could well be in the future.

This lack of consensus regarding national objectives and the weak sense of national interest account in part for the failure of parliamentary regimes in all but a few countries. Again, discussion of the political problems and prospects of Asian and African countries is deferred until Chapter 5. Here, this and other political consequences of the particularism of the transitional society may simply be noted.

The forms of parliamentary democracy and representative government introduced into these societies during the period of colonial rule operated essentially as they do in the West only so long as they were supervised and protected by European rulers. Since independence, they have been overwhelmed by the divisiveness of parties, factions and personal cliques and by the refusal of ethnic groups and sects to compromise their differences. Further, those in possession of office have been unwilling to risk an election, lest an opposition group be voted in, which, in its turn, would balk at holding subsequent elections. Freely elected parliamentary regimes with active opposition parties have continuously survived and been able to govern with reasonable effectiveness only in a handful of countries and then because of special circumstances.

Closely related to this early failure of Western-type democratic institutions in all but a few Asian and African countries is the third major consequence of the particularism of the transitional society —authoritarianism. This is the means by which Asian and African countries have been able to hold themselves together as political entities and in some cases to adopt and pursue a reasonably consistent set of national objectives and policies. This minimum degree of national consistency and sense of direction has been maintained by the persistence of, or the reversion to, the authoritarianism of the traditional society, although it generally takes new political forms.

The traditional society was authoritarian in nature. Within each of its constituent units, and within the hierarchy of these units as a whole, status determined who had power, and custom defined the purpose, norms and limits for the exercise of power. Emperors and kings were often believed to be divine, and disobedience to them and to lesser authorities was shunned as a transgression of the divine order of the universe, which was generally regarded as identical with the natural and social orders. When rulers flagrantly transgressed the bounds of custom or when precedents provided no guide for dealing with novel problems, there were mechanisms to formulate and express a consensus of those immediately below the ruler at each social level—e.g., the king's ministers or council in ethnic kingdoms and multi-ethnic empires, the council of clan or village elders in tribal societies, and in some cases the village community itself, as in parts of India before the British conquest. When traditional kings and tribal chiefs lost the confidence of their subjects, they were replaced through palace revolutions and changes of dynasty. Also, at all social levels, powerful religious sanctions operated psychologically to bring about the self-destruction, through enervation or excess, of an authority whose subjects had conscientiously withdrawn their confidence and support because he had transgressed custom and lost "the mandate of heaven."

These mechanisms of consensus and condemnation are sometimes considered a form of organic democracy, and hence as constituting a basis for a modern democratic political system. This view, however, is sentimental and erroneous. These traditional mechanisms lacked any concept of popular sovereignty, and they did not express or foster secular ideas concerning the rights and obligations of the individual. Both their sources and their sanctions were transcendental and religious.

In the transitional society, traditional forms of authority persist within the old social units that have continued relatively intact. In addition, the concepts, attitudes and relationships that characterize traditional authoritarianism have frequently been transferred to the new social groups and institutions. The new national governments, political parties, trade-unions, private and state enterprises and cooperatives, educational institutions, etc.—all tend in some degree to embody attitudes toward authorities, habits of obedience, and quasi-religious sanctions operating on both leaders and subjects which are adapted from those of the traditional society. Although the titles of rulers and leaders may be Western, the powers they exercise, the obedience they are accorded, and the sanctions that reinforce and circumscribe their power are still influenced by the attitudes and practices of the traditional society.

In this connection, a word should be said about "charismatic leaders." The term "charisma," first used by Max Weber in a rather precise sense, has become very fashionable during the past fifteen years and is applied in popular usage to any authoritarian political leader with a colorful personality. However, Weber distinguished among traditional, charismatic and rationalized types of authority, reserving the term "charismatic" for leaders who obtained political power without the legitimacy either of traditional inherited status or of modern constitutional procedures. Thus, to Weber, the charismatic leader is an innovator, whose possession and exercise of political power break the accustomed norms of the society and who thereby could and sometimes does open the way for social change.

However imprecise the term has become in popular usage, its significance has been partly retained in the focus on the element of personality and of affect involved in charisma. Lacking either traditional status or constitutional sanction, Weber explained, the charismatic leader legitimizes his power through his ability to generate the people's belief—and usually his own as well—that he possesses capabilities far transcending those of ordinary men by virtue of his personality or his office, or both. In primitive and traditional societies, such powers are always perceived as magical and religious, and this aura of the sacred—and therefore omnipotent—persists to considerable degree even in more secularized transitional societies. Although he now holds the modern office of president, prime minister or party chairman—rather than the traditional office of king, chief or priest—the charismatic leader in Asian and African countries is still widely believed to wield superhuman power over his domestic and foreign opponents, over the obstacles that impede his country's progress toward its objectives, and even over the forces of nature. In all societies, such faith in the leader's charisma expresses and makes bearable deeply rooted fears, anxieties and needs, and therefore always takes the form of a strongly emotional relationship between him and his followers.

The charismatic element appears in varying degree in the types of leaders prevalent in Asian and African countries in the post-independence period. The most dramatically conspicuous type is the leader whose charisma contains pronounced tendencies toward megalomania and paranoia. These powerful psychological processes—which are his own means for coping with his personal anxieties and needs—serve also to infuse him with the psychic energy and determination required to win and hold power, and at the same time enable him to evoke the necessary affective responses in his followers. Another, less flamboyant type of leader —more numerous in Asia and Africa today—is the military dictator usually projected into power by army discontent with the ineptitude or paralysis of quasi-parliamentary regimes. Charismatic qualities are less pronounced among the leaders of these military regimes owing, no doubt, to the more rationalized character of military organizations and training. But, where charismatic characteristics are evident, they are also based upon personal psychological processes, frequently reinforced by overt commitment to the beliefs and practices of the traditional religion.

Regardless of whether authoritarian regimes are civilian or military or are headed by leaders with more or less charismatic personalities, the tenure of office of any particular faction or clique at the national level—and even of individual leaders at subnational levels—is usually precarious owing to particularistic and personal rivalries and conflicts. This precariousness motivates in part their more or less conscious efforts to invest themselves with the sanctity of traditional rulers and thereby to obtain greater stability of tenure through the awe and devotion of their subjects.

Finally, the particularism of the transitional society expresses itself not only in the conflicting interests of social groups and individuals and the absence of an adequate sense of national identity and purpose but also in deep inconsistencies among the values, norms and standards by which the society operates. In government, in the economy, and in the relations between the individual and the new and old social groups and institutions in which he participates, tradition confronts innovation in the purposes and goals that motivate action, in the norms by which these activities are carried on, and in the standards by which performance is judged.

In all societies, there are inconsistencies among values, norms and standards, and the realization of some in varying degrees precludes that of others. In different ways, both the static traditional society and the dynamic Western society have been able to deal with this "existential" problem more or less effectively. The traditional society excludes or strongly subordinates values and aspirations which might conflict with those that support its stability and homogeneity. Pluralistic Western society operates by continuous efforts to achieve compromises and temporary accommodations among competing values and aspirations, although this process breaks down in periods of revolution or of other severe social stresses.

Neither method is effective in the transitional society. Innovating values and norms can no longer be excluded or subordinated, as in the traditional society. The inconsistencies between innovating and traditional values are too large and conspicuous, and the mechanisms of reconciliation are too new and weak for Western-type pluralistic compromises and consensus to be achieved easily or frequently. Thus, the particularistic transitional society is riven by much deeper and more intractable conflicts of values, norms and standards than is Western society. This problem lies at the root of the difficulties of the transitional process—the subject of the next chapter.

CHAPTER FOUR

The Nature and Outcome
of the Transitional Process
in Asia and Africa

There has long been a tendency in the West, and particularly in the United States, to regard the traditional society as dead and to assume that Western institutions and values have already extensively replaced, and will in the future even more rapidly supersede, those of the traditional society. Westerners anticipate that the outcome will be the spread of their own distinctive type of society to all parts of the planet. In short, the transformation that Asian and African countries are now undergoing is regarded as a rapid and inevitable movement from traditional to Western society. These views are among the major premises, explicit or implicit, of the foreign-aid policies of the Western countries. They also underlie the theoretical formulations and the practical prescriptions of many development experts. To assess the validity of this way of thinking, we need to look more closely into the nature and probable outcome of the transitional process through which Asia and Africa are now passing.

A Model of the Transitional Process

The discussion of the particularism of the transitional society and its consequences in the preceding chapter was too general to enable us to appreciate the complexities and interrelationships of the psychological and social processes involved. For that purpose, it would be helpful to have a simplified model of the transitional process that would reveal its key elements and their interactions. However, all models in the social sciences—even where the terms of the model can be quantified—are at best only conceptual devices that enable us to isolate certain elements or factors from the complexities of objective reality so that their interactions and implications can be more readily perceived and analyzed. Thus, social-science models inevitably oversimplify the phenomena they purport to explain, and there is also a related tendency—against which model builders are not always sufficiently on guard—to sacrifice their relevance to reality to their logical elegance.

With these reservations in mind, this chapter presents a model of the transitional process that attempts to take its multidimensional character into account. The model endeavors to describe simultaneously several inextricably interrelated processes in the transitional society: the formation of individual personality and sense of self-identity; the transmission and learning of social roles and culturally determined patterns of feeling, seeing, believing, acting and aspiring; the methods of handling the anxieties and conflicts generated by the inconsistencies within and among these processes; the interactions among the disintegrative and the integrative forces operating in the transitional society; and the ways in which they inhibit and stimulate the emergence of a new sense of cultural and national identity. Accordingly, the model begins with the individual in the transitional society and then deals with the social process as a whole, focusing upon the ways in which social change occurs, its most significant manifestations, and the factors that influence it.

Our starting point is the process of socialization, which constitutes the essential link between the individual and society. From the viewpoint of society, it involves the internalization within the individual of the distinctive concepts, values and norms comprising the culture. First analyzed at the end of the nineteenth century by the great French sociologist Émile Durkheim and more fully explored in recent decades, this process of internalization of values and norms constitutes the mechanism by which the characteristic institutions and relationships of a society are preserved and transmitted from one generation to the next, and the child learns how to feel, believe and act as a member of his society. From the viewpoint of the individual, internalization is part of the psychological process of personality formation. While there is much disagreement among psychologists and sociologists regarding the specific mechanisms involved in personality formation, the model employs in greatly simplified form the analysis first formulated by Sigmund Freud to explain the development in the child of the ego and superego and later extended and incorporated into social theory by Talcott Parsons.[1] Finally, the model adopts and extends the conceptual framework developed by Benjamin Nelson for dealing with the problems of alienation, *anomie* and crises of identity in contemporary Western society.[2]

Before considering Nelson's conceptual framework, the process may be briefly described by which each society presents to the child what Nelson calls "paradigmatic figures," who provide the model, or template, on whom the child can pattern his own feelings and actions, his conception of the roles he is to play as an adult, and his expectations of future status or achievement. For a boy, the main paradigmatic figure is the dominant male in his nuclear family group—the father in Western society but, in some primitive and traditional societies, the maternal uncle or another adult male relative if the nuclear family is part of a matrilinear or matrilocal variety of the larger extended family. In the Freud-Parsons analysis, it is the dominant male who constitutes the paradigmatic figure most important for the socialization process. By the example of his own activities and by precept, the father points beyond the inward-oriented nurturing and protecting relationship of mother and child to the outward-oriented and differentiated roles which the child must learn to play in the wider society as he passes through adolescence and into adulthood.

In the traditional society, behind and reinforcing the male head of the family are other paradigmatic figures—the village elders, the clan and tribal chiefs, the leaders of castes and sects—whose roles

---

[1] See particularly the papers collected in Talcott Parsons, *Social Structure and Personality* (New York: The Free Press, a division of Macmillan Company, 1964), pp. 17–111 and additional references on p. 79, fn. 2.

[2] Benjamin Nelson, "Actors, Directors, Roles, Cues, Meanings, Identities," *The Psychoanalytic Review,* V. 51, no. 1, Spring 1964; pp. 135–160.

are perceived as more remote but wholly consistent versions of that of the father or maternal uncle. By modeling himself upon these similar figures, and, through their mediation, identifying his own interests and aspirations with those of the organic social units in which he participates, the boy in the traditional society acquires during childhood and adolescence a sense of his own identity as an integral member of his particular family, clan, caste, sect and tribe.

In contemporary Western society, this process has been modified by the greatly increased importance of individualization, which is in continuous dynamic tension with social identification. The main paradigmatic figure in Western society is the father, although, if he is absent or ineffective, his role may be played by another adult male significant to the boy (e.g., an older brother, uncle, teacher or youth leader). While he is learning to pattern his feelings, attitudes and behavior upon those of the paradigmatic figure, and thereby identifying with him, the boy in contemporary Western society is also striving to become an individual in his own right. Indeed, as we have seen, the values and institutions of Western society compel him to behave as a separate, self-instigating and self-responsible individual, whether he wishes to or not. In these circumstances, the process of personality formation and maturation in contemporary Western society is ambivalent. On the one hand, the boy identifies with a paradigmatic figure and through him with the diverse social units in which they both participate. On the other hand, particularly during adolescence, the boy is also asserting himself against and differentiating himself from this figure. The achievement of a sense of self-identity and self-confidence is a resultant of these two intertwined yet conflicting processes, which the existentialist theologian Paul Tillich distinguished as "the courage to be as oneself" and "the courage to be as a part" of the many different and competing social groups and institutions in which the individual participates.

The development of an adequate sense of identity and purpose is inherently more difficult in a differentiated dynamic society, such as that of the West, than in the static and homogeneous traditional society. Indeed, in contemporary Western society, it has become more difficult and uncertain than ever before, a development that has given rise to the problems of alienation, *anomie* and crises of identity. These phenomena in Western society are paralleled in the transitional society by analogous processes of social disintegration and resulting inadequate individual sense of identity.

As we have seen in the preceding chapter, the differentiated particularism of the transitional society contrasts sharply with the homogeneity of the traditional society. This difference has important implications for the processes by which maturing individuals achieve a sense of identity and learn their roles in social groups and institutions. Participating as he does in a growing number of contrasting and often conflicting old and new social units—on the one hand, the traditional extended family, village, tribe, caste and sect; and, on the other hand, the modern nuclear family, productive enterprise, trade-union, political party, social club and atomized urban mass—the individual in the transitional society tends to have more diffuse identifications with them than with the organic social institutions of the traditional society. But, precisely because the heterogeneous groups and institutions of the transitional society compete for his loyalty and cannot provide him with the all-enveloping, mutually consistent, and strongly supportive social identifications of the organic traditional society, they are all the more important in the formation of such sense of self-identity as he can develop. His need for a sense of identity impels him to become more conscious of his social affiliations—diffuse and competing as they may be—and to express them more fervently than in the traditional society.[3] At the same time, he relates more and more as an individual to the new political and economic institutions, which deal directly with him as a taxpayer, worker and consumer, and this further diffuses and confuses his sense of social identification.

So far, the process of personality formation and social identification in the transitional society closely parallels that in Western society. But, a complication of major importance in the transitional society must now be taken into account. This is the fact that, in the transitional society, the paradigmatic figures on which the maturing individual must model himself, and the social roles and institutions with which he must identify, are often radically in-

---

[3] This is the psychological aspect of the "life-or-death" intensity of the particularism of the transitional society described in the preceding chapter.

consistent. True, inconsistencies exist in the highly differentiated Western society, and are in part responsible for its problems of alienation, *anomie* and identity. But in Western society, however conflicted models and roles may be, they are nevertheless still parts of a single culture, share a common history, and have developed organically within the same social system. This is not the case in the transitional society, which contains, in effect, two sets of paradigms, roles, values and standards. One set is indigenous, static and familiar; the other set is alien, dynamic and strange.

We can now turn to Nelson's conceptual framework in order to see more clearly the operation and significance of this radical dichotomy characteristic of the transitional society and its culture. Nelson distinguishes four aspects or systems in the cultures of all types of societies.[4] First, cultures are infused with a "dramatic design" by which they invest the apparent meaninglessness of physical and social existence with a sense of "aim, purpose and historical form." Second, cultures contain a "defensive system comprising an array of beliefs and attitudes which help to defend against . . . the anxieties, fears and aggressions generated in the lives of individuals and societies. . . ." Third, every culture is permeated by a "directive system," which instructs people how to perceive, feel, think and perform in desired ways. Fourth, a culture can also be regarded as a "symbol economy," that is, "all groups aspiring to pre-eminence of authority, power, influence, prestige necessarily contest with one another for control" of the symbolic cultural representations by means of which the values and objectives of the society are expressed and recognized.[5]

Societies communicate to their members their own particular sense of meaning, their prescribed defensive mechanisms, and their chosen directives regarding attitudes and actions through elites of various kinds who compete in, control and manipulate the symbol

[4] All quoted passages are from Nelson, cited.

[5] In other words, each society has its own particular forms of power, wealth, prestige, fame and approbation which it accords to groups and individuals by virtue of their status or achievements. Such rewards obtained by birth or effort are symbols in the sense that they represent an implicit or explicit social convention to recognize them as valuable and to accord obedience and respect to their possessors. Groups and individuals compete among themselves for these symbolic distinctions, since the demand for them must, by their nature, exceed the supply. Hence, by analogy, Nelson designates this system a "symbol economy."

economy of the society. Nelson refers to these elites as "officers or agents of induction" and to their function as "mediating" between the symbols of the culture and the individuals and groups that comprise the society. This function is in large part carried on by means of "cues" or "directives," which Nelson groups into six categories.

Nelson's first set consists of the cues to *perception,* that is, the basic categories of thought by which, in each culture, people perceive one another, their social roles and the institutions in which they participate, and even their physical environment. As Nelson points out, "hardly an hour passes in the socialization process without the child being told what and how to see, hear, smell, touch and construe." The second set—the cues relating to *feeling* —inform or direct people about how they are to feel with respect to the persons, objects, institutions, situations and events they encounter in the course of their lives. Such feelings vary from one culture to another. Third, Nelson identifies a set of cues prescribing the particular ideas, possibilities, explanations and aspirations in which people must affirm or deny their *belief.* The fourth set contains the cues indicating the persons, symbols, acts and events at which people are directed to *marvel* or wonder, or which they are to deem sacred and to hold in awe. They differ from the *belief* cues in that they have little or no intellectual content and are characterized instead by "a passionate non-reflective commitment . . . and lose their force and attraction if they are excessively scrutinized." These cues play a major part in charisma.

Nelson's fifth set is the *action* cues, that is, the directives to actions that people are expected to perform or to avoid in their relationships with one another and in the social roles appropriate to their status or accomplishments. These acts comprise the full range of individual and social activities and prohibitions, for which each society establishes its own "positive and negative incentives mediated by the officers of induction with varying resorts to power and persuasion." The sixth and last cues are those of *emulation,* which point to and identify the paradigmatic figures in each society whose attitudes and behavior people are directed to imitate. Nelson explains that "wherever there is mediation of any cue, the person who is engaged in the act of mediation is either presenting himself or someone else as a model for imitation. It is this paradigmatic element in all interpersonal situations which proves to be so critical."

It is apparent that, while Nelson's six sets of cues may be conceptually distinguished, in real-life situations they are often only different aspects of a multifaceted psychological and social process. More important, it is apparent that in all societies, even in the most homogeneous—i.e., primitive and traditional societies—there are bound to be some inconsistencies within and among the different cue sets. In addition, in the more heterogeneous and dynamic societies—i.e., transitional society, Western society—there is some degree of instability in the cue sets, since they change over time, as well as some degree of incongruity between them and people's sense of reality and of the "fitness of things," as this sense is biologically and culturally derived in each society. Nelson points out that there is a continuum or scale—ranging from perfect consistency, stability and congruence at one end, to complete inconsistency, instability and incongruence at the other end—along which societies can be ranged, although none can ever be at either extreme. Societies which tend toward the inconsistent-unstable-incongruous end of the scale are bound to suffer from crises of identity, excessively conflicted motivations and attitudes within individuals and groups, ambivalent behavior, apathy and depersonalization.

Nelson's conceptual framework helps us to grasp the nature and significance of the dichotomy characteristic of the transitional societies of Asia and Africa. By definition, all must be ranged toward the inconsistent-unstable-incongruous end of Nelson's scale, although many are moving slowly in the other direction. The mediatory elites in these particularistic societies are themselves divided into traditional and modern groups, which compete with one another. The cues they communicate to others in the society and the paradigms they set for them express values, interests, norms and standards that are equally ambiguous and inconsistent. Many of these symbols are alien in origin, and are often communicated directly from Western society and not through the indigenous traditional or modern elites. Moreover, the ability of people in these transitional societies to comprehend and respond to cues and paradigms is often limited by cultural discontinuities, language barriers, educational inadequacies, and deficiencies of health and nutrition.

Ambiguity and Conflicted Personality in the Transitional Society

At this point in the presentation of the model, it would be useful to explore more fully the significance of the inconsistent, unstable and incongruous characteristics of the transitional society for the process of personality formation and the social performance of individuals. Before doing so, however, a point emphasized in the preceding chapter should be reiterated. It is that there are large numbers of people in Asian and African countries—indeed, well over half in most of them—whose personalities are still formed and whose adulthood continues to be lived more or less completely within the social structure and culture of the traditional society. And, even for many who are beginning to participate in modern sectors and activities, the momentum of the traditional society still carries them along without significant psychological strain or conflict. Nonetheless, each year, more and more Asians and Africans experience, in one way or another, the psychological effects of participating simultaneously in competing old and new social groups and institutions, of trying to realize contradictory traditional and modern values, and of regulating their behavior by disparate and often conflicting norms and standards.

Those most severely affected by conflicting cues, paradigms and mediating authorities are the members of the new elite groups who are themselves the main agents of the modernizing influences. They include political leaders and government administrators, entrepreneurs and managers of the modern types of private and state enterprises, and professionals and intellectuals. For this reason, the most useful illustration of the effects of conflicting models and cues in the transitional society would be a summary description of the process of personality formation and role determination of these modernizing elites in Asia and Africa.[6]

[6] For a specific and much more detailed example, see Theodore Geiger and Winifred Armstrong, *The Development of African Private Enterprise* (Washington: National Planning Association, 1964), especially Chapter II and Appendices I and II.

On the one hand, most of them have been born and have spent their childhood in some form of the traditional extended family, even though they may have been brought up in towns or cities rather than in the countryside. They have, therefore, had some experience during their formative years of the affective personalized relationships characteristic of the institutions of the traditional society, and throughout their lives they are reluctant to relinquish the emotional and economic support derived from the psychological warmth and security provided by the extended family and its broader kinship and lineage affiliations. They are habituated to recognizing without question the authority and example of the traditional head of the household (father, maternal uncle, older brother or cousin) and of the other elders of the village, tribe, caste or sect with which their family is traditionally affiliated. As adults, they continue to acknowledge, or to feel uncomfortable in denying, the traditional family obligations of mutual sharing of output or income, of defending and advancing relatives' interests, and of according these claims a priority that overrides even their own self-interest. They are expected to provide jobs for relatives regardless of their employment qualifications and to divert often substantial portions of their own earnings or capital—and sometimes of their employer's or the government's property—to help parents, brothers, uncles, cousins and other relatives to live better, to start a business, to send their children to school, to pay their taxes and fines, and in other ways to share freely with anyone who falls within the degrees of kinship recognized by custom.

On the other hand, upon reaching adulthood, most members of the new elites found small nuclear families of their own, although not always physically separated from the traditional extended-family household. They support their nuclear families through various types of modern occupations carried on in the impersonal, rationalized institutions of the government, the economy, the educational system, the mass media, etc. Therein, they acquire a new set of cues and paradigms mediated in new ways by new agents of induction. Inevitably, they come to feel that the achievement of modern living standards and upward social mobility for themselves, their wives and their children is a primary obligation. Their ability to fulfill it depends in great measure upon their personal performance in their modern-type occupations and upon meeting, at least minimally, the responsibility of advancing the interests of the modern public or private institutions in which they work. The authorities they recognize, and whose examples they seek to emulate, have either been Westerners, particularly in the pre-independence period, or the indigenous political leaders, administrators and managers who now direct the new impersonal institutions of the society.

Similar inconsistencies characterize the value systems of these societies. A pervasive example in Asia and Africa is the competition between pecuniary and nonpecuniary values, which significantly inhibits the economic growth of these countries. On the one hand, new economic activities are pursued both as ends in themselves—i.e., work itself is a good—and as the means for maximizing incomes and productive investment to achieve improved material living standards, greater economic security, and more prestige and power. On the other hand, the traditional values of leisure (i.e., waking time not spent in work), of prestige derived from conspicuous consumption and other nonproductive uses of economic resources (e.g., expenditures on weddings and funerals, religious endowments, ceremonial and ritual gift giving), and of avoidance of physical labor continue to be sought as ends in themselves even by people engaged in the most modern forms of economic activity. Traditional educational and religious goals—such as preservation of venerable theologies and ethical-legal systems, contemplation, transcendence of individuality and of physical reality—compete with the new desire to achieve mastery over nature, to reconstruct society, and to realize individual potentialities. And, throughout the particularistic transitional society, the traditional ideal of the exclusive tribal or caste brotherhood continues to oppose the new ideal of universal equality expressed in the imported Western religious and political concepts.[7]

These examples are perhaps sufficient to indicate the depth and tenacity of the conflicting cues, paradigms and roles to which the new elites—as well as others—in Asia and Africa are exposed in the course of their life experiences. The next question is how individuals handle these conflicts. In many cases, they do not. Al-

[7] See Benjamin Nelson, *The Idea of Usury: From Tribal Brotherhood to Universal Otherhood* (Princeton: Princeton University Press, 1949).

though very few studies have as yet been made of psychiatric disorders and their incidence in Asian and African countries, the little evidence at hand indicates a high percentage of the particular kinds of psychiatric illnesses that could be expected in such circumstances: psychosomatic headaches and gastrointestinal symptoms, neuroses of the anxiety and depressive types, and schizophrenic psychoses. However, most people in the transitional society cope with these ambiguities and conflicts by trying to compartmentalize their lives and, where—as is often the case—they fail to do so, by accepting and living with contradiction and incongruity in their own feelings, beliefs and actions. Either way, a psychic effort is required, and a personal and social price is paid.

Westerners often complain of what they consider to be irrational, inconsistent or irresponsible attitudes and behavior on the part of Asians and Africans, and tend to attribute the persistence of such phenomena to a perverse unwillingness to think or act "rationally." Westerners themselves often exhibit similar tendencies; and in any case, such a view utterly fails to recognize either the nature of behavior of this kind or the strength of its resistance to conscious control. Such conduct is often in reality a defense mechanism for coping with the deep personality conflicts resulting from the inconsistency, instability and incongruity of the directive system of the transitional culture. Asian cabinet ministers who consult astrologers before making important decisions; African presidents and prime ministers who use witchcraft to protect themselves and defeat their rivals; high government officials and managing directors of private companies who propitiate local spirits and deities when modern bridges, power plants and factories are dedicated—these and many similar phenomena may be labeled meaningless superstitions by Westerners but, more significantly, they are ways of relieving the anxieties and accepting the ambiguities of living simultaneously in two worlds.

Colorful as they are, these mechanisms have comparatively less importance in the transitional society than do other manifestations of its ambiguities and conflicting values and cues. Of much greater significance are their effects on the role performances of members of the new elites and, hence, on the capacity of the new political and economic institutions to function with reasonable efficiency. The most important of these effects are: a diffuse sense of personal and social identity; inadequate self-confidence and willingness to exercise initiative and judgment; impulsive—and often irresistible—drives for immediate gratifications with insufficient regard for longer-term personal consequences and social implications; lack of sustained effort in achieving realistic individual and social goals; diversion of attention and energy to the pursuit of peripheral or irrelevant objectives; and susceptibility to emotional appeals and to domination by authoritarian figures. Some or all of these effects can be discerned in a majority of the elites in Asian and African countries today.

In sum, the elite-group member in the transitional society is impelled to model himself upon both traditional and modern paradigmatic figures, whose different patterns of feelings, attitudes and actions are largely conflicting. He continues to participate in affective personalized traditional social groups while becoming increasingly involved in the rationalized, impersonal and atomizing institutions of modern political and economic systems. His social identifications tend to be diffused by the growing number and diversity of the social groups and institutions, old and new, in which he participates. He is confronted with a multiplicity of conflicting values and inconsistent cues regarding the things he must perceive, feel, believe and do. He senses that the indigenous set of institutions, roles, values and behavioral norms has been failing to maintain its integrity under the impact of the alien set which, however, embodies a standard of performance requiring capabilities and a degree of plasticity that are extremely difficult for him to develop, since he has not been born and adequately educated in them.

The difficulty in these circumstances of developing a sufficiently integrated personality and sustained life orientation saps both the willingness and the ability to act consistently over long enough periods to achieve realistic personal ambitions, to carry on efficiently the functions implicit in new social roles and tasks, and to achieve the aspirations that the elite groups seek for their countries. And, the more the individual resolves these conflicts in favor of modern values and behavior, the less he may be able to communicate with, and evoke the active support of, the great mass of the people, who still live wholly or substantially within the institutions and norms of the traditional society.[8]

These personality problems express and reinforce the adverse effects of other characteristics of the transitional society: its particularistic conflicts; its inadequate supply of the technical skills, cultural conditioning and practical experience necessary to attain effective standards of performance in modern economic and political activities; and the immense passive resistance of the continuing institutions and behavioral norms of the traditional society. Thus, Asian and African countries approach the gigantic task of modernization with severe handicaps in all dimensions of their societies, particularly in the process of personality formation and socialization, in the defensive and directive systems of their cultures, in their capacity to define and sustain coherent and effective social roles, and in their ability to administer their new political and economic institutions and to mobilize popular energies to achieve national goals.

How Social Change Occurs in the Transitional Society

Having sketched the implications of the dichotomous character of the transitional society for personality and individual performance of social roles, we may now explore the ways in which qualitative social and cultural changes occur—in other words, the

[8] For example, contrary to Western expectations, the most Westernized members of the new elites—who in many cases provided the initial leadership of independence movements during the colonial period—were often unable to maintain their dominant positions for very long after independence was achieved. While ineptitude and insufficient personal motivation were sometimes responsible for their loss of political power and social influence, their failure has also been owed in important degree to the fact that they were more Westernized than their rivals. Their personalities and behavior were felt to be too alien by the great majority of the politically active and socially aware portions of the population; and they themselves were often neither willing nor able to evoke the kinds of affective responses from their followers on which a charismatic relationship depends. In many cases, the most Westernized members of the new elites, particularly among the professionally and technically trained groups, have eventually migrated to Western Europe or North America not only because they could thereby improve their living standards and work satisfactions but also because they felt more at home in the West despite overt or tacit racial and ethnic discrimination.

processes by which innovations are introduced and become self-perpetuating and the resulting inconsistencies, instabilities and incongruities in the directive system are mitigated and the modernized ways of perceiving, feeling, believing and acting are given greater scope. It is sometimes alleged that Freudian psychological theory and Parsonian social theory—on which the model depends —do not adequately allow for qualitative changes in individual personality, once formed, or in functioning social systems. Since space does not permit detailed refutation of this criticism, it must suffice to indicate briefly the ways in which innovations do appear and become established in individual attitudes and behavior and in the institutions, values and norms of the social system.

In the traditional society, the process of qualitative social change is initiated by events that weaken or impede the ability of the established paradigmatic figures and agents of induction to inculcate the traditional values and norms in the customary ways. Everett E. Hagen has described in detail a multigenerational process exemplifying probably the main way in which the internalized values and behavioral norms of traditional societies begin to change.[9] Particular groups within a traditional society suffer loss of customary status as a result of the kinds of events described in the preceding chapter: colonial rule, economic penetration by the market economy, introduction of new facilities disseminating modern knowledge and ideas, etc. After several generations of progressive frustration and impaired self-confidence among hitherto authoritarian fathers, they are inclined to become withdrawn, passive and uncertain. Eventually, the wives are impelled to seek compensation for such inadequate husbands by motivating their sons to engage in more assertive, innovative and achievement-oriented behavior. While aspects of Hagen's analysis have been questioned —particularly its reliance solely upon status deprivation as the source of impairment of the traditional authoritarian paternal role—it does provide an explanation, consistent with Freudian and Parsonian theories, of the process whereby new attitudes and norms are inculcated over several generations in a hitherto stable and static traditional society.

[9] See Everett E. Hagen, *On the Theory of Social Change: How Economic Growth Begins* (Homewood, Illinois: The Dorsey Press, Inc., 1962).

The multigenerational mechanisms of social change continue in the transitional society. In the still very large traditional sector, they probably constitute the major psychosocial process by which, particularly in the countryside, individuals become motivated to release themselves from traditional modes of living and working together. This is one reason why the transitional process is so much slower in rural areas. But, there are also ways in which social change occurs more rapidly—within the life careers of individuals —in the transitional society. Such rapid social change is typical of the dynamic Western society, and the mechanisms by which it takes place can be best illustrated by reference to Western experience.

The history of Western society is characterized by individuals who, as adults, experienced major qualitative changes in the patterns of feeling and behavior internalized during their childhood and adolescence. These personality changes have resulted either from processes of self-discovery analogous to Freudian psychoanalysis—from what Nelson has called "journeys within"—or from processes of voluntary or enforced adjustments to drastic modifications in their social or physical environments analogous to Darwinian natural selection. Examples of the first type are the changes in attitudes and roles induced by religious conversions and systems of confession and spiritual direction, traumatic personal experiences, identification with innovating political and intellectual leaders, and deliberate efforts at self-improvement and education.[10] Examples of the second type are the adjustments in behavior necessitated by alterations in social institutions during wars, revolutions, and economic and political crises, and the modifica-

[10] With respect to this type of rapid personality change, it is relevant to note that, by a process of self-examination and testing essentially psychoanalytic in nature though much more limited in scope and duration, David C. McClelland has helped selected groups of Indians significantly to change their motivations and self-conceptions with respect specifically to economic activity. These programs were, of course, controlled exposures of the participants to values and standards stressing high individual achievement in entrepreneurial roles. However, such experiences occur naturally in the dynamic Western society and also, through its influence, in the transitional society. For a brief report on these programs, see David C. McClelland, "Achievement Motivation Can Be Developed," *Harvard Business Review*, V. 43. no. 6, November–December 1965, pp. 6 ff; for a detailed account of McClelland's views on motivation and social change, see his *The Achieving Society* (Princeton: D. Van Nostrand Company, Inc., 1961).

tions in attitudes and actions induced by engaging in new occupations, migrating from a rural to an urban area or to a culturally different country, and loss of status or wealth.

As is evident from these examples, rapid social change may be defined as significant qualitative modifications in attitudes and behavior occurring within individual lifetimes. As such changes at the individual level become sufficiently extensive, they manifest themselves at the social level as changes in institutions, that is, in the roles played by individuals, in the ways in which these roles are related to each other in specific patterns of cues and responses, and in the relations among existing and new patterns. Conversely, changes in institutions and in their interrelationships induce or require changes in the attitudes and behavior of the individuals composing them. In effect, therefore, the two types of rapid social change are opposite faces or aspects of the same process. This is also true of the relationship between changes in attitudes and changes in behavior. Although actions are inherently much more specific and concrete than feelings, behavior can be considered to be in part the externalized social manifestation of an attitude and, conversely, an attitude may be considered to be in part the internalized psychological form of the behavior implicit in a particular social role or patterned response to cues. Both can change simultaneously as well as sequentially, and neither necessarily has to precede the other.

The capacity for rapid forms of social change is inherent in the nature of the transitional society—in the inconsistency and instability of its cues and directives. The existence side by side—and often within the same paradigmatic figures or agents of induction —of both traditional and Western values and norms provides for people exposed to them the knowledge of, and the opportunity to adopt, changes in customary attitudes and behavior. It is no longer possible for the traditional sector of the transitional society to exclude or suppress the alien Western values and norms which, as we have seen in the preceding chapter, have sooner or later undermined those of the traditional society whenever they have been in direct competition with them. Hence, traditional values and norms are unstable and can be replaced or transformed. Because the differences between the traditional and Western sets of values and norms are so wide, the range of possible combinations of old and new is correspondingly varied.

These opportunities to innovate are realized either by unconscious identification with paradigmatic figures or by conscious imitation of their example or conformity to their directives. The incentives to do so are both positive and negative. The positive include the desire for material rewards in terms of property, incomes and living standards, for political rewards in terms of power and influence, and for social rewards in terms of approbation and prestige. The negative incentives include fear of the loss of such benefits already obtained, of the denial of opportunities to obtain more, and of punishment, legal or otherwise, for failure to conform to directives and norms.

Thus, the inconsistencies and instabilities within and between the two sets of values and norms in the dichotomous transitional society open the way for individuals to experience various kinds and degrees of change in their attitudes and behavior and for institutions to undergo change in the roles and patterned relationships of which they are composed.

At the same time, however, the nature of the transitional society also limits the extent and the rate of rapid social change. Where the values and behavioral norms of the traditional portion of the society are not in direct competition with those of the West, their inertia tends to restrict social changes to slow multigenerational processes such as that described by Hagen. Also, as we have seen, traditional loyalties and obligations continue to be felt by members of the modernizing elites, which tends to weaken their commitment to Western values and their capacity to behave in accordance with Western norms. This tendency is aggravated by the alien character of Western values and norms and by inadequate educational preparation in the knowledge and skills required for effective performance of them. In consequence, Western values and norms are also unstable and are limited in the extent to which they induce fundamental and permanent changes in individuals and institutions.

Moreover, as Talcott Parsons has explained, societies are characterized by "pattern maintenance"—the tendency to make the minimum necessary changes in roles and their interrelationships and to re-establish an equilibrium as soon as such alterations have been absorbed. A prime example of pattern maintenance was described in the preceding chapter: the tendency of the peasant economies of Asia and Africa to stagnate at the first and least productive stage in the development of commercial agriculture.

Thus, in the transitional society, the factors fostering and inhibiting social change are in continuous tension. Innovations are always occurring, but their effects on individuals and institutions are often incomplete or transient. The traditional sector passively resists change; the modernizing sector has a divided and weak commitment to it and, in addition, lacks the knowledge and skills required for manifesting it effectively. In consequence, even though the capacity for and the mechanisms of rapid social change exist in the transitional society, their operation is limited and their effects are not always permanent.

For these reasons, the transitional society has a much slower rate of social change than does the dynamic Western society. The latter is so dynamic because the formerly generational and the rapid processes of social change have, in effect, merged. People born and educated in Western society are habituated to rapid social change within their own lifetimes and, by and large, are both willing to experience and able to adjust to it. Nonetheless, so rapid a rate of change imposes great psychological stresses and social strains. But, because rapid change is one of its intrinsic characteristics, Western society is much better able than are the transitional societies of Asia and Africa to cope with the resulting tendencies to social disintegration and to feelings of alienation, *anomie* and inadequate identity in individuals.

The transitional society is continually undergoing social disintegration as the values, norms and institutions of its traditional sector are eroded and disappear and as those of its modernizing sector only incompletely or transiently replace them. Conversely, such order and coherence as contemporary Asian and African societies possess are still largely those of the traditional society, as it is protected and supplemented by the new political and economic institutions that have not yet been in direct competition with it and, therefore, have not yet fatally undermined it. However, social reintegration cannot be made to occur by reconstructing the traditional society. Individuals can and do return to the traditional sector of their transitional societies as one way of resolving their conflicted feelings and inadequate sense of identity. But, the transitional society as a whole cannot resolve its inconsistencies and instabilities by returning to its past. It can do so only by moving forward to its future, however protracted and arduous the journey may be.

That the process will be long, difficult and at times without a clear and consistent direction is implicit in the nature of the transitional society. Many Asian and African countries will mark time for long periods, or will zigzag back and forth in abortive starts in various directions, or will even retrogress. Already it is evident that there will be many periods of internal turmoil resulting from traditional religious, ethnic and racial conflicts and civil wars; from Communist and other modern forms of political subversion; and from nativistic messianic and redemptive movements, religious and secular. It is because of such concurrent processes of social disintegration and reintegration that the transitional societies of Asia and Africa will experience only a slow transformation in the foreseeable future.

The Search for Identity

The identity problems of individuals in the transitional society are related to and paralleled by those of the society as a whole. In contemporary Asian and African countries, what Nelson calls the "dramatic design" of the culture lacks clear definition and coherence. In their traditional past, the meaning of existence and the aims of society were expressed in the symbol systems of the religions of each region. And, to most people in these societies, including many of the modern elites, these traditional symbols still have power to give some sense of meaning and direction to their lives. But, side by side with the traditional dramatic design, another symbol system exists to which they also respond in greater or lesser degree. This second symbol system—derived in large part from the alien Western society—expresses a radically different dramatic design, as we have seen. In consequence, the culture of the transitional society has little identity of its own. Rather, it is an unintegrated and inconsistent mixture of weakening traditional symbols and vaguely perceived and partially absorbed alien symbols. The fact that there is no coherent dramatic design that is *sui generis* in the transitional society accounts for the absence of a clear and strong sense of national identity and purpose in Asian and African countries.

This absence of a clear sense of national identity is more or less consciously felt to be intolerable by the new elites of these countries, and efforts to create distinctive identities for their societies are among the most central phenomena occurring in them. Called by such terms as "nationalism" and "socialism," this search for identity is similar in its significance to the process by which Western society evolved its own distinctive dramatic design. However, contemporary Asian and African efforts exhibit certain characteristics that differ importantly from the experience of the West.

In Western society, the development of national consciousness and a sense of identity was a slow process that began in the late Middle Ages and reached its fullest expression in the late nineteenth and early twentieth centuries. Politically, the development of Western nationalism consisted of the consolidation of nation-states, which—as a result of long centuries of dynastic wars, territorial shifts and emancipation efforts—are today fairly homogeneous in language, culture and historical continuity. More important, the cultural content of Western nationalism has always been indigenous, expressing the dynamic evolution of the dramatic design of Western society.

In contrast, the evolution of Asian and African national consciousness is impeded not only by the particularism of the transitional society and the arbitrary character of many national boundaries but more fundamentally by the ambiguity of and the conflicts within its culture. No Asian or African country yet possesses a dramatic design and directive cue system sufficiently consistent, stable and congruent with realities and needs to provide the cultural content for a clear and strong sense of national identity and purpose. There are essentially two processes by which Asian and African countries will evolve such an articulated and distinctive cultural content and, hence, an adequate sense of national identity.

The first consists of preserving and renovating the elements of the traditional culture that still retain significance. Although transitional societies cannot regress to their past, they can draw upon traditional elements that continue to have meaning and a sense of direction for their people. In all societies, this has been one of the major social functions of religion, and it is natural that, in southern Asia and the Middle East, Buddhism, Hinduism and Islam should be generating a succession of revival and modernization movements.

During the colonial period, such movements were usually protective in nature and were largely motivated by the need to find something enduring and valuable in the traditional culture that could be reasserted in the face of the intruding Western culture. This helped Asians and Africans to ward off or assuage the sense of inadequacy and loss of self-confidence resulting from the failure of the traditional society to maintain its integrity under the impact of the West. Since independence, these religious revivals have had a dual character. On the one hand, they have been encouraged and used by traditional ruling elites to prevent or retard the process of social change. On the other hand, they have been used by radical regimes and left-wing parties, as in Burma, Ceylon and Indonesia, to foster national consciousness and to enlist majority support by exacerbating ethnic and sectarian hostilities toward minority groups. At the same time, the religious organizations have been endeavoring to fit themselves better to cope with conditions in the transitional society through improvements in the organization and training of the religious elite; arrangements for greater mass participation; efforts to adapt doctrines, rituals and ethical and legal regulations to the needs of modernizing economic and social systems; and the formation of political parties and quasi-political movements dominated by religious sects.[11]

However, as they develop, the new dramatic designs of Asian and African societies are likely to be less and less religious in content, even though they may be so in origin. Ultimately, modernization will mean substantial secularization, as it has in the West. There, Judaeo-Christian concepts and expectations of individual

[11] On modernizing movements in the traditional Asian religions, see Robert N. Bellah, ed., *Religion and Progress in Modern Asia* (New York: The Free Press, 1965).

salvation and social renovation both in and from this world could be and were translated into modernizing secular forms because, as we have seen in Chapter 2, they were themselves a major source and expression of Western dynamism. But, with their lack of millennial expectations and their denial of the value of nature and society, neither Buddhism nor Hinduism has played such a role in the past, and neither is likely to do so in the future. Such an autonomous development is even less likely in tropical Africa where, except for the spread of Islam in the northern tier of sub-Saharan states, great historical religions never evolved or took root. The indigenous animistic tribal cults of the region have little capacity today for independent development into higher forms, even though certain of their elements—e.g., witchcraft, "bush medicine," the secret societies—continue to flourish among all social groups, including the modern elites, in part as a means of assuaging the ambiguities and anxieties of the transitional society.[12] In both Asia and Africa today, the capacity of the indigenous religions to serve as sources of dynamic renovative concepts and motivations depends upon the extent to which they have been—and will in the future be—influenced by Western religious ideas and expectations. Islam may have the greatest potentiality for responding to such influences precisely because of its original Judaeo-Christian affinities.[13]

The importance of Western society as the source of dynamic redemptive concepts and expectations brings us to the second—and much more significant—of the two processes by which Asian and African countries are gradually evolving new dramatic designs and clearer senses of identity. Elements drawn from the traditional society are likely to be meaningful less by themselves than fused or infused in novel ways with the alien concepts, values and institu-

[12] On the animistic African religions, see Daryll Forde, ed., *African Worlds, Studies in the Cosmological Ideas and Social Values of African Peoples* (London: Oxford University Press, 1954).

[13] Indeed, throughout its history and in all parts of its vast territory, Islam has generated renovative movements. Their aim was generally to purge the religion of corrupting elements and to return to the pure and simple faith of the Prophet. But, unlike the Protestant Reformation and other renovative movements in Christianity, the asceticism of these puritanical Islamic sects did not foster worldly achievement, to which—aside from warfare—they were generally hostile or indifferent. An exception has been the Ismaili sect.

tions imported from Western society. A few examples may help to clarify this second process.

Let us consider, first, the way in which Western religious concepts have already influenced developments in Buddhism, Hinduism, Islam and the African animistic cults. During the colonial period, the loss of independence, the failure of anti-colonial revolts, and the awesome superiority of the conquering Western culture led not only to reassertive and modernizing efforts in the indigenous religions but also to receptivity to the messianic and redemptive ideas disseminated by Christian missionaries and from other Western sources. Under their inspiration, a local leader would proclaim himself (sometimes herself), or would be proclaimed by his followers, a prophet or messiah destined to expel the hated foreign rulers by his supernatural powers and to inaugurate a reign of peace and plenty for all who believed in his mission and magic. Such messianic movements of freedom and recompense within and alongside the indigenous religions can be found wherever Western rule was imposed in the past century and a half—and not least among suppressed minorities within Western society itself.[14] Most of these nativistic cults arose suddenly, flourished briefly, and then disappeared as organized movements. But they generally left behind a residue of redemptive ideas and messianic expectations that continued to inspire equally transient successors. In the post-independence period, the specific anti-colonial content of such cults naturally abated but those that survived or developed subsequently have generally continued to be more or less hostile to Westerners on racist grounds.

Over the longer term, the influence of Western redemptive and renovative concepts is likely to be significant in Asia and Africa not only through the activities of these messianic sects, but also more pervasively through the other types of religious, political and social movements that are stimulated by, and help to mitigate the personal ambiguities and social disintegration of, the transitional process. One rather extreme example of such a development was the effort made in Indonesia under Sukarno to merge traditional

[14] These numerous movements in Asia, Africa, Latin America, the Middle and Near East, Oceania, among the Indians of the United States, etc., are surveyed in Vittorio Lanternari, *The Religions of the Oppressed: A Study of Modern Messianic Cults* (New York: Alfred A. Knopf, Inc., 1963).

and Western religious and political concepts in a highly nationalistic religiopolitical synthesis.[15] More typical and eventually more significant is the influence of Western redemptive and renovative ideas in disseminating new values stressing achievement in this world and norms of behavior conducive to it. The inculcation of such values and norms in both religious and secular forms would be analogous to, though not necessarily identical with, what Max Weber called the "worldly asceticism" of the Protestant Reformation—frugality, abstinence, thrift, prudent investment, hard work and rationalized pursuit of entrepreneurial success—in its effects on economic growth and social improvement in Asian and African countries.[16]

In time, such changes in attitudes and behavior would inevitably generate awareness of the wide disparities between the new expectations for social and economic improvement and the limited capabilities of Asian and African societies to fulfill them. When such perceptions and feelings become sufficiently widespread, a development will then have occurred that could validly be called a "revolution of rising expectations." The resulting restlessness and ferment could lead, however, to opposing consequences. On the one hand, they could stimulate increasingly effective efforts to accelerate economic growth and social reform within these societies. On the other hand, they could produce increasingly dangerous outbreaks of revolutionary messianism, religious and political, not only within Asian and African countries but also directed against other nations in these regions and elsewhere in the world.

Another major example of the second process by which Asian and African countries are beginning to develop new cultural designs and senses of national identity is through adaptation of the Western concept of socialism. Since independence, most of these countries have declared themselves socialist states or have proclaimed that socialism is their ultimate objective. The economic

[15] On the traditional religion, see Clifford Geertz, *The Religion of Java* (Glencoe, Ill.: The Free Press, 1960); on the religiopolitical synthesis, see Herbert Luethy "Indonesia Confronted," *Encounter,* V. 25, NO. 6, December 1965, and V. 26, NO. 1, January 1966.

[16] On the influence of Western concepts and norms on Asian religions, see Robert N. Bellah "Reflections on the Protestant Ethic Analogy in Asia" in the *Journal of Social Issues,* V. 19, No. 1, January 1963.

and political significance of socialism will be analyzed in the next chapter. Here, we are concerned with its more general social significance in the search for identity.

Today, the commitment to socialism in Asian and African countries is not motivated and justified primarily by Marxist-Leninist doctrines and expectations. True, virtually all of these countries have indigenous Communist parties, whose leaders have usually been trained in Moscow or Peking, and which articulate the full range of Marxist-Leninist doctrines. But, even in Indonesia, where the Communist party was before its suppression the largest political group in the country and participated in the government, these doctrines have not been widely accepted in their orthodox forms among the non-Communist members of the elites, much less among the great mass of the people. The chief attraction of Marxist-Leninist concepts has been as a means of expressing resentment against the West ("imperialist aggression," "neocolonialism"). Otherwise, communism's specific prescriptions are felt to be largely irrelevant to the actual economic and social problems, internal and external, with which Asian and African countries are confronted.

Instead of trying to institute Marxian socialism, most Asian and African countries have been seeking to express and rationalize their socialist commitment in concepts and organizational forms adapted from those of the traditional society. In addition to the establishment of state enterprises and some nationalization of private enterprises, much stress is placed, especially in Africa, upon efforts to foster cooperatives of farmers, of artisans producing light consumer goods and providing services, and of wholesalers and retailers, as well as consumer and credit cooperatives. Cooperative enterprises of these kinds are regarded as modernized versions of the traditional joint production and consumption of the subsistence household or village community. Similarly, this type of indigenous socialism is believed to express in a modern form such traditional values as sharing, mutual help, and communal activity in work and leisure.

These organizational forms and values derived from the traditional society represent attempts to provide an indigenous content for the borrowed Western concept of socialism. Indeed, these countries have sought to emphasize the indigenous character of their adaptations of Western socialism by calling their own versions "Arab socialism," "African socialism," "Indian socialism," "Burmese socialism," "Indonesian socialism," etc. Regardless of their variety and despite the paucity of their achievements, these efforts at developing indigenous forms of socialism are significant because—like nativistic messianic cults and other renovative movements—they, too, help to inculcate the sense of the worthiness of activity in this world, the desire for social and economic improvement, and the norms of individual and collective behavior conducive to conscientious performance of the new social roles and occupational tasks. In these ways, the infusion of the alien Western concept of socialism with elements derived from the traditional society contributes to the process of creating a distinctive national consciousness and sense of identity.

In Africa south of the Sahara, the new elites have been absorbed in a broader search for what is called "the African personality" in the English-speaking countries and *"négritude"* in the French-speaking nations. Their search—and the absence of a similar effort in Asian countries—reflects the fact that the traditional cultures and animistic cults of Africa are simpler and less articulated than those of Asia. Because the traditional African society has less to contribute, the elements that can be adapted from it are all the more strongly emphasized by the African elites. At the same time, because so few features of traditional African society are relevant to modern expectations, institutions and techniques, the imported Western concepts and activities are likely to play a significantly larger role in the eventual new dramatic designs of African cultures than in those of Asia.

These examples of the two processes—the reassertion and modernization of traditional elements and the fusion of traditional elements with imported Western concepts and institutions—may suffice to illustrate their fundamental importance in the transformation of transitional societies. In both Asia and Africa today, it is much too early to discern the results of the search for national and cultural identity. But, regardless of the expectations of the modernizing elites in these countries, it is clear that the transitional process is both limited by, and dependent for its development upon, the traditional society and culture. Hence, despite the intentions and efforts of some Asian and African elites, conscious and comprehensive policy measures cannot enable them to break completely with the traditional past and to construct new societies in accordance with different values and institutions.

Two attempts at such gigantic "social engineering" have been under way in the contemporary world—one for half a century in Russia and the other for two decades in China—but neither has succeeded in this respect. Both Russia and China experienced violent social revolutions that swept away many aspects of their traditional political, social and economic institutions and relationships. Both then embarked upon deliberate and accelerated processes of social change in accordance with somewhat different versions of Marxist-Leninist doctrine. However, despite the intention of the ruling Communist elites in both countries to break with the past and to build completely new societies fulfilling the redemptive predictions and embodying the utopian prescriptions of their respective orthodox doctrines, many innovations have occurred through adaptation to or fusion with major elements of traditional values, expectations and relationships, although often under different names and in different forms. Indeed, the adoption of many of the most important innovations was possible largely because they were consistent with the pre-existing attitudes, relationships and sense of national identity and purpose.

Thus, there are important elements of continuity between Russian society under the czars and Russian society under the Communists in values and expectations, methods of social integration and control, and the attitudes of the Russian people. For example, the expectation of Russian Orthodox Christianity that Moscow would be the "Third Rome" destined to rule the world in the new age of redemption was secularized into the Leninist-Stalinist expectation that Moscow would be the center of the world revolution destined to lead the international proletariat into the world-wide socialist utopia. The czarist autocracy, with its centralized bureaucratic regulation of economic activity and attempts to control social institutions and cultural expression, has been perpetuated in the Soviet autocracy, with its more pervasive and effective centralized direction of all of the major systems of the society. The willing conformism of the Russian people and, conversely, their anxiety when individual responsibility and initiative are expected of them, as well as their concomitant need for identification with prepotent, semi-divine leaders, continue to be evident under the Communist regime as they were in the days of the czars.

The continuity between neo-Confucianism and communism in China is equally apparent. The concept of China as the "middle kingdom," occupying a mediating position of example and tutelage between heaven and the barbarian kingdoms comprising the rest of mankind, is today translated into the conviction that China is the only legitimate interpreter of Communist doctrine and the natural exemplar of its prescriptions for correct revolutionary behavior. The Confucian bureaucratic state, with its hierarchy of centrally appointed and directed officials and its method of self-selection and self-perpetuation through rigorous examinations limited to orthodox interpretation of the Confucian classics, is matched by the Communist bureaucratic state, with its successive levels of cadres and party officials and its analogous system of selection and perpetuation through a carefully observed novitiate and periodic retesting and reindoctrination. In place of the unquestioned parental authority within the traditional family and reverence for the ancestors of neo-Confucian society, there are today the authoritarian socioeconomic organizations in city and countryside and the reverent obedience to political leaders—above all to Mao Tse-tung, combining in one person the new Confucius and the successor to "the son of Heaven." Neo-Confucian contempt for and intolerance of other religious and philosophical-political doctrines foreshadowed Communist scorn for individualistic values and its suppression of all types of intellectual and artistic dissent.[17]

[17] One crucial difference, however, between neo-Confucian China and Communist China is that between the former's static world view and the latter's dynamic evolutionary conception. As Nelson points out, this is the first instance of one of the world's major non-Western cultures adopting an eschatological redemptive religion originating in the West. Whether this unique event temporarily or permanently commits China to a dynamic redemptive conception of its own destiny will be one of the important factors determining China's future role in world affairs. See Benjamin Nelson, "Religion and Development" in Theodore Geiger and Leo Solomon, editors, *Motivations and Methods in Development and Foreign Aid* (Washington, D.C.: Society for International Development, 1964), pp. 67–68.

Only a few Asian and African countries are attempting to engineer social change as comprehensively and rapidly—and with as little regard for the cost in terms of human lives and suffering—as the Russians and the Chinese have been trying to do. The great majority have limited their efforts to stimulating, directing and assisting the processes of social change that are largely occurring naturally in these transitional societies in the ways explained earlier in this chapter. In consequence, reassertion, modernization and transformation of traditional indigenous elements are likely to play even more important roles in their search for identity than they have in Russia and China, whose ruling Communist elites have been hostile to so many of their countries' inherited values and institutions.

There is a widespread view in the West—especially in the United States—that, because such processes of social change in Asian and African countries will sooner or later involve increasing industrialization and urbanization, their societies and cultures will more and more come to resemble those of North America and Western Europe. In this view, it is only a question of time before the entire planet is Westernized. These expectations express a kind of unconscious and unintentional Marxism: in effect, they imply that the mode of production determines the nature of society and culture.

Industrialization consists of a distinctive set of attitudes, roles, patterned responses, skills and techniques which can be embodied not only in manufacturing activities but also in agriculture, and which constitutes the most productive type of economic system yet evolved by human societies. Because it is so productive, it will sooner or later spread to any society which desires to increase its productivity and which possesses the minimum conditions necessary for its establishment. Because industrialization consists of a distinctive set of attitudes, roles, responses, skills and techniques, societies that have been industrialized must *ipso facto* resemble one another in these respects. Moreover, the conditions necessary for the introduction and successful growth of an industrial system —urban population concentrations, transportation and power systems, integrated national markets or easy access to foreign markets, impersonal economic relationships, rationalized producing and distributing organizations, and many others—mean that industrialized societies will tend to resemble each other in these respects as well.

However, these areas of similarity, important as they are, do not by any means exhaust the significant aspects and dimensions of society and culture. It is enough to recall that Japan successfully industrialized itself without loss of its distinctive cultural identity in order to appreciate how great the differences are likely to be between the West and the countries of Asia and Africa even after the latter have made substantial progress in industrialization. Thus, despite the resemblances to Western society that will inevitably result from industrialization and urbanization, Asian and African countries will in time evolve new national and cultural identities with their own distinctive values and norms, political and social institutions, and cultural expressions.

This discussion of the two processes by which Asian and African countries will gradually evolve their new dramatic designs and senses of identity illuminates another important function of the traditional sector of the transitional society. In addition to providing the major system of order and coherence in these unstable societies during much of the transition, it is the source or raw material for a large part of the content of the new and modernized values and institutions that these societies will develop in their search for national and cultural identity. However, the inertia of the traditional sector—the difficulty of moving it from the course in which it has been fixed for millennia—constitutes a major obstacle preventing easy or rapid completion of the transitional process. Thus, neither the present nor the future of Asian and African countries can be adequately understood unless the crucial, though deeply ambivalent, role played within them by the traditional sector is fully recognized.

The New Integrative Elements in the Transitional Process

In the transitional society, the gradual reintegration of individual personalities through the growing predominance of modernizing values and norms in individual attitudes and behavior proceeds parallel to and in continuous interaction with the gradual emergence of a new sense of national and cultural identity that can integrate the many conflicting particularistic groups and interests and orient them toward a reasonably consistent and compelling sense of national purpose. Thus, a crucial role in this process is played by common values, norms and standards that can transcend—although they need not suppress or supersede—individual and group interests and behavior patterns. Talcott Parsons calls them "universalistic" values because they are meant to be common to the society as a whole and are believed to apply to all individuals composing it.

Historically in the West, and elsewhere in the contemporary world, particularistic and traditionalistic societies have undergone some form of the transitional process. Regardless of major cultural divergences among them and of important differences in the extent and nature of their efforts to direct and accelerate the modernization process, the nations of Western Europe and North America, the Soviet Union, China and Japan have all had to develop certain common features. These include a conviction of the worth of achievement in this world and a belief in the possibility and desirability of social improvement; the gradual prevalence in certain crucial respects of universalistic values over particularistic interests and loyalties; greater and sharper differentiation of the various roles played by individuals, involving a major reduction in the relative importance of kinship arrangements and a concomitant replacement of the traditional affective personalized relationships by rationalized impersonal relationships; and the determination of individuals' life careers much more by personal achievement than by ascribed status. These social and cultural changes have both reflected and supported increasing coherence and stability within the directive systems of these cultures and greater congruence between them and the physical and social realities of the environment within which these societies have to operate. In consequence, more and more distinctive dramatic designs have evolved within their cultures, characterized by a heightened sense of national identity and purpose. In turn, this development—and the concomitant and concurrent changes in individual personality described above—has decisively strengthened the willingness and ability of the people, particularly the elite groups, to increase and make more effective use of their society's resources. In these ways, the processes of innovation and of social integration have become self-reinforcing and the definitive new identities and dramatic designs of these societies have emerged.

The case of Japan is instructive because it is the only non-Western society that has so far successfully completed the transitional process and because it illustrates the crucial integrating and motivating role played by indigenous factors in its success. Unlike Communist China, which has borrowed its motivating and integrating doctrine from the West, Japan has achieved its development through the evolution of a system of universalistic values and norms that is largely indigenous in origin. True, Japan's culture has borrowed heavily from China's throughout its history. But, by the beginning of the Tokugawa period early in the seventeenth century, the borrowed elements had been adapted and integrated into Japanese society and culture in a distinctive manner. Two crucial features of this period (which immediately preceded modernization) were the distinctive Japanese form of Zen Buddhism, with its emphasis on individual experience and performance in this world, and the revival of older Shinto concepts of the Emperor's symbolic role in expressing national purpose and of the subject's duty of obedience and sacrifice.[18] From these and other indigenous elements, a set of universalistic values and behavioral norms had evolved by the end of the Tokugawa period which motivated enough samurai, merchants and wealthier peasants to respond dynamically to their increasing knowledge of the achievements of Western society and their awareness of the fate of other traditional Asian states unable to cope with Western military power and political and economic influence.

During the ensuing Meiji period and, indeed, until after World War II, Japan employed an authoritarian development strategy reflecting the authoritarian and oligarchical nature of its inherited social system. However, Japan's development strategy was never as totalitarian in aim or in performance as the strategies of the Soviet Union and China. While central government authorities

[18] See Robert N. Bellah, *Tokugawa Religion* (Glencoe, Ill.: The Free Press, 1957).

have played a major role in planning, directing and assisting economic growth, private decentralized economic decision making and activity have always been not merely permitted but encouraged. Rival political parties have been active since the late nineteenth century, although they have become major influences in national politics only since World War II. Scientific inquiry was never warped by the officially favored religious-political doctrine, and freedom to express political and social dissent was never wholly suppressed even during the most militaristic period between the world wars. Since World War II, under a more representative and popularly responsive political regime, Japanese society has been becoming increasingly pluralistic, but the transformation of its inherited paternalistic and personalistic social relationships is not yet assured, and its democratic institutions still operate rather ineffectively and continue to be quite precarious.

Over the past hundred years, without loss of cultural and national identity, Japan has attained and sustained a rate of economic growth and of political and social modernization that has been unique among non-Western societies. This achievement has resulted in large part from the fact that its motivating and integrating system of dynamic universalistic values has been predominantly indigenous in origin and, despite its essentially authoritarian character, has fostered a substantial and growing degree of diversified decentralized initiative and activity, particularly in economic affairs. Except for Japan, no non-Western country has yet evolved from indigenous sources a system of universalistic values capable of preserving or generating a sense of national identity and purpose, an alignment and coordination of particularistic interests and loyalties, and elite groups willing and able to cooperate in stimulating and directing economic growth and the modernization of political and social institutions.

Japan's example illuminates a fundamental problem faced by the transitional societies of Asia and Africa. For the people of an Asian or African country—particularly its elite groups—to develop the willingness and the ability to move decisively ahead in the transitional process, they must feel that they belong to a society with a sense of unique identity, a sense of effective effort, and a sense of self-accomplishment. But, these are precisely the qualities most difficult for these transitional societies to develop. Their traditional cultures have failed to maintain their integrity under the impact of the West and, unlike Japan and even China, virtually all of these societies failed to maintain their political independence as well. Since the end of colonialism, they have been trying to reassert and modernize elements of their traditional cultures and to merge them with imported Western institutions, norms and standards, but these processes are still in their formative phases and are, indeed, inhibited by the continued dependence of Asia and Africa upon the West. For, the more that Asian and African countries have to depend upon the West—or for that matter upon the Soviet Union or China—for the necessary concepts, values and institutions, as well as for financial and technical assistance, the longer and more difficult will it be for them to achieve the requisite sense of self-confidence and identity. This consideration has important implications for Western relationships with these countries, particularly for the foreign-aid activities of the United States.

The elites of Asian and African countries are more or less aware of the basic problems posed by their dependence. Whether consciously or unconsciously, their response to it has been an intensified political nationalism. Through it, a sense of identity and of self-confidence may gradually be generated by symbols expressing national consciousness, values defining the national interest and the obligation to advance it, and behavioral patterns stressing individual and group achievements in working toward it. Thus, the fostering of political nationalism is the major means by which universalistic values are likely to be developed within the directive systems of Asian and African cultures.

Introduced into Asia and Africa by the encounter with the West, political nationalism was stimulated by the largely political nature of their efforts to obtain and preserve national independence, and it has been reinforced by the subsequent political preoccupations, foreign and domestic, of these new nations. In today's polycentric system of world politics, even the most geographically remote Asian or African country is inescapably affected by the rivalries of the superpowers and by the pressure and example of its neighbors. Within the country, the governmental system plays the most active and pervasive role not only in development strategy but also in holding together such divisively particularistic societies. Participation in national politics, in the control of the machinery of government, is the key factor determining the present welfare and the future prospects of contending tribes, sects, parties and economic interest groups. Consequently, the institutions and processes commanding the widest attention in these countries are those comprised in their political systems.

So far, Asian and African countries have expressed their political nationalism more strongly and clearly in their external relationships than in their internal relationships. As we have seen in Chapter 3, there is as yet a very weak sense of common identity among the particularistic groups within most Asian and African countries. Since independence, however, many Asian and African countries have been endeavoring to play an active role in international affairs; in many cases, a more active role than is warranted by an objective assessment of their power or their needs. There are several specific motives for their participation in regional and world politics: to protect themselves against external aggression; to avoid becoming involved in or injured by cold-war conflicts; to obtain economic benefits from trading partners and capital-exporting nations; to pursue territorial or hegemonic ambitions; and to divert the attention of their people from domestic problems and frustrations. But, permeating and reinforcing all of these motivations is the fact that active participation in international affairs is one of the most important ways by which Asian and African countries can foster their sense of national identity and of self-confidence. Just as individuals strengthen their awareness of self-identity and their self-confidence by interacting with others, so, too, can societies be stimulated to a heightened sense of their national identities and capabilities through encounters with other countries in the arenas of regional and world politics.

The Model Completed:
The Role of the West in the Transitional Process

In achieving this purpose, the effectiveness of such international encounters, both negative and positive, is increased when the relationship not only involves the pursuit of specific interests, real and imagined, but also bears directly upon the crucial psychological and social processes of the transition. For this reason, the external relationships of Asia and Africa with the West are among the most profoundly significant experiences that these countries are undergoing today. We can now complete the model of the transitional process by considering the role that the West plays in it.

In essence, the West provides the countries of Asia and Africa with the example of a society that has succeeded in achieving high and rising living standards for the great mass of its people; in developing governmental systems able to carry out effectively the increasingly diverse and difficult functions required in the contemporary world; and in maintaining the capacity to defend itself against possible external enemies with the most scientifically advanced weapons yet devised by mankind. For many centuries, Western society has been the source of most of the planet's scientific discoveries and technological innovations, as well as of its major new movements in philosophy, literature and the arts. In all of these fields of human activity, the West provides the standard of performance by which other societies, consciously or unconsciously, measure their own accomplishments.

Moreover, the West is not a remote or passive model for Asian and African countries. As we have seen, their encounter with the West has been the direct and active force that has propelled them out of the historical course in which, as traditional societies, they have been fixed for thousands of years. Although they are now politically independent, the West is still actively and directly involved in Asian and African countries. It is the leading protagonist with which they seek to cope in their efforts to play a distinctive part in world politics, as well as their main trading partner and the source of most of the financial and technical assistance needed to supplement their own resources of capital and skills.

In effect, the West plays a paradigmatic role for Asian and African countries analogous in significance to that ascribed earlier in this chapter to paradigmatic figures in the process of socialization and individualization. On the one hand, Asian and African countries follow the example and adopt the methods of the West in seeking to develop their economies, to improve the effectiveness of their governments, and to raise the living standards and educational qualifications of their people. On the other hand, Asian and African countries are continually impelled to assert their individuality and independence vis-à-vis the West by reacting against its influence and opposing its interests. The relationship is, therefore, deeply ambivalent, compounded of emulation and rejection, admiration and denigration, attraction and hostility.

By its nature, an ambivalent paradigmatic relationship of this type is of a fundamental—and not a superficial—character and presents great difficulties for both sides. The significance and problems of this relationship for the West have already been suggested in Chapter 2. For the elite groups in Asia and Africa, it is a profound experience which permeates virtually all aspects of their consciousness and behavior. In all fields of their activity— politics, government, economy, defense, science and technology, literature, art, religion and philosophy—they are constantly faced with the model set by the West and are always conscious of its standards of performance. Wherever they look at home, they are confronted with the evident failure of their traditional indigenous societies and cultures to withstand the dissolving impact of the West. Wherever they look abroad, they are confronted with the power and influence of the West and with its evident ability to defend and further its own interests. Whenever they seek to advance their own interests in world affairs, they are made aware of their dependence upon Western financial and technical assistance and upon Western restraint in not pressing its own advantage too far to the detriment of theirs.

In such a profound, pervasive and ambivalent relationship, neither the West nor the countries of Asia and Africa are able to limit their interactions to those that involve predominantly rational calculations of self-interests and mutual interests. All sorts of other impulses and responses, conscious and unconscious, are inevitably present on both sides, but more intensely so on the part of Asian and African countries because the relationship is more important for them. This is why Asian and African countries can simultaneously denounce the West in United Nations forums and solicit increased aid from Western governments. This is why they can express sincere admiration for Western social and intellectual achievements yet at the same time believe and publish the most inprobable allegations regarding Western motives and actions. This is why Western generosity and forbearance are accepted by Asian and African countries as no more than their due, while Western mistakes and misdeeds, even the most trivial, are excoriated as unexpected and unpardonable sins. This is why the significance to them of their own "third world" activities and conferences lies less in the practical benefits to the participants than in the opportunities thereby afforded to relieve their ambivalences and express their resentments vis-à-vis the West. These and many other conflicted reactions and incongruities are inherent in the nature of a relationship with so many dimensions.

One manifestation is the widespread appeal which the charge of "neocolonialism" has for Asians and Africans. Neocolonialism is not only a Communist slogan to sustain hostility against the West after colonial rule ended. It also—and more significantly—expresses the feeling of Asian and African countries that, even though they are now politically independent, they are still not their own masters. They point to the occasions when Western diplomacy pressed them into serving its purposes or frustrated their own initiatives. More subtly, the activistic and directive nature of Western efforts to help them plan and execute their development programs emphasizes their dependence and keeps alive their sense of continuing to be under colonial-type influence and control.

A somewhat similar psychological process is involved in their racist feeling vis-à-vis the West. In part, of course, it is an understandable reaction to the West's own racial prejudices. But, anti-white feeling in Asia and Africa is also a way of asserting a separate and different identity against that of the paradigmatic figure. This aspect could make racial hostility to the West a significant component of Asian and African attitudes and actions in the years to come.

Compared with the depth and emotionality of their relationship with the West, that between Asian and African countries and the Soviet Union and China is superficial and relaxed. This difference baffles many Westerners who correctly point out that it is the Communist states and not the West which are the main threats to the independence of these countries.

However, in Asia and Africa today, with the exception of

those countries directly confronted by external aggression or internal subversion, the threat of conquest or domination by Peking or Moscow is not regarded as unmanageable or as of the same order of importance as their relationship with the West. In most cases, Asian and African countries have either suppressed their indigenous Communist parties or have been able to control them, and they implicitly or explicitly rely upon Western power and self-interest to protect them from external Communist aggression. No independent Asian or African country was ever a colonial dependency of Russia, and Chinese imperial control in Southeast Asia ceased to be effective at least two centuries ago. Hence, neither Russia nor China has played a role in the dissolution and transformation of the traditional societies of these regions.

Despite Communist propaganda—and the fears of many Westerners—the Soviet Union and China have not become models for the great majority of Asian and African countries. Indeed, for reasons discussed in the next chapter, most of them have deliberately chosen not to adopt such distinctive Communist prescriptions as comprehensively and centrally planned state socialism; totalitarian methods of social and political control; officially enforced orthodoxies in science, philosophy, social thought, literature and the arts; and messianic ambitions in world politics. The few that have tried to copy these Communist methods—at one time or another, Algeria, Egypt, Ghana, Guinea, Indonesia, Mali and Syria—have done so only in limited respects, with significantly less resort to terroristic methods, and without using their local Communist parties as the instrument of decision making and control. At the same time, even these countries still look to the West as a source of ideas, assistance and standards, and the vehemence of their frequent denunciations and hostility bespeaks the depth of their continued emotional involvement with the West as a paradigmatic figure.

I have no intention of belittling the importance of the relationship between Asian and African countries and the Communist states, and the danger that frustration may impel them to accept, or ineptitude to fall under, the domination of Communist parties oriented toward Moscow or Peking. Nonetheless, this relationship differs in kind as well as in degree from that between Asian and

African countries and the West. The Communist countries play a paradigmatic role only to a minor extent; their relationship with Asia and Africa lacks multidimensionality—the complex and contradictory blending of rational, emotional, historical and cultural elements—and it does not involve the ambivalences and difficulties that characterize the relationship with the West.

In sum, the role that the West plays is a crucial element in the transitional process through which the countries of Asia and Africa are slowly resolving their ambiguities and developing their senses of identity. As this process advances, the conflicted character of the relationship should gradually be resolved. But whether in this resolution the positive or negative aspects of the relationship will come to predominate will depend upon the outcome of the transitional process—upon the kinds of societies that will eventually emerge in these regions—and upon the way in which the West consciously and unconsciously carries out its paradigmatic role.

The model of the transitional process is now complete. It has, however, at least one major limitation. Because its purpose is to illuminate the nature of the transitional process as a whole in terms of its implications for Western concern with "development," it is a *macro* model, indicating only in broadest outline some of the many different and conflicting values, institutions, relationships and movements comprising the transitional society. The disaggregation, or breaking down, of such a *macro* model into the many separate, interacting *micro* processes of which societies are composed would be a task well beyond the purpose of this book and well beyond the resources that could be provided by the available research. As Westerners become more willing to discount the effects of the perceptual biases and the motivations of their own culture, and as the large amounts of necessary data are accumulated through empirical investigation, the realities of Asia and Africa will become much better known and the nature and probable outcome of the transitional process far more profoundly understood.

CHAPTER FIVE

Development Strategies in Asia and Africa and Their Limitations

The purpose of this chapter is twofold: to outline the main types of policy measures by which Asian and African countries are endeavoring to accelerate and direct the transitional process, and to describe the limitations imposed by the nature of the transitional society upon their willingness and ability to do so. Because we will be concerned with deliberate measures of policy rather than with social processes per se the term "development strategy" will be used to designate such conscious directive efforts without, however, rescinding the reservations expressed in Chapter 1 regarding the misleading connotations of current usage of the word "development."

In the West, particularly in the United States, it is widely believed that development is simply a matter of rational decision making—a technical problem of choosing the most desirable and practicable objectives and of selecting and applying the most effective means to attain them. True, such rational decision making is one of the major elements involved. But, the analysis in preceding chapters has been intended in part to demonstrate that decision making in Asia and Africa, as in all societies, reflects not only technical considerations but also the perceptual and conceptual biases of the culture and the past history and existing structure and modes of functioning of the society. Thus, while conceptually distinguishable, the technical and the sociocultural aspects of development strategy are inextricably linked in any process of national decision making.

The model of the transitional process presented in the preceding chapter was designed to reveal the individual psychological and the collective social aspects of the transitional process and their main interrelationships. Here, we shall be concerned with two major dimensions of the social aspect, the political and the economic, which are the principal components of the development strategies of Asian and African countries. However, it must be emphasized that, just as the psychosocial aspects of the transitional process are separable only in rational analysis and not in reality (societies are always composed of individuals and individuals can exist only in societies), so, too, are the various systems within a society inseparable from one another.

In effect, the social process is an integral mechanism of mutually interacting parts. Its essence can perhaps best be represented by a dimensional metaphor. The process by which institutions, attitudes and relationships change consists of concurrent modifications along some or all intersecting dimensions—political, social institutional, economic and cultural. Thus, for example, economic growth involves not only changes in the economic system but also concurrent changes in the political, social institutional and cultural systems, or dimensions, of the society. Generally, few of these changes are logically prior to one another, nor does it always matter chronologically in which dimension an innovation is initiated. In most cases, unless the concurrent modifications in the other relevant dimensions, or systems, occur simultaneously—and often spontaneously—the initial innovation is abortive or soon largely dissipated.[1]

Conceiving of the transition as a multidimensional process, whose past history and present characteristics set the limits within which possible choices can be made, has two important related implications for understanding development strategy. First, the process is neither wholly determined nor wholly free. Second, every development experience will contain both common and unique elements. The common elements usually reflect the general form of the transitional process, which the model in the preceding chapter

[1] Thinking of the social process in terms of a dimensional metaphor also avoids the possible error of reductionism which lurks in the use of a metaphor of levels. This is the temptation to regard the lowest level as *ipso facto* the most important and, therefore, as determinative of the others.

endeavored to describe. However, to say that the transitional process has everywhere a common general form does not mean that there is a necessary sequence of stages through which a transitional society must pass, nor that there is a single set of specific institutions, attitudes and relationships which every society must possess before it can develop at a satisfactory rate. The unique elements are reflected in the particular substantive content of each transitional experience. They are especially relevant to the specific development decisions made consciously or unconsciously by each country, since such choices are always within the limits fixed by its particular history and culture.

Types of Development Strategy

Despite their variety, the many different sets of choices, or development strategies, that Western and non-Western countries have adopted, consciously or unconsciously, in past centuries and in the contemporary period can be classified into two types, which may be designated as the "totalitarian" and the "pluralistic." Each is here sketched as a Weberian "ideal" type in order to illuminate its distinctive characteristics, and it should be kept in mind that the experiences of actual societies only approximate to them in varying degrees.

The category of totalitarian development strategies comprises largely conscious efforts to achieve total integration of the society and maximum mobilization and expansion of resources through the motivation of universalistic values systematized in the form of a quasi religion; through the detailed control of all major dimensions of the society by centralized authorities; and through the suppression of all competing—and even merely diversionary—particularistic interests and loyalties. The category of pluralistic development strategies consists of efforts—in past centuries largely unconscious, but much less so today—which involve looser social integration and which mobilize and improve the use of resources mainly through decision making and initiative by diverse individuals and groups in accordance with their interests. This decentralized diversified decision making is, however, constrained and transcended in a variety of ways by universalistic religious or secularized values, and supplemented, coordinated and regulated by broadly representative governmental authorities. The differences between totalitarian and pluralistic development strategies are most evident in their respective systems of universalistic values, in their methods of social integration and control, and in their attitudes and practices regarding diversity, competition and dissent. Their differences in the two latter respects are familiar enough and need not be further discussed here. However, a brief analysis of the differences in their systems of universalistic values is necessary both because they are less well known and because of the importance of such integrating and motivating elements in the transitional process in Asia and Africa.

Except in Japan, the universalistic values that have evolved in the historical manifestations of both types of strategy have all been derived from the dramatic design of Western society—from its concepts of the nature and destiny of man as embodied in the Judaeo-Christian tradition. Although there have been variations in the scope and emphasis of those considered important in each type of strategy, both have been redemptive, seeking to achieve social justice and economic plenty in this world, and stressing the obligation of individuals and groups to work toward these social goals. Hence, messianic and utopian expectations have been present in both types of strategy, although they have been much more explicit and crucial in the totalitarian value system. In contemporary examples of both types of strategy, the originally religious formulation of the system of universalistic values has been secularized and, in effect, refocused upon the nation as the symbolic expression of the society's sense of purpose. Thus, in Western Europe and North America, as well as in Eastern Europe, the Soviet Union and China, the sense of national identity has provided the central symbol around which other universalistic values have crystallized and from which they have derived their proximate sanction and legitimacy.

However, there have been important differences between the two kinds of strategies particularly regarding the ultimate validation of the values each has sought to realize and the methods each has employed in its efforts to achieve them. It is these differences which justify the view that totalitarian strategy embodies a quasi religion while pluralistic strategy does not. Totalitarian strategy replaces the will of a transcendental and immanent God by a self-contained and self-determined historical process as the ultimate sanction for its system of universalistic values and for the legitimacy of its methods. Moreover, just as divine grace guarantees salvation, so these laws of social evolution are believed to guarantee the inevitable coming of a state of society embodying equality and plenty for all. Faith in this inevitable redemption by social forces is buttressed by an intricate socioeconomic and philosophical doctrine, rigorously protected against heresy and doubt by continual indoctrination and punishment. Attitudes and actions expressing individuality and self-interest are *ipso facto* condemned as immoral, and only those feelings and behavioral patterns are sanctioned that involve selfless participation in the common effort to achieve the goals toward which the laws of history (e.g., dialectical materialism) are believed inexorably to be working.

In contrast, pluralistic strategies sanction and legitimize their system of values and their methods in heterogeneous and much less intense ways. Historically, motivating and integrating values have been directly religious in character, as exemplified by the role of the "Protestant ethic" in the development of the nations of northern Europe and North America. Today, in all parts of Western society, even in its East European Communist variety, many individuals continue to feel the validity of a specifically religious sanction for their attitudes and actions. However, for the most part, values and behavioral patterns in the pluralistic countries of Western Europe and North America are sanctioned by various naturalistic philosophies and humanistic ethics. Despite their variety, they all stress the positive values of freedom of thought and expression, of mutual toleration of differing views and diverse behavior, and of the right of individuals and groups to act in their own self-interest and on their own initiative consistent with the right of others to do the same and with the welfare of the society as a whole. Thus, by their nature, pluralistic value systems cannot be expressed as a set of orthodox doctrines and behavioral norms commanding unquestioned faith and uniform obedience.

The effectiveness of totalitarian development strategy depends in part upon the ability of the ruling elite to enforce a unanimism, or singleness of purpose, on the society in carrying out the activities prescribed by it. The effectiveness of pluralistic strategy depends in part upon the capacity of the governing elite to harmonize and orient the diverse and competing activities of individuals and groups and upon the latter's willingness in turn to accept such regulation and to restrain their own self-interests in the interest of the society as a whole. In a sense, totalitarian strategy tries vainly to recapture the organic unity and stability of the traditional society despite the increasing diversification of roles and the plasticity inherent in the transitional process. Pluralistic strategy aims, in effect, to convert a paralyzing particularism into a dynamic pluralism.

These two types of development strategy and their differences are relevant to both the present choices and the future prospects of Asian and African countries. For our purpose, it is useful to conceive of the two types as the opposite ends of a continuum along which the actual development strategies of Asian and African countries can be ranged. Two countries—North Korea and North Vietnam—are committed to Communist-type totalitarian strategies and are, therefore, close to that end. A number of others— e.g., Algeria, Burma, Egypt, Ghana under Nkrumah, Guinea, Iraq, Mali and Syria—can be placed toward the totalitarian end, although not so close to it as the two Communist states. The great majority of Asian and African countries can be ranged from them toward the middle of the continuum because neither in aim nor in performance are they totalitarian states. Nonetheless, the development strategies of the many countries in this median category all involve an active and authoritarian role for the central government —even in the few that have not proclaimed themselves socialist states.

This conception of the government's role reflects not only explicit commitments to socialism but also the characteristics of these transitional societies. The authoritarian and paternalistic behavioral norms of both the old and the new ruling elites in these countries are matched by the scarcity of individuals in the other social groups who desire and are able on their own to initiate substantial innovations in the social institutional, economic and political dimensions of the society. Hence, the ruling elites must—and, of course, are usually eager to—meet the need that exists for a preponderant authority to accelerate and direct the transitional process. In the economic system, the still limited number of indigenous private entrepreneurs, their frequently inadequate innovative capabilities and managerial skills, and the scarcity of resources throughout the private sector mean that governments have had to undertake a much more extensive range of functions than in the Western private enterprise economies. Even the few nations committed to predominantly private enterprise systems, such as Lebanon, Liberia, Taiwan, Thailand and Turkey, have been unable to implement a completely pluralistic development strategy.

Nor have Asian and African countries been able to follow thoroughgoing totalitarian strategies. Except for the two Communist states, which have received the necessary direction and resources from Moscow and Peking, even the countries noted above with indigenous totalitarian-type regimes have been unable to impose upon their societies the degree of unanimism characteristic of Russia and China. While competing interest groups, political factions and personal cliques within the governing elite, as well as the disparate tribes, sects and particularistic groups within the society as a whole, have had to submit to authoritarian political and economic control by the ruling party, they have been strong enough in most cases to resist the degree of suppression and enforced uniformity characteristic of the Communist states. For its part, the ruling party has not had the motivating doctrine or symbol, the trained and fanatical personnel, the knowledge and techniques, and the economic resources required to implement a more thoroughgoing totalitarian strategy.

Thus, the particularism and authoritarianism of Asian and African countries and the limited capabilities of their regimes, on the one hand, make it unlikely that any of them could at present effectively implement a predominantly pluralistic strategy and, on the other hand, inhibit them from carrying out—though not from attempting—a thoroughgoing totalitarian strategy. In consequence, the development strategies of most of them will continue to be more or less mixed. They will continue to allow—and, hopefully, more and more of them will actively encourage—diversified decentralized decision making and initiative to complement the initiative and activity of the central government and to compensate for the latter's inability to mobilize sufficient human energies and economic resources through the public sector and to administer efficiently those which it can. But, the greater the scope for initiative and energy outside the central government and the ruling political party, the more important it is, if the country is to achieve increasing political effectiveness and adequate economic growth, for it to evolve a set of universalistic values able gradually to restrain and orient the pursuit of individual and group self-interest. Such effective universalistic values constitute the essence of the differences between particularism and pluralism.

For the great majority of Asian and African countries, as we have seen, political nationalism and, to a lesser extent, economic socialism provide the symbols around which the new integrating and motivating universalistic values are most likely to crystallize during the transitional process. In consequence, under the terms "political development" and "economic development," they constitute the major portion of the development strategies that most Asian and African countries are attempting to implement.

Relation of Political and Economic Development

A popular assumption in the United States today—and to a lesser extent in Western Europe—is that economic growth and rising living standards will lead automatically to the development of democratic political regimes in Asia and Africa. True, as Aristotle explained, there are certain economic preconditions for the various forms of government; and democracy is more likely to flourish where citizens can earn adequate and reasonably assured incomes and the extremes of wealth and poverty are absent. However, from the Hebrew prophets through the Greek philosophers, the Roman historians, the medieval theologians, and the modern social and political theorists, until the spread of Marxist ideas in the second half of the nineteenth century, no one questioned that good government—under any of Aristotle's three main types of regime —was a precondition for economic progress and prosperity. Economic growth may be a necessary—though it can never be a sufficient—condition for the eventual evolution of democratic regimes in Asia and Africa. But, Westerners tend to underestimate the importance of good government as, in turn, an essential condition for economic growth.

In other words, there is a reciprocal relationship between the political system and the economic system, which are really different dimensions or aspects of a total process consisting of innumerable interactions. Changes in the political system translate themselves into changes in the economic system, and vice versa. In all Asian and African countries, the acceleration of economic growth requires, among other factors, an increased capacity on the part of the political system both to make more relevant and realistic policy decisions regarding national goals and resource allocations, and to administer such decisions more effectively. The particular political changes necessary to achieve such improved capabilities are, therefore, prerequisites for the increase and more effective allocation of resources needed for accelerated economic growth. For its part, economic growth involves the evolution of new and more efficient forms of economic organization and of more dynamic attitudes and expectations regarding economic activity. These are, in turn, essential for the development of more effective and more representative political systems.

In the absence of the political capacity to resolve the issues involved in accelerating economic growth and to administer the resulting policies and programs, little if any lasting and cumulative economic growth is likely to be achieved. In this sense, good government is the prerequisite for economic progress. At the same time, unless the economic system is increasingly differentiated into more dynamic and self-reliant producing, investing and consuming units—both individuals and corporate and cooperative entities—the political system is not likely to evolve effectively functioning institutions responsive in various ways to popular needs and expectations and capable of coordinating and orienting the activities of a more pluralistic society.

For the great majority of Asian and African countries, the immediately relevant innovations are those in the political system required to initiate the process of interdependent and interacting economic and political changes. In a very few countries, of which

India is the leading example, the system of national politics inherited from the period of British rule has been capable thus far of generating a consensus regarding national goals and the allocation of resources for achieving them. However, even in India, the administrative system is not yet able to implement effectively the resulting policies and programs, for reasons discussed below. Virtually all other Asian and African countries have even less administrative capability for carrying out the governmental policies and programs needed to stimulate economic growth and, in addition, have not yet been able to achieve systems of national politics that can make the requisite decisions and can maintain a consensus for a sufficient time among the contending particularistic groups comprising the national society. Thus, in greater or lesser degree throughout Asia and Africa, some improvements in the political system are prerequisites for achieving and sustaining a higher rate of economic growth. For this reason, the problems and prospects of political development are discussed before those of economic growth.

The Characteristics of Transitional Political Regimes

In all of Asia and Africa, there have been only four countries —Ceylon, India, Malaysia and the Philippines—in which, since independence, two or more political parties have continued to operate and more or less free elections have been held without interruption of such characteristically democratic procedures by military coups and dictatorships or the imposition of single-party rule. In only two of these countries—Ceylon and the Philippines —have there as yet been actual transfers of political power from one political party to another through reasonably free elections in accordance with constitutional procedures.

The wonder is not that so many Asian and African countries have been unable to maintain democratic institutions and procedures but rather that even a few have managed to preserve those established under their former colonial rulers. In Western society, functioning democratic institutions required centuries of development during which their preconditions were established: the predominance of universalistic over particularistic values and interests; a strong sense on the part of individuals of self-restraint and social responsibility; the ability to disagree over specific issues, policies and priorities without impairing the national consensus on fundamental principles and general goals; and sufficient confidence on the part of rival political parties, factions and leaders in the continuity of the democratic process to make them willing to abide by the decisions of the electorate regarding their tenures of office. Even within the West, countries vary in the degree of effectiveness and continuity of their democratic institutions. Indeed, only in the English-speaking nations, the Low Countries, Scandinavia and Switzerland have all of these preconditions been fulfilled in sufficient degree to have prevented periodic interruptions of democratic processes by authoritarian or totalitarian regimes.

The single-party regimes characteristic of many Asian and African countries have been formed either by the suppression of rivals or by their more or less voluntary absorption into the dominant organization. The single party tends to be a coalition of uneasy and shifting alliances among ethnic groups, religious sects, ideological factions and personal cliques. Most of these single parties are designed to include the politically active and reliable members of elite groups and, in some instances, are explicitly modeled on the Communist type of elitist party, as in Algeria. Others—for example, in Guinea and Mali—are intended to be mass parties embracing as large a portion of the population as possible in an effort to supersede the traditional and modern particularistic groups and organizations or to subordinate them to the all-embracing universalistic party. Some, though not by any means all, single-party regimes are, or have been, headed by prepotent or charismatic leaders, such as Kenyatta, Nasser, Nkrumah, Sihanouk and Touré, who have tended to exercise autocratic powers.

The dictatorships also characteristic of Asian and African countries are of two types. The first consists of autocracies headed, actively or nominally, by traditional rulers, as in Ethiopia, Iran, Nepal, Saudi Arabia and Thailand. The second type is headed by military leaders, as in Algeria, Burma, the Central African Republic, the Congo, Dahomey, Ghana, Indonesia and Pakistan.[2] While some military dictatorships have held power continuously,

---

[2] An exceptional situation existed under Sukarno in Indonesia which had neither a single-party regime nor a military dictatorship. Sukarno enjoyed a quasi-traditional autocratic status through his charismatic personality and his ability to balance contending political parties and the military.

the more frequent pattern has been for them to supersede civilian regimes from time to time in order to prevent national paralysis and disintegration, left-wing or Communist seizures of power, or to resolve stalemates between rival political leaders. The intermittent character of military dictatorships reflects their lack of legitimacy. In contrast to the traditional autocrats, the exercise of power by the military is not sanctioned by custom or validated by constitutional arrangements. As temporary saviors of the nation, they usually feel compelled to promise the restoration of civilian rule, however long delayed it may be in fact. A few—Nasser, for one—have succeeded in transforming themselves from military dictators into autocratic leaders of civilian-type regimes.

The great majority of Asian and African countries have not solved the problem of political succession. There are, of course, two kinds of exceptions to this generalization: the two countries in which political power has passed from one party to another through democratic procedures, and the larger group of countries actually or nominally ruled by traditional autocrats, who usually succeed one another in accordance with customary procedures. In most Asian and African countries, however, succession is determined either by a palace revolution or by a military *coup d'état*.

Moreover, all of these regimes tend to be not only precarious but also erratic. On the one hand, the civilian or military leader in power must seek to preserve and enhance his authority by eliminating or closely controlling his rivals. On the other hand, in order to rule effectively, he must enlist wider support than his personal clique or military colleagues through alliances and compromises with other factions and groups within the dominant party or among the politically active portion of the population. Thus, these regimes tend to fluctuate between repressive and conciliatory actions.

Major Limitations on Political Development

Owing to the nature of the transitional societies of Asia and Africa, all types of political regimes in these countries—even the few with functioning democratic institutions—are more or less authoritarian. As we have seen, the more particularistic its society and the weaker its sense of national identity, the more a nation must rely upon its central authority to maintain a minimum degree of cohesiveness and sense of direction. But, for the same reasons, the more limited is the ability of the central authority to contain and resolve particularistic conflicts, to define and express a consensus on national goals, and to stimulate and coordinate individual and group efforts for their achievement. Thus, authoritarianism is inherent in the nature of the society but the power of the central authorities is always restricted in greater or lesser degree by the other characteristics of the transitional society. This reciprocal relationship is crucial for political development in Asia and Africa, and it involves three kinds of limitations on the power and capacity for decision and action of authoritarian regimes.

The first major limitation is the particularism of the transitional society. This characteristic has already been amply discussed in other chapters, but it would be well to emphasize again that an understanding of the nature and consequences of particularism is fundamental for grasping the magnitude of the difficulties confronting these countries and for assessing the pace and direction of their development over the decades to come. Because they have been habituated throughout their lives to political processes in pluralistic and not in particularistic societies, many Westerners fail to appreciate the extent to which particularism limits the capacity of authoritarian—and even of totalitarian—governments to make difficult decisions and to enforce them.

The second type of limitation is the inertia of the traditional sectors in Asian and African countries. Again, this characteristic of transitional societies has already been discussed. We may, however, note one point that is especially important for political development: the fact that the great mass of the people are not yet accustomed to an active and pervasive government that seeks to regulate and direct as many aspects and details of their individual and group behavior as are covered by development strategies. In traditional societies that had developed multilevel political hierarchies, the central authorities were remote from the people and directly touched their lives only for certain limited purposes: warfare, the levying of taxes and tithes, and the exaction of labor services for large-scale construction projects. Even during the colonial period, European administrators dealt directly with the great mass of the people almost exclusively to collect taxes and to maintain law and order. Hence, particularly in the countryside where the preponderance of Asians and Africans still continues to live, the influence of the central authorities is limited by the people's unfamiliarity with the kinds of responses that government initiatives are intended to evoke from them. The unresponsiveness of this relationship is both aggravated and perpetuated by the persistence of traditional values and norms and by the adverse effects on individual and group performance of the conflicts between the old and the new.

The third type of limitation arises from the particular characteristics of the ruling elites in these transitional societies. As we have seen, they feel the conflicts in their attitudes and expectations more sharply and more consciously than do the great majority of the people, in most of whom traditional values and norms still tend to predominate. Insofar as the political capabilities of the elites are concerned, their conflicted attitudes and expectations express themselves in three main forms.

The first, already discussed in Chapter 4, is impaired performance resulting from the conflicting cues to which they are expected to respond and from the psychic drain of coping with these ambiguities and with their inadequate sense of identity.

The second is the confusion among personal, group and national interests that permeates most individuals in the elite groups. As explained earlier, a characteristic of the transitional society is the emergence of a sense of individual interest distinct from the interests of the traditional and modern groups in which people participate. At the same time, the interests of and loyalties to both the old and the new particularistic groups continue to be felt strongly and are often in conflict with one another. Finally, as members of the ruling political elite, they are developing a sense of the interest of the nation as a whole which, in turn, conflicts in many respects both with their individual interests and with the interests of the particularistic groups to which they belong. Thus, in all of their social roles and in all of the dimensions of their experience, they encounter conflicts of interest and of loyalty.

The problem is that the mechanism for resolving such conflicts is not yet adequate for the function which it must perform. As we have seen, these countries have not yet evolved a set of universalistic values which would yield a generally accepted order of priority among these multiple interests and loyalties and which, in turn, would be conducive to increasing political effectiveness and economic growth. Nor have these transitional societies yet generated both a sense of obligation eliciting voluntary conformity to such priorities as can be fixed by a particular regime and the parallel ability to enforce them either through legal-juridical systems, as in pluralistic societies, or by coercion.

Moreover, the order of priorities natural to transitional societies tends to inhibit political development since it accords the highest priority to the interests of particularistic groups, both old and new, and the second priority to the advancement of individual interests, with the national interest subordinated to both. Such an order of priorities also characterized Western Europe and North America at comparable periods in their development. A widespread manifestation of this transitional order of priorities, then and now, is the diversion of government resources and the granting of special privileges to the families, tribes, sects, factions and other particularistic groups to which political leaders and government officials owe loyalty, as well as their proneness to expect and to accept bribes and favors for themselves. These practices are, of course, further aggravated by the frequent disparities between the rising consumption expectations of the elites and official salaries at all levels of government. Favoritism, bribery and corruption are not, however, unique to Asian and African countries. But, where they occur today in pluralistic Western countries or totalitarian Communist states, the influence of universalistic values and socially responsible behavioral norms—however differently they may operate—substantially offsets the wasteful and diversionary effects of favoritism, bribery and corruption.

The third form of expression of conflicted elite-group attitudes relates to their conceptions of the national interest. It is generally assumed in the West, particularly in the United States, that the ruling elites of Asian and African countries are single-mindedly and passionately committed to political and economic development as the overriding national goals. However, this is nowhere the case.

In countries where the ruling elites are still composed of or dominated by the traditional groups, there may be no interest in political or economic development at all; or, if external and internal pressures for them have grown too great, the traditional elites may undertake development efforts but always subordinated to the maintenance of their superior social status and the preservation and increase of their property and incomes. In countries where modern elites predominate, other national goals may be accorded a priority greater than, or at least equal to, economic growth and the development of effectively functioning political institutions.

Chief among these other national goals in most countries is the fostering of the sense of national identity through heightened political consciousness and activity, particularly in external relationships. As we have seen in Chapter 4, this is an essential element in the transitional process. However, in the short term, an overriding priority given to creating national identity by such means can be detrimental to economic growth and the evolution of more effective political institutions. Indonesia under Sukarno has probably been the most extreme example of a country whose then ruling elite was so committed to fostering the sense of national identity that it not only neglected economic development but deliberately pursued foreign and domestic policies that resulted in disinvestment, declining living standards, and a substantial reversion to subsistence economic activities. To a lesser extent, Algeria, Burma, Egypt, Ghana under Nkrumah, Guinea and others have also placed a significantly higher priority on forging a sense of national unity and uniqueness through aggressive foreign policies and doctrinaire socialistic reorganizations of their economies than on accelerating economic growth by the most efficient means.

In many Asian and African countries, economic development also competes, in some degree, with such other national goals as acquiring national prestige for its own sake and to play an important role in world and regional politics, achieving territorial ambitions, disseminating ideological doctrines, and expressing resentment and hostility against the West. Moreover, as we shall see later in this chapter, the economic growth of Asian and African countries requires that a greater percentage of the available resources be devoted to investment rather than consumption. Yet, if higher priorities are assigned to such other national goals as increasing economic welfare and greater equality of incomes, then resources will be diverted from investment to consumption. Thus, economic development is only one of the national goals pursued by Asian and African countries, and it may not be, and often is not, given the highest—in some, not even a high—priority in the allocation of national resources and of elite-group efforts.

The inhibiting effects on political and economic development of the conflicting interests and loyalties of elite groups and of their commitments to competing national goals are increased in most countries by lack of experience and training for decision making and administration. Except in the very few countries never ruled by the European powers, neither political leaders nor civil servants have had much more than a decade and a half of experience in making decisions regarding major national policies, and most of them have had considerably less. Moreover, only a small minority has as yet had the requisite formal education and training in public administration, economics, accounting, public law, personnel management and other disciplines and techniques required to analyze policy problems, to recommend policy decisions to responsible ministers and senior officials, and to carry them out effectively.

Inadequate experience and training are in part a result of—and their adverse effects are aggravated by—the fact that, at all levels of the civil service, bureaucratic attitudes and practices originally established by the British and French colonial administrations did not encourage—indeed, usually did not permit—initiative and latitude for discretion on the part of their Asian and African employees. This reflected both the colonial rulers' lack of interest in fostering political development and economic growth and the inexperience and inadequate training of their Asian and African employees. Instead, virtually all of the activities of government were conducted in accordance with prescribed procedures designed to cover in detail all situations that might arise. This routinization of decision making and administration has been perpetuated in the post-independence period and constitutes a major impediment to development. It is especially serious in countries, such as India, which place the heaviest burdens of decision making and administration on political leaders and government employees in conse-

quence of economic development strategies that involve comprehensive and detailed planning, extensive state enterprises, and a
multiplicity of administered controls over private economic
activities.

Prospects for Political Development

The characteristics of transitional societies and of their elites
inhibit the development of greater political effectiveness in several
ways. The lack of consensus regarding the goals that the nation
should pursue and their relative order of priority means that policy
decisions are much more difficult to make in transitional societies
than in the Western pluralistic nations and the totalitarian Communist states. Because of the inadequate administrative capabilities of the ruling elites, policy decisions are not translated effectively into relevant and practicable measures, and they tend to be
carried out with insufficient consistency and flexibility. The effects
of these administrative weaknesses are aggravated by the limited
responsiveness of the people to the much broader and unfamiliar
range of governmental activities in the post-independence period.
And, throughout these societies, the government's authoritarian
role has the contradictory effect, on the one hand, of providing at
least the minimum necessary sense of national purpose and mobilization of resources and, on the other hand, of inhibiting both
within the elite groups and among the people generally the initiative, innovation and enterprise required for fostering greater political effectiveness and faster economic growth.

Although the nature and pace of political development in Asia
and Africa are constrained by these limitations, it should also be
recognized that the severity of the difficulties measures the achievements of the ruling elites in many countries. Their courage, intelli-
gence and shrewdness have outweighed the effects of their
conflicted attitudes and other limitations, enabling them to hold
their societies together and to impart some sense of purpose and
direction to their national efforts. Year by year, the small groups
of dedicated and capable people within the ruling elites become
larger and more experienced in coping with the problems confronting them. Each new generation of the ruling elites will be better

equipped by the experience of its predecessors and by the improved education and training it receives to make more relevant and realistic policy decisions and to administer more effectively the governmental measures necessary to implement them. Although changes at the popular level—particularly in the countryside—occur more slowly, the people generally will also be better able in time to respond appropriately to the government's initiatives.

Progress of this kind is consistent with the nature of transitional societies and of the external influences to which they will continue to be exposed. Fortunately, too, it is a cumulative process; the more that has been achieved along these lines, the more rapid and extensive further development is likely to be. However, during the decades when it is getting under way, not much can be done to accelerate it by deliberate decisions and actions. Basically, such an acceleration would require the deliberate inculcation of new attitudes and behavioral norms on a scale too great to be feasible with the means available to these countries. Hence, as explained in Chapter 4, the decades immediately ahead will witness extremely slow—in many cases, imperceptible—progress, and it will often be erratic with periods of retrogression. There are several dangers that will be particularly important during these coming decades.

Today, it seems less likely than in the immediate post-independence years that Asian and African countries would voluntarily opt for totalitarian communism—a possibility of major concern to the West, and an outcome which its aid has in large measure been intended to prevent. There are several reasons for this trend. The search for national identity is so fundamental a characteristic of transitional societies and so important an element in their development strategies that it deters most members of elite groups from subordinating themselves to an externally directed discipline and limiting their freedom of action by dependence for outside aid solely upon Moscow or Peking. Thus, their nationalism constitutes the major barrier to the voluntary adoption of communism by Asian and African countries.

Moreover, the credibility of communism as the panacea for the problems of society is considerably less than it was some years ago. The deficiencies and ineffectiveness of totalitarian development strategy, not only in the Soviet Union, China and Cuba but also in non-Communist totalitarian countries, such as Algeria, Burma, Ghana under Nkrumah, and Guinea, are becoming more widely recognized throughout Asia and Africa. While the realization of indigenous forms of socialism will continue to absorb the interest and energies of elite groups, communism of the Russian or the Chinese variety is becoming less attractive and its appeal will probably continue to decline further in the future.

However, there are other important factors involved in determining whether Asian and African countries will succumb to Communist regimes. Communist seizures of power could well be the outcome of ineptitude or folly on the part of the ruling elites, and of their inability to resist invasions or civil wars. Indonesia before the end of the Sukarno regime was so preoccupied with other national objectives that it permitted serious economic deterioration and political disintegration to occur and thereby opened the way for a rapid Communist advance toward power. Traditional ruling elites, by adamantly resisting the reforms and development efforts demanded by the modern elites, could push them into joining or allying themselves with Communist elements as the only hope of acquiring the strength and unity necessary for achieving their objectives.

The possibility of Communist seizures of power as a result of situations of these kinds has already been demonstrated by the experiences of the post-independence period. There are also more speculative possibilities that could in the future open the way to Communist regimes. It seems clear that the increasing rivalry between Moscow and Peking will result in greater efforts by each side both to win the support of and to subvert Asian and African countries. On the one hand, such intensified efforts are likely to strengthen nationalist resistance to communism; on the other hand, they are likely to be more effective in undermining incompetent non-Communist regimes.

Even if some Asian and African countries do succumb to communism in the decades to come, such regimes are likely over the long term to become less and less firmly committed to following the dictates of Moscow or Peking not only in their foreign policies, but also in their domestic affairs. This tendency would result from their compelling search for a sense of national identity, whose essential political precondition is the maintenance of national independence and the preservation of the largest possible degree of external and internal freedom of action.

Although it is unlikely that the great majority of Asian and African countries will succumb to communism in the foreseeable future, this does not mean that they will necessarily evolve, either rapidly or slowly, into pluralistic societies with effectively functioning democratic institutions similar to those of the West. Indeed, the survival of democratic institutions is by no means assured in the four countries where they have functioned continuously since each achieved its independence.

Disintegration into independent linguistic-ethnic states is already, and will continue to be, a threat to the future of a united India. It would probably lead to single-party regimes in the successor states, since fanatical elements would almost certainly be in control of them if such a division were to occur. Even if India continues to be united, the gradual decline that has been occurring in the electoral strength of the Congress party could eventually result in loss of its preponderant majority in the federal legislature. Owing to the size of this majority, India has in effect had the equivalent of a single-party regime. If continuing Congress party rule were seriously threatened, it is by no means beyond the limits of the possible that the opposition parties would be suppressed and other measures taken to ensure perpetuation of the existing regime.

Malaysia has already expelled one of its constituent states— Singapore—owing to the fear that the more dynamic Chinese minority mobilized by that city's ambitious leaders would dominate the slender majority of Malays in the federation as a whole. In the Philippines, continued preoccupation with partisan rivalries and factional disputes, with attendant widespread corruption and diversion of resources to local political purposes, could in time lead to intermittent military dictatorships, as has been the case in Pakistan, Turkey and other Asian countries in which civilian regimes have lost public confidence for these and other reasons. Ceylon has been bedeviled with ethnic and religious disputes and political factionalism, and resultant economic deterioration. In-

deed, in Ceylon, the survival of democratic institutions has been
little short of a miracle; by the same token, their ability to survive
strains of such magnitude could very well mean that they have a
better chance of persisting in Ceylon than in the other three countries. For the great majority of Asian and African countries, the
most probable outcome is that authoritarian regimes will continue
for the foreseeable future. The rapidity with which the Western-
type democratic institutions established during the last years of
colonial rule have become ineffective attests to their lack of roots
within these societies. Neither in their traditional past nor in their
current transitional state of divisive particularism, popular passivity and elite-group insecurity and conflicted feelings is there a basis
for the attitudes and constraints necessary for Western-type democratic institutions.

Instead, the cultural heritage of the traditional society and the
attitudes, relationships and behavioral norms characteristic of the
transitional process predispose Asian and African countries to
evolve oligarchical political systems which, hopefully, would in
time be able to handle the succession from one administration to
the next peacefully and in accordance with constitutional procedures. As part of this process, single-party regimes would become
coalitions more broadly representative of the increasingly differentiated elite groups and better able to reach agreements on national
goals and policies by compromises and mutual concessions, as has
been the case in Mexico for the past three decades. The basis for
such representative and effectively functioning coalition regimes is
already implicit in the practice of many of the existing dominant
parties of absorbing rather than suppressing their oppositions.

The next step would be increasing willingness and ability to
moderate and constrain the competition of particularistic groups,
partisan factions and personal cliques by two broader considerations: the interest of the coalition as a whole in its own survival
and increasing effectiveness; and the interest of the regime as a
whole in its continued survival through improved capability to
define and implement a reasonably consistent and realistic set of
national goals representative of popular needs and expectations. A

national consensus would in this way emerge initially among the elite groups and would win wider and wider popular support as the regime became better able to work toward such representative and practicable national objectives. But, whether or when these more representative authoritarian regimes might evolve into functioning democracies cannot now be foreseen.

For the indefinite future, then, the course of political development in most Asian and African countries will be neither rapid, smooth nor continuous. Palace revolutions, assassinations and military *coups d'état* will be the most prevalent ways in which administrations succeed one another, although they will usually seek subsequent legitimization through elections, plebiscites or other forms of expression of popular acceptance. Civilian and military autocrats with prepotent or charismatic personalities will alternate with more collective types of authoritarian regimes. Civil wars between ethnic, religious, partisan and other particularistic groups will continue to erupt, as they have already in a number of countries since independence was achieved. Messianic and renovative movements, religious and secular, will punctuate periods of comparative calm with domestic turmoil and sometimes with aggressions against other countries in the name of their particular redemptive missions.

Thus, the domestic political history of many Asian and African countries is likely to be chaotic and violent in the years to come. In this respect, it will resemble the political history of Latin American countries during the century and a half since they achieved independence, although a major political difference should be noted between Latin America and Asia and Africa. This is the fact that, in Latin American countries, opposition political parties have always existed and single-party regimes have never been permanently established in the region. Even in Mexico, small opposition parties exist today, although their activities are somewhat restricted.

In their political relationships with one another, as well as with the West and the Communist states, the policies and actions of Asian and African countries will continue to be dominated by nationalism. Their search for national identity, however, runs counter to their expressed desire to achieve greater unity with one another on the basis of geographical proximity, ethnic relationships, and common interests and problems. Movements for greater solidarity among Asian and African nations were particularly prominent during the years immediately before and after independence, and expressed their common struggle against colonial rulers and their continuing fear of neocolonialist domination. But, neither the agitation over neocolonialism nor the positive devotion to ideals of racial, cultural or geographical solidarity has been sufficient to generate much significant progress toward realization of Pan-African and Pan-Arab unions—the two leading concepts of this kind.

Indeed, the current trend is away from regional arrangements involving formal political or economic unification, as exemplified by the repeated narrowing of the scope of the economic union among Kenya, Tanzania and Uganda, despite decades of beneficial operation under British rule; the abortive efforts at political mergers between Egypt and other Arab states; and the lack of interest among the countries of southern Asia in proposals for even the limited economic integration of a free-trade area or a customs union. Instead, groups of African, Arab and South Asian countries have been willing to join only intergovernmental arrangements that do not require appreciable integration, with concomitant loss of political and economic sovereignty, but simply involve mutual cooperation with respect to certain common problems and needs. Included in this category are the African and Arab organizations to coordinate policies on regional political problems, the United Nations regional economic commissions for Asia and Africa, and the new Asian and African development banks.

Despite these arrangements for intergovernmental cooperation and the restraining influence of the United Nations and of world opinion, the kinds of mutual suspicions, conflicts of interest and ambition, and armed hostilities that have already manifested themselves among Asian and African countries since independence will recur during the foreseeable future. In consequence, Asia and Africa will continue to be major sources of disorder in the world political system, providing opportunities for conflicts among the superpowers and thereby threatening world peace.

The Economic Implications of Development Strategies

Since the beginning of "development" aid, the most widely accepted view in the West has been that the rates of economic growth of Asian and African countries could be directly and correspondingly accelerated by providing them with increments of economic resources and by helping them to improve their technical and managerial skills. Thus, scarcities of resources and skills are believed to be the factors limiting the rate of economic growth in these countries. Certainly, without resources to invest or the skills to use them effectively, economic growth is not possible. But, our survey of the problems of political development indicates that, more fundamental than the question of resource and skill availabilities, are the difficulties of decision making and administration imposed on these countries by the characteristics of their transitional societies and elite groups. In particular, the inability to agree on the priority to be assigned to economic growth and to adopt the necessary policies, and the inadequacy of the governmental and private efforts to carry out such policies as may be adopted, constitute more inhibiting limitations on rates of economic growth in Asia and Africa than do scarcities of capital and technical skills per se.

These noneconomic limitations on the rate of economic growth once again emphasize the fact that economic institutions and relationships do not constitute an autonomous system but are an aspect or dimension of a society inextricably interacting with its other major dimensions. In other words, economic development strategy cannot be devised in isolation. Efforts to do so by development theorists and practitioners have generally resulted in prescriptions that are either irrelevant to actual situations or impossible to implement.

This does not mean that economic theory cannot provide insights into, or indicate prescriptions for coping with, the economic problems of Asian and African countries. The difficulty usually arises from failure to abandon the *ceteris paribus* principle when moving from theoretical analysis to applied prescription. To be effective, theoretical analysis must abstract from the complexities of reality, and it does so by assuming that some of the relevant factors involved in a problem will not change and, hence, can be discounted in arriving at the solution. However, in real life—and particularly in societies as inconsistent, unstable and incongruent as those of Asia and Africa—the "other things" cannot be assumed "to remain equal" and, therefore, must be taken explicitly into account in drawing operational conclusions from theoretical analysis. In consequence, this discussion of economic development strategy will focus on the limitations imposed by both noneconomic and economic factors on the capacity of Asian and African countries to tackle their economic problems more effectively.

In seeking to enlarge the scope of their ability independently to direct and accelerate their economic development, Asian and African countries are confronted with both policy choices and technical choices. The policy choices relate to the goals they seek to achieve by economic means. The technical choices relate to the ways of bringing about the changes in economic institutions, activities and methods necessary to increase resources and allocate them more effectively. In all societies, however, goals are to some degree in competition with one another, and the technical means chosen for achieving them may also be inconsistent with one another and with the objectives they are supposed to serve.

For example, in low-productivity economies, the more effectively market incentives and governmental measures direct resources away from consumption and into investment, the more rapid economic growth will be, other things being equal. However, in Asian and African countries today, achieving greater justice and welfare through more equitable distribution of incomes and rising living standards would require a shift of resources from investment to consumption and the relaxation of the incentives and pressures to save and invest. Again, the rate of economic growth in these countries would be higher and hence future welfare would be greater if differential rewards were offered for superior individual and group performances and if people had a substantial degree of freedom to make their own decisions regarding production, investment and consumption. But, such differences in income would be inconsistent with the goal of equality, and the greater the freedom for individual and group initiative, the more inhibited the society would be in seeking to mitigate injustices. Thus, such values as equality, freedom, justice and welfare cannot all be realized fully and simultaneously.

The choices among goals, the relative weights assigned to each, and the ways in which they are reconciled with one another and with the means adopted for achieving them are expressed, implicitly or explicitly, in economic development strategies. Each of the two general types of development strategy employs different institutions and techniques for producing and allocating the necessary economic resources. Totalitarian strategy characteristically involves the detailed planning and supervision by central authorities of all significant economic activities, and state ownership or management of all or most economic facilities. Because this strategy tries to prohibit or narrowly circumscribes decentralized decision making through the market process, it is by nature highly bureaucratic, operating by prescribed procedures and tending to restrict initiative to, and to concentrate policy making at, the highest levels within the central government. Totalitarian strategy is also autarchic by nature, because the more dependent the economy is upon foreign trade, the less freedom of action the central authorities have with respect to domestic economic activities.

In theory, the simpler an economic system, the less difficult it should be for central planners to make and enforce detailed decisions regarding production, investment and consumption. In practice, however, the planners in such relatively undifferentiated and largely subsistence economies lack the data and skills for making effective decisions and the means for implementing them. Conversely, the more differentiated and complex an economy becomes, the less effective central planning will be. The information needed by the planners is always incomplete and often incorrect and out of date; significant events frequently occur which the planners cannot possibly foresee; and their judgments are inevitably affected by personality factors, by the conceptual and perceptual biases of the culture, by institutional constraints, and by the pressures of partisan and factional interests. Thus, for a system of comprehensive and detailed central planning and state enterprise to operate effectively in a complex industrialized economy, the planners need to be omniscient, prescient, infallible, omnipotent and incorruptible. Nor can the use of computers and of advanced econometric techniques endow the planners with greater capabilities in these respects than their human limitations permit.

Finally, a characteristic problem of totalitarian economies is the difficulty of obtaining adequate economic motivation. As we have seen, individuals and groups are not expected to engage in economic activities in their own interests but only in those of the society as a whole as defined by the ruling elite. However, except in periods of crisis, such transpersonal motivation is usually neither powerful nor pervasive enough to induce the great majority of workers, farmers and managers of state enterprises voluntarily to maintain—much less to increase—their productivity and to forgo their own consumption and leisure in favor of those of future generations. In consequence, various forms of coercion are imposed in an effort to ensure a minimum efficiency of performance and to restrict consumption so as to maximize saving and investment.

In pluralistic development strategy, substantial freedom is allowed to workers, farmers, investors and consumers to make their own decisions regarding production, consumption, saving and investment in accordance with their conceptions of their own interests in relation to the opportunities, incentives and pressures embodied in the market process. In effect, the market process makes, and signals in appropriate ways, coordinated decisions regarding the allocation of resources. Owing to the decentralized and nongovernmental nature of decision making and to the need for the individual producing and consuming units sooner or later to balance their expenditures and incomes, pluralistic economies tend to operate with greater efficiency than do totalitarian economies, provided that the allocation of resources by the market process is stimulated, supplemented and regulated by appropriate government policies and activities. Also, such economic systems tend to be more open to the world economy and hence to participate to a greater extent than do totalitarian economies in the international division of labor based on comparative advantage. In consequence of the substantial latitude for voluntaristic choice and of the more or less direct perception of their self-interests by the producing, consuming and investing units of the economy, the motivations of individuals and groups tend to be more conducive than in totalitarian economies to conscientious performance of work tasks and managerial responsibilities and to increases in productivity and incomes.

However, pluralistic strategy also has its difficulties and limitations, particularly in transitional societies. Because of the persistence of traditional attitudes and expectations in Asian and African countries, entrepreneurs tend to lack competitive vigor, often preferring to share tacitly or deliberately a static market and to maximize short-term profits at the expense of reinvestment for long-term growth. Many social and cultural factors also inhibit farmers and workers from responding adequately to market incentives and pressures. Moreover, even if the attitudes of these groups were more dynamic, they usually lack the skills and the capital to take advantage of the opportunities for expansion and innovation that arise automatically or under the stimulus of governmental measures.

The other major difficulty in successfully applying a pluralistic strategy in transitional societies arises from the limitations of the market process. Left to itself, the market does not normally allocate resources to the construction or operation of certain facilities and services which are essential for sustained economic growth and increasing economic welfare. For example, entrepreneurs in Asian and African countries are not likely to possess the capital and the skills to construct and operate power and transportation systems, irrigation and water projects, and port facilities, as well as schools and hospitals. Nor are consumers always able or willing to buy at economic prices the goods and services provided by such facilities. Further, in many of these countries, certain types of manufacturing plants require large investments or sophisticated production and management techniques which only governments can finance or obtain from abroad. Hence, if resources are to be allocated for such purposes and the necessary capital and skills obtained, governments have to undertake the responsibility for engaging in these activities themselves or for stimulating and assisting private entrepreneurs to do so.

In addition, governments have to be willing and able to guide, stimulate and regulate the market process for several essential purposes. One is to ensure that private activities will be broadly consistent with the priorities regarding investment and production that are necessary to achieve national goals and, as a corollary, to supply private organizations with the financial resources and technical knowledge they may lack but which are required if they are to conform to national priorities. Another is to maintain the fullest use of productive resources compatible with a reasonable balance between supply and demand within the economy and between the inflow and outgo of foreign exchange in its external economic relations. Others are to preserve a significant degree of competition to the extent permitted by the size of the market; to prevent private activities from leading to the exploitation of or the denial of opportunities to the weaker groups in the society; and to protect the health and safety of the people generally.

The difficulty is that, in most Asian and African countries, the governments do not themselves possess adequate resources and skills for carrying out these varied responsibilities. Nor, as we have seen, are they usually willing or able to resolve the particularistic rivalries and the conflicts of interest involved in adopting and implementing the required national goals, economic policies and measures of governmental assistance. Nonetheless, despite these limitations, Asian and African countries have significantly less difficulty in trying to carry out a pluralistic than a totalitarian strategy because the former places on them a much lighter burden of decision making and administration and the incentives it offers for reasonably efficient and productive private behavior are much greater. In consequence, except in the few nations committed on doctrinal grounds to a totalitarian approach, most Asian and African countries have been trying various kinds and degrees of government planning and state enterprise, on the one hand, combined with more or less extensive private initiative and activity in accordance with market incentives and pressures, on the other hand.

More specifically, the many countries in this median category of development strategy have relatively large public sectors in the modern (i.e., nonsubsistence) portions of their economies embracing social facilities (e.g., schools and hospitals) and infrastructure (e.g, transportation and power systems) but also, in some cases, certain extractive and manufacturing industries (e.g., petroleum and coal, steel and chemicals). These public-sector investing, producing and distributing activities are generally planned in some detail by an appropriate government ministry or coordinating agency, and various devices are employed to ensure that approved public programs and projects will obtain a prior claim on available resources of capital and skills and of imported or domestically produced raw materials, components and capital equipment. The stronger and more explicit the commitment to socialism, the larger is the public sector and the more numerous and varied are the activities conducted by state enterprises.

Nongovernmental decision making and activity usually prevail in agriculture, wholesale and retail distribution and the service trades but tend less often to predominate in manufacturing industries for the reasons explained above. The appropriate governmental authorities endeavor by various means and in varying degrees to stimulate and assist the private sector to diversify, to increase productivity and production, and to expand exports. However, in the more socialistically inclined countries, the cooperative form of nongovernmental enterprise tends to be favored over individual and corporate enterprises, owing to the belief that it is less "capitalistic" and represents a modernized version of the traditional communal organization of production.

In a growing number of countries, the private sector is included in the national development plan, usually in aggregative terms as part of a national accounts projection. However, a few countries endeavor to specify targets for some or all of the activities included in the private sector, and to implement these goals both by detailed controls over investment, production and distribution and by financial and technical assistance. India is the leading —but by no means typical—example of this practice. In addition, India has employed detailed controls over domestic prices and access to foreign exchange in order to check inflation and hold down urban living costs, and to stimulate exports and restrict imports so as to conserve scarce convertible currencies.

The capacity of Asian and African countries to plan and implement such a median economic development strategy largely reflects, as we have seen, their political, social and economic limitations. It would be hard to find an Asian or African country in which national development planning is fully achieving the results expected of it. The necessary economic data are not generally available and the planning personnel usually lack the required technical skills. Satisfactory techniques have not yet been devised for translating aggregative and sectoral targets into specific investment projects and functional programs and for ensuring that the necessary funds for construction and operation of those in the public sector are included in annual governmental budgets. Even in India, which has the best record in the foregoing respects, procedures for progress reporting and periodic plan review and revision are rudimentary. Moreover, the few countries, such as India, which also engage in detailed planning and regulation of the private sector have been unable to cope with the extensive bureaucratic decision making involved and, in consequence, have inhibited private initiative, misallocated resources, and unintentionally encouraged "black-market" activities, bribery and corruption.

These weaknesses of economic development planning are compounded by the inefficiency of many state enterprises, particularly in extractive and manufacturing industries. In part, this inefficiency reflects the persistence in their managers and employees of the same traditional attitudes as characterize many of their counterparts in the private sector. In part, however, it reflects a greater propensity on the part of state-owned and state-managed enterprises to uneconomic policies and practices. These include: the bureaucratic tendency to continue to rely upon standard operating procedures even when changing circumstances require discretion and innovation; the delays in decision making resulting from unwillingness to assume responsibility and from the concomitant tendencies both to refer decisions to the highest authority and for the latter to prohibit decision making by subordinates; and the propensity to rely upon subsidies, monopoly privileges and other forms of governmental resources and powers to cover deficits and compensate for competitive inadequacies. While private enterprises—particularly the older type of family firm, which still predominates in most transitional societies—also tend to have these deficiencies, there is a significant difference of degree between them and state enterprises because they are much less likely to obtain large continuing subsidies or permanent monopoly privileges from the government and, therefore, must sooner or later be able to earn their own way under market conditions or face bankruptcy.

Limitations on Economic Policy Decisions

The inhibiting effects on the rate of economic growth of this limited ability to use existing institutional means and potentially available techniques effectively are compounded by the difficulty of resolving constructively the major issues of policy involved in increasing and more efficiently allocating economic resources. These issues are familiar, since they constitute the major concern of the expanding literature on economic development. However, we may briefly survey the major problems in order to illustrate the difficulties of resolving them in transitional societies. Those discussed are consumption versus saving; agriculture versus industry; import substitution versus export promotion; and inflation versus monetary stability.

A universal policy problem in all countries seeking to redirect resources in order to accelerate economic growth is the rate of saving and investment. Its relevance has already been noted to the conflicts among the goals of equality, freedom, justice and welfare that are intrinsic in decisions regarding the allocation of available resources. There are also specific social and economic problems involved, which some economists have called the "low-income trap." With incomes at or near subsistence levels, the capacity to forgo consumption is small and, therefore, the rate of saving will be low. At the same time, rates of population growth have been increasing in many countries, and all or most of the expansion of output resulting from such net new investment as they have been able to achieve is needed to provide minimum subsistence for the additional people. Any increases in per-capita incomes are likely to stimulate offsetting Malthusian increases in population. Either way, there may be no long-term increase in per-capita income and hence in the rates of saving and investment.

As noted in Chapter 3, there are as yet only a few Asian and African countries in which population pressures at present, or in the near future will, condemn them to the "low-income trap." Too often it is assumed that India is representative of Asian and African countries generally. In this respect, as in others discussed in this and preceding chapters, India is the extreme case and not the average. Only Egypt, Indonesia and Pakistan now have population problems approaching India's in magnitude. However, because these four countries contain a majority of the people of Asia and Africa, mitigation of their population pressures—as well as of China's—is essential not only for their own future welfare but also for the security of the rest of mankind.

A high rate of population growth does not necessarily constitute a problem in countries which have unused arable land and nearly static consumption expectations, as is the case in much of tropical Africa. More important, the "low-income trap" is not inescapable, although the process may be both long and difficult. It is possible to do so even where population pressures are serious because increases in productivity result not only from new capital investment—which may not in certain situations even be a necessary condition—but also from greater food consumption and better nutrition, changes in attitudes and expectations, increases in knowledge and skills, improvements in economic organization and management, and reforms in government policies and practices. Also, it may be possible to reduce the rate of population growth through the spread of more effective methods of contraception. Thus, countries can and do escape the "low-income trap," but the means of doing so generally consist of precisely those social and cultural changes that are the slowest to occur and the most difficult to accomplish.

If and as increased resources can be saved from consumption and used for investment, a second issue arises regarding their allocation between agriculture and industry. There is a series of more specific problems subsumed under this general policy issue. All Asian and African countries are still agrarian in character, with at least half—and in most cases considerably more—of the population engaged in agriculture, both subsistence and commercial, and in processing, distribution and service activities directly related to it. Thus, the agricultural sector generates—directly and indirectly through exports—by far the largest proportion of the personal savings, government revenues and foreign-exchange earnings available for financing investment. Moreover, in virtually all Asian and African countries, the agricultural sector will continue to provide employment and income for a majority of the population for decades to come. This is because, even on the most optimistic assumptions, the nonagricultural sectors are not likely to grow fast enough to absorb both the future increase of population and a large enough proportion of the existing numbers of people so as to employ a majority of them.

These considerations argue that, in Asian and African countries, agricultural development should have the highest priority in terms of official attention and a preferred claim on the required resources, although not necessarily the largest share of capital investment. This has not, however, been the case for a variety of reasons. The elite groups in virtually all of these countries tend to identify agriculture with the traditional past and industry with the modernized future, and to believe that only rapid industrialization, presumably by freeing their countries from reliance upon foreign trade, could enable them to achieve economic independence.

These attitudes and expectations are reinforced by the fact that the productivity of capital and labor tends to be higher in industry than in agriculture because of the greater scope for mechanization and economies of scale and the greater effect of external economies. Hence, the more capital and labor that are shifted from agriculture to industry, the faster the gross national product will grow and the greater the resources that will be available for increasing both consumption and investment. Moreover, it has been generally believed that, in countries in which the ratio of rural population to arable land is high, the marginal productivity of agricultural labor would be zero and that, in consequence, the only means of relieving rural unemployment and underemployment would be by accelerating the growth of the nonagricultural sectors. In addition, the growing migration to the cities resulting from the disintegration of the traditional agrarian society and from inadequate incomes and employment in the countryside has focused attention upon the need to increase employment opportunities in urban areas.

For all of these reasons, the development of the nonagricultural sectors, particularly manufacturing industry, has been given the highest priority in the allocation of resources in virtually all Asian and African countries. The various considerations involved on both sides of this issue are of such a nature as to make a reversal of the relative priorities of agriculture and industry quite difficult to accomplish. True, intellectual misconceptions and deficiencies in knowledge are involved, but they are the least difficult obstacles to overcome. An example of the first is the widely prevalent opinion that the marginal productivity of agricultural labor is zero in countries with a high ratio of rural people to arable land—a conclusion based largely upon *a priori* reasoning. Recently, however, empirical investigations have provided evidence for believing that, even in India, substantial additional labor could be productively employed in agriculture provided more adequate market incentives and improved managerial competence made farmers more willing and better able to undertake the additional effort and the risk entailed in achieving higher output and higher incomes.[3] The two major deficiencies in knowledge are the insufficiency of experimental work designed to improve the biological and technological aspects of tropical agriculture, and the dearth of empirical studies of the cultural, social and psychological factors involved in the acceptance and spread of innovations and of changes in attitudes and norms in the countryside.

Although greatly increased applied research in these fields is certainly necessary, the major obstacles to accelerating agricultural development cannot be overcome solely by empirical investigation and experimentation. The institutions, attitudes and behavioral norms of the traditional society have naturally persisted with greater vitality and on a more extensive scale in the countryside than in the urban areas. Chapter 3 has already described the tendency of peasant agriculture to stagnate in the first phase of commercial development. Unaccustomed to innovation and too unproductive and close to bare subsistence levels to take the risk of innovating, the bulk of the rural population in most countries is capable, even under the most favorable conditions, only of a slow rate of social and cultural change. And, in many countries, such

[3] See Morton Paglin " 'Surplus' Agricultural Labor and Development: Facts and Theories," *The American Economic Review*, V. 55, no. 4, September 1965; pp. 815–834.

changes are inhibited by the open or covert opposition of landlords and moneylenders, sheiks and tribal chiefs, superior castes, dominant sects, ruling ethnic minorities, and other particularistic groups, whose property, incomes, power and privileges depend in part upon continued stagnation or barely perceptible progress in the countryside.

Difficult as it may be, the transformation of agriculture is nevertheless the most important task of development strategy in most Asian and African countries for the specific reasons indicated above. They may be generalized and restated in terms of the socio-cultural model of the transitional process presented in Chapter 4. The traditional agrarian sector still provides the major system of order and meaning in these transitional societies. To allow it to continue to stagnate through neglect would only hasten its dissolution and reduce its capacity to provide economic resources and market demand for the growth of the modern industrialized sector in both manufacturing and agriculture. In these circumstances, the modernizing sector in town and countryside would be even less likely to develop fast enough to generate the new system of order and meaning that will evolve in the course of the transitional process. Thus, the probability is increased that the disintegrative tendencies will overwhelm the new integrative factors, thereby indefinitely prolonging the transitional process and augmenting the danger of internal and external disorder.[4]

Agricultural development depends fundamentally upon the willingness and ability of the farmers themselves. Their initiative can be stimulated by adequate incentives and by the successful and sustained examples of the innovators among them. Government programs for providing technical assistance, low-cost credit, im-

---

[4] Some development economists have advocated a "big push"—i.e., massive and rapid investment in infrastructure and industry—to raise incomes quickly enough to escape the "low-income trap" and to provide employment for large-scale migration from the countryside to urban areas. "Big-push" theorists tend to underestimate or overlook the importance of the traditional agricultural sector, whose modernization is essential for sustained economic growth. Moreover, this technocratic prescription is highly unrealistic. Such massive capital investment would require increasing severalfold the foreign aid obtained from the United States and Western Europe—a very unlikely prospect. Even if the capital were made available, investing it productively would require Asian and African countries to perform prodigies of efficient decision making, organization and management—an even less likely prospect.

proved seeds, fertilizers, and other inputs required to increase productivity, as well as irrigation projects, farm-to-market roads and other capital investments, are necessary supplements to, *but not substitutes for,* such pervasive and powerful incentives and paradigms. The latter are especially important in the larger countries, where the sheer size of the rural population makes it all the more difficult for government programs and projects to reach every village.

However, neither adequate market incentives nor effective government programs are easy to provide. In many countries, farmers' incomes from the principal cash crops are determined, first, by the state of export markets and, second, either by the rate at which the government taxes export proceeds or by the difference between the export price and that paid to the farmers by government marketing agencies. In recent years, increases in the output of such major export crops as coffee, cocoa, cotton, rubber and sugar have tended to exceed the growth of demand for them in the importing countries. The resulting declines in prices have meant lower incomes in the countryside and reduced government revenues available for administrative expenditures and development investment; but rising prices would probably stimulate another round of increased output in excess of the growth of world demand.

A similarly unsatisfactory situation, although for different reasons, exists in the internal market with respect to the prices of domestically produced foodstuffs and agricultural raw materials. Governments have been constrained by urban unemployment and by actual or threatened urban unrest to keep down the retail price of food. Also, efforts to reduce the high production costs of both state and private enterprises have sometimes entailed restrictions on the prices of the domestically produced raw materials required by these manufacturing industries. In consequence, in most Asian and African countries, it has hitherto proved impossible to reconcile the need for higher prices to stimulate increases in agricultural productivity, on the one hand, and the lower prices enforced by the world market and by internal urban and industrial constraints, on the other hand. As a result, both the international and the internal terms of trade have been unfavorable to agriculture in most Asian and African countries during recent years.

Mitigating these problems presents major difficulties. Stabilizing world prices and stimulating import demand for tropical agricultural products cannot be undertaken by the exporting countries alone. Such measures require not only the active participation but also the financial assistance of the major importing countries of North America, Western Europe and Japan. However, even if effective international commodity stabilization schemes could be devised and adopted by the importing and exporting countries concerned, there would still remain a major problem of preventing overproduction. In those Asian and African countries significantly dependent on the export of agricultural staples, the primary need is not to expand production of the crops already in oversupply, or likely again to be, but to increase productivity on the farms engaged in raising them so that farmers' incomes will rise and some productive resources can be shifted to other potential export crops and to domestically required foodstuffs and raw materials. Such changes in agricultural techniques are in part dependent, as we have seen, upon adequate and effective government-assistance programs and capital investments. But, both the willingness and the ability of Asian and African governments to undertake such efforts are limited by the economic and noneconomic factors discussed above.

The third major issue is that of import substitution versus export promotion. In broadest terms, it relates to the allocation of resources between activities which increase exports and those which reduce imports. This issue has important implications for the pattern of domestic investment and production; for the capacity to earn foreign exchange and to finance the imports of goods and services required to accelerate economic growth; and for the balance of payments and the exchange rate and convertibility of the national currency. Import-substituting activities should, by definition, include not only manufacturing but also increased domestic production of foodstuffs and other agricultural commodities required at home. In particular, many countries have been importing increasing amounts of food, which they could raise themselves, thereby saving scarce foreign exchange for other imports more directly useful for economic growth. However, the concept of import substitution has usually been limited to producing at home manufactured goods that have hitherto been imported. This narrowing of the meaning of import substitution stems largely from the notion that industrialization means economic independence.

Another reason for the preference for import substitution as compared with export promotion is the greater difficulty involved in producing commodities efficiently enough to enable them to be sold competitively in the world market and, in the case of manufactured goods, to surmount the barriers imposed by importing countries desiring to protect their own "infant" industries or long-established but noncompetitive enterprises. In contrast, import-substituting activities do not have to penetrate either rigorously competitive or highly protected markets. In order to supersede imports, "infant" industries only require—and usually receive—the protection of high tariffs, quotas and other devices. Such measures generally have the effect of substantially raising the domestic prices of these goods.

The tendency for the prices of domestically manufactured commodities to exceed by an appreciable margin those of the imports which they have superseded is aggravated by the fact that, in many countries, the competition of traditional handicrafts has long since disappeared and few, if any, additional modern-type competitors are likely to be able or permitted to establish themselves within these still small domestic markets. Thus, new industrial enterprises, both private and state, frequently have monopoly positions in their markets. In addition, the small scale of production, the inexperience of the new enterprises, the high cost of some raw materials and other production inputs, and the lower efficiency of labor in most newly industrializing societies result in high production costs, which may sometimes not even be covered by the high domestic prices that can be charged in the absence of competition from imports. In consequence, the new industries may require subsidies or the granting of monopoly status by the government. This is usually the case with state enterprises. For these reasons, import-substituting industries are generally less difficult to establish and maintain than are export-promoting activities.

The process of industrialization must of necessity involve the substitution of domestic production for actual or potential imports.

However, the rate and pattern of industrialization need to be determined on the basis of such realistic considerations as the size of the existing market and its probable rate of growth; the availability at economic prices of the necessary raw materials, components, fuel and operating supplies; the cost of recruiting and training the required labor and supervisory and technical personnel and their likely future level of productivity; and the extent and duration of the protection and possible subsidization which the new industries would need. In many Asian and African countries, adequate weight has not been given to these criteria, with several adverse consequences for economic growth.

The increase in internal costs and prices has generally meant a decline in living standards for the consumers who previously relied upon lower-priced imports. The higher domestic price level is directly or indirectly reflected in higher prices for exports, which often impair the country's capacity to earn needed foreign exchange. Moreover, the reduction in foreign-exchange expenditures may not be as large as anticipated because the cost of importing the necessary raw materials, components, fuel and operating supplies for the new industries is frequently overlooked or underestimated by proponents of import substitution. Hence, excessive or premature import substitution usually has an adverse effect upon the balance of payments and, at least in the shorter run, does not substantially reduce dependence upon the international economy.

One way of making the process of import substitution more economic would be to enlarge the size of the market by the formation of free-trade areas or customs unions among Asian and African countries. Indeed, if the many small countries in these regions, particularly in tropical Africa, are to attain a significant degree of industrialization, they can do so only by participating in arrangements of this type. However, as noted earlier, the single existing free-trade arrangement—the East African common market—has suffered several reductions in scope and its continued existence is now in doubt. Only a few of the French-speaking West African countries have been seriously discussing the formation of a free-trade arrangement. The main obstacle to free-trade arrangements is, of course, the political and economic nationalism characteristic of these transitional societies.

The fourth major issue is that of inflation versus monetary stability. Rising prices in Asia and Africa result not only—and not mainly—from excessive import substitution and other "cost-push" factors but more importantly from the pressure of excess demand generated principally by large and continuing budgetary deficits. In countries seeking to mobilize scarce resources for accelerated economic growth, there is an inevitable bias toward recurrent or persistent inflationary pressures, which are difficult to suppress or offset. Planned goals usually exceed resource availabilities in consequence of inadequate information, errors in judgment, the necessity of satisfying the demands of powerful and competing particularistic groups, and the natural human tendency to be influenced more by the urgency of need than by the limitation of capability. Even when adverse developments diminish available resources, governments are prone to maintain expenditures on the assumption that the setback is temporary; but the deficit usually turns out to be larger or longer lasting than anticipated. For all of these reasons, deficit spending by governments is endemic. In certain countries, owing largely to domestic political pressures and particularistic rivalries, it may get out of hand, as has been the case repeatedly in Latin America during the past hundred years. As yet in Asia and Africa, only Indonesia has been experiencing an inflation of this kind, although Algeria, Egypt and several other countries have been under increasing pressure.

This brief review of these four key economic policy issues illustrates some of the difficulties of arriving at clear-cut resolutions of them. Not only are the purely economic considerations equivocal, but there are serious conflicts involving both economic and noneconomic objectives. Hence, these issues would be difficult to resolve effectively even in countries with a basic consensus regarding national goals and the priorities among them, and with effective mechanisms for reconciling and harmonizing the conflicts of interest involved. Indeed, within all Western nations, domestic politics is in large part concerned with issues of this type, and national decision making regarding them is usually neither easy nor rapid. Because of the lack of a consensus on national goals and priorities and of effective mechanisms for harmonizing conflicting interests, the process of national decision making on complex and ambivalent economic issues is all the more difficult and prolonged in Asian and African countries. In addition, their scarcity of resources means that they have much less freedom of action in dealing with such problems than do Western nations.

Thus, the ability of Asian and African countries to accelerate their rates of economic growth depends fundamentally upon their willingness and capacity to make the relevant decisions regarding national goals and priorities, and to administer these decisions effectively. True, a greater availability of resources might ease the difficulties of decision making, but it would not remove them. Only the progress of political development, as sketched above, is likely to make the crucial difference.

Prospects for Economic Development

With this basic qualification in mind, we may now try to look at the prospects for economic development in Asia and Africa in the decades immediately ahead. Customarily, such forecasts are made quantitatively by means of long-range projections in national accounts terms for individual countries or for groups of countries. These projections usually estimate future economic growth by forecasting the rates of increase in gross national products or national incomes, or in per capita incomes.

However, aggregative projections generally do not provide a picture of *what is most likely to happen* in Asian and African countries individually or collectively. When made by or for the countries themselves, their purpose usually is to show *what should happen,* assuming that appropriate policies are adopted and implemented and the required additional resources are obtained. When made by international organizations or by Western governments and scholars, the purpose generally is to demonstrate *what more is needed* to achieve an assumed desirable rate of growth in order to make a case for obtaining the additional resources through increases in foreign aid. In contrast, to show how much economic growth is likely to occur, long-range projections would have to be made on the basis of demonstrated capabilities, realistic estimates of the additional resources likely to be available, and the effectiveness of the policy changes that these countries could most probably adopt and implement given the limitations imposed by their capacity for decision making and administration and their social and cultural characteristics.

Even if projections of probable economic growth over the longer term were to be prepared on the latter basis, they would still give a misleading picture for two reasons. The first is that, for most Asian and African countries, the data on past performance and present and prospective capabilities are still seriously deficient in comprehensiveness, detail and accuracy. In addition, the quantitative effects on the major economic variables of unforeseeable developments could be quite substantial—plus or minus—over the long term. Hence, the margin of error in such long-range projections is very much greater than the errors implicit in long-term projections for countries, such as those of North America and Western Europe, in which the statistical data are much more complete and reliable.

The second reason relates to the fact that the quantitative economic variables of which such projections are composed are neither individually nor as a system autonomous. Their magnitudes are dependent not only upon their interactions with one another and upon such quantifiable noneconomic factors as population growth, but also upon social, political and cultural developments which cannot be expressed in quantitative terms and which, in many cases, cannot even be foreseen. The assumption that the economic variables covered by such quantitative projections can be regarded as an autonomous system is another example of the misapplication of the *ceteris paribus* principle. Indeed, in any country in which sustained economic growth is occurring, these noneconomic factors are almost certainly not going to remain the same.

Nonquantitative assessments of the probable future course of economic growth are much less rigorous or satisfying than are quantitative projections, but they are the only way in which the nonquantifiable factors can be taken explicitly into account. Moreover, a nonquantitative approach makes it possible to focus attention upon the fact that economic growth is in essence a social process, involving the spread of institutions, values and norms which are conducive to increased productivity.

Chapter 4 has already sketched the ambivalent character of values and norms in Asian and African countries as they affect economic behavior. Here, the institutional aspect of the process of economic growth may be briefly discussed. Assuming that values and norms are conducive to productive economic behavior, the growth process takes the form, in the economic dimension of the society, of the generation of opportunities for new and expanded economic activities and of the operation of positive and negative incentives which induce or coerce people to engage in them. However, the less differentiated an economy is, the slower will be the rate at which new opportunities are generated. With their large subsistence sectors, the low productivity of their commercial agriculture, and the rudimentary nature of most of their industrial systems, Asian and African countries generate new economic opportunities slowly and intermittently, and potential opportunities are often unrecognized and unrealized. Moreover, as we have seen, neither their incentives nor their pressures operate very effectively. In consequence, even though they may be able to sustain a high rate of investment in aggregative terms, it does not have an effect comparable to that which the same rate would have in more highly differentiated economies, such as those of the West. In other words, the process does not become self-multiplying until it has been going on for quite a long time.

For example, as we have seen, new manufacturing industries in Asian and African countries tend to rely upon imports for the necessary raw materials and components, and do not usually stimulate their production locally because the market for them is too small. The converse tends to be the case in the United States, Western Europe and the Soviet Union. Therefore, the establishment of a new factory in an Asian or African country does not automatically involve "backward and forward linkages," as Albert O. Hirschman [5] calls them, to anything like the extent that happens more or less automatically in already differentiated economies.

Thus, economic growth is very much a case of "to him that hath shall be given." The more differentiated an economy is, the greater its capacity for further and faster growth. The more that

[5] Albert O. Hirschman, *The Strategy of Economic Development* (New Haven: Yale University Press, 1958).

the elite groups in particular and the people in general are willing to take initiatives, to innovate, to subordinate particularistic interests to universalistic values, to carry out conscientiously their official duties and productive work tasks, the faster their countries will develop the required human skills and material resources and the more effectively will they allocate and use these means of economic growth. The many countries in which traditional values and institutions still predominate are more or less severely handicapped in this fundamental respect. In contrast, the few Asian nations that already have significant modern sectors in town and countryside have a natural advantage.

In sum, the great majority of Asian and African countries will, at best, be able to achieve and sustain only modest rates of economic growth. Even in the few in which economic expansion is likely to be appreciable—say, an annual average increase of from 5 to 7 percent in real terms—the characteristically high rates of population growth (averaging 2.4 percent a year in Asia and Africa) mean that their per capita increases will be correspondingly less. Moreover, the ability to *maintain* high rates of increase in per capita gross national product or national income for periods of significant length is the essential measure of economic advancement. As we have seen, political difficulties, particularistic conflicts, administrative inadequacies, ideological prejudices and other adverse developments characteristic of these transitional societies are from time to time likely to nullify the gains made during years of substantial economic growth through disinvestment or economic stagnation while increases in population continue. Thus, economic growth in the majority of Asian and African countries, like other aspects of the transitional process, is bound to be slow, uncertain and erratic for the foreseeable future.

Also, it is important to recognize that the result of deliberate policies and programs designed to accelerate the economic-growth process is never simply a direct impact upon the availability and allocation of human skills and material resources. Their effect on the willingness and ability of the elite groups and the people to use available skills and resources efficiently and to increase them is more fundamental and of greater significance for future development.

I have characterized as authoritarian the median type of development strategy that is expressed in the specific policies and programs by which the great majority of Asian and African countries are seeking to accelerate their economic growth. This strategy reflects the particularistic nature of transitional societies and their conflicting attitudes and behavioral norms, comprised of both traditional and modern values and expectations. Owing to its authoritarian character, it tends to inhibit the development of precisely those attitudes and norms required to accelerate economic growth. It does so by concentrating most significant economic decision making in the central government and by expanding public-sector investments and state enterprises. This tendency exists even in countries that do not have a commitment to socialism because economic initiatives and activities outside the control of the central authorities or the ruling political party are suspect. National development planning and public investment in necessary activities which the private sector is unwilling or unable to undertake are certainly required for accelerating economic growth. But, too much or the wrong kind of central government planning, and the preemption by inefficient state enterprises of activities which private entrepreneurs have already undertaken successfully or could be induced to start, result not only in loss of time and waste of skills and resources but, more fundamentally, in impeding or insufficiently stimulating initiative, innovation, conscientiousness and other values and norms required for accelerated economic growth.

However, the inhibiting effects of authoritarian development strategy are gradually being recognized in more and more Asian and African countries. In most of them, the elites have been committed to socialism, negatively to express their opposition to capitalism—which they identify with their former colonial rulers—and positively as a means of developing their national identities through reassertion and modernization of the communalism of the traditional society. But, their efforts to develop socialist economies have been increasingly frustrated by the inherent inefficiencies of detailed central planning and widespread state enterprise, compounded by their own limited skills and political and administrative capabilities for making and enforcing the myriad decisions required. Hence, despite their continued commitment to socialism, an increasing number of countries—including even India—have been explicitly encouraging or covertly permitting a growing scope for diversified decentralized initiatives and activities, and the resultant market-type incentives and pressures are stimulating a significant degree of increased efficiency.

This trend is likely to continue over the foreseeable future and, indeed, holds out the greatest promise for accelerated economic development in Asia and Africa. On the one hand, the fear of a return to a more rigorously authoritarian development strategy and the gradual acceptance and spread of universalistic humanitarian values and of a sense of social responsibility—which, however ill expressed in practice, have always been the justification for socialism—are likely in time to exercise an increasingly significant influence in restraining and orienting particularistic interests toward national goals. On the other hand, the greater dynamism and efficiency inherent in diversified decentralized initiative and activity under an effective system of market incentives and government action and regulation are likely to foster more rapid and substantial economic growth than these economies would otherwise have been able to achieve.

CHAPTER SIX

Latin America:
History and Heritage

Despite the many differences in aspects of their cultures and social structures, Asian and African countries were grouped together in the preceding chapters because they are all essentially traditional societies in process of transition as a result of their encounter with the West. But, the countries of Latin America cannot be included in the same category. Although they have certain resemblances to Asia and Africa, they have not been traditional societies nor is their current transformation the consequence of an unprecedented and socially corrosive encounter with a more powerful, dynamic and alien culture.

True, the indigenous Indian communities of the New World were traditional societies in much the same sense as those of Asia and Africa, and they were conquered by comparatively as dynamic and powerful Westerners in the sixteenth century. But, their encounter with the West had entirely different consequences than that of Asia and Africa. Even the three most complex indigenous New World societies—those of the Aztecs, Mayas and Incas—were rapidly shattered by the conquistadores and their institutions, relationships and values were soon replaced by those brought from the Iberian peninsula by the Spanish settlers. Although in the mountainous countries from Mexico south to Bolivia and Paraguay, many Indian communities have survived, preserving their indigenous languages and impoverished variants of their original cultures, they have constituted, in effect, passive and shrinking "enclaves" within the dominant and expanding Latin American society. In Asia and Africa, the reverse has been the case: Western institutions and values have constituted active and expanding "enclaves" within the indigenous societies, radiating powerful influences through them. Thus, both the nature and the effect of the enclaves have been radically different in Asia and Africa as compared with Latin America.

For more than four and a half centuries, Latin America has been an integral part of Western civilization. Despite certain elements derived from the traditional Indian societies, Latin America's social institutions, cultural values and norms, and economic and political systems have been Western in character, derived directly from Western antecedents and continuously influenced by developments within other parts of Western civilization, notably Western Europe and the United States. Thus, Latin America has constituted one of the great subcultures of Western civilization.

In endeavoring to understand Latin America's history and current problems and prospects, it is essential to recognize that Latin American society is derived from a period in Western civilization prior to the Protestant Reformation, the Age of Enlightenment, the French Revolution, the industrial and democratic revolutions of the nineteenth century, the rise of modern science and technology, and the secularization of Western culture. Hence, these great determinative movements in Western civilization have not been experienced by Latin America at firsthand; that is, Latin America has neither been an innovator nor an active participant in these dynamic processes. Instead, they have been diffused to Latin America from their sources in Western Europe and North America, constituting the outside influences on Latin America's evolution. However, they have not been alien influences, as in the case of Asia and Africa. Although originating outside the Latin American subculture, they have been developments within Western civilization as a whole—of which Latin America has been an integral part—and hence have not been incompatible with Latin American culture in any fundamental sense.

Latin Americans often comment upon the mimetic character of their society, deploring the fact that Latin America has not initiated any of the great movements in Western civilization since the

Renaissance but has imported them. Nonetheless, Latin American borrowings from other parts of Western society were selected, adapted and incorporated into its culture in accordance with its own distinctive conceptual and perceptual biases. Thus, in order to understand the evolution and prospects of Latin American society, it is not sufficient to view them only within the context of Western civilization. The purpose of this chapter is to sketch in broad outline those aspects of Latin America's own history and heritage that play a significant role in motivating and impeding its current efforts to accelerate its political and economic modernization.

The Iberian Background

The distinctive institutions, values and attitudes established by Spaniards and Portuguese in the New World during the sixteenth century were those of Iberian-Catholic culture from which they had come. Although over the past four and a half centuries Latin American society and culture have been substantially secularized and partially adapted to the different social, economic and political conditions of the mid-twentieth century, the major elements of the dramatic design of contemporary Latin American society still embody many of the essential features of the values, expectations and norms which the conquistadores, settlers and royal officials, as well as the Dominican, Franciscan and Jesuit missionaries, brought to the New World during the initial period of conquest and settlement.

The societies of the Iberian peninsula have been integral parts of Western civilization since antiquity. But, from the early eighth century until the end of the fifteenth century—a period of nearly eight hundred years—the region experienced a combination of social changes and cultural influences unique in the history of the West. This set of experiences was occasioned by the Mohammedan conquest and settlement of the peninsula, and by the long centuries of Christian reconquest and reconversion. Space does not permit, nor do our purposes require, an analysis of the many ways in which these experiences produced in the Iberian peninsula a unique variant of Western society and culture. Suffice it to say that the discovery of the New World at the end of the fifteenth century coincided with the completion of the Reconquest, and marked the beginning of the most dynamic and creative century in the history of the peninsula—the *siglo de oro,* as it is called by Spanish historians.

The long centuries of the Reconquest both expressed and strongly reinforced the Spanish will to power and sense of self-confidence. With its resources consolidated by the union of the kingdoms of Aragon and Castile under Ferdinand and Isabella, Spain was prepared to embark upon a period of geographical and political expansion during which it was the leading power in Europe. Under its sixteenth-century Hapsburg rulers—Charles V, the grandson of Ferdinand and Isabella, and his son, Philip II—Spain dominated European politics, ruling directly over large parts of Italy, Germany and the Low Countries, and established its authority over the largest portions of the New World. Throughout the sixteenth century, Spain was almost constantly at war to round out and defend this empire—in the Mediterranean and Eastern Europe against the advancing Turks; in Italy, Germany and the Low Countries against the rising French monarchy and the Dutch struggling to achieve their independence; and on the seas against English, Dutch and French freebooters eager to capture Spanish treasure ships and to win footholds on the islands of the Caribbean and the shores of Central and South America. In addition, Catholic Spain—the most orthodox and devout country in Europe in consequence of its centuries-long crusade against the Moslems—assumed the major responsibility for trying to suppress and, when it failed to do so, to contain the Protestant Reformation.

Spain's performance during its century of greatness was remarkable in view of the difficulties of defending such widely scattered territorial possessions with the relatively slender resources at its disposal.[1] The task of Charles V and Philip II might ultimately have proved less difficult and Spain's period of pre-eminence might have endured considerably longer had its economy and social structure undergone a transformation as rapid and profound as that upon which other European countries were

[1] It is generally supposed that the gold and silver captured from the Aztecs and the Incas and subsequently mined in Mexico and Peru provided ample resources for Spain's century of greatness. However, large as American treasure may have been in absolute terms, it was quite inadequate to finance the new responsibilities which Spain assumed during the sixteenth century.

embarked in the course of the sixteenth century. Instead, for reasons beyond the scope of this study, Spanish society did not undergo, or even commence, a fundamental transformation, although there was considerable economic expansion during the first half of the sixteenth century under the stimulus of the opportunities provided by the conquest and settlement of the New World and Magellan's circumnavigation of the planet in 1519–21.

The system of large landed estates worked by serfs in some parts of Spain and by free tenants in other regions continued to dominate the economy and to provide the largest portion of the incomes supporting the aristocracy and the Church, Spain's ruling elite groups. Inherent in such institutions was the determination of social roles largely by inherited status and the persistence of social relationships that were personalistic and paternalistic. Regardless of the varying degrees of responsibility that have been assigned to the inflationary effects of American treasure and to the inhibiting effects of the Crown's mercantilist policies and interventions, it was nevertheless the case that neither commerce nor industry grew to become major sectors in the Spanish economy.[2] In consequence, the Spanish middle class never became large or dynamic enough to seek and obtain the political power and the influence on national policy achieved by its Dutch, English or even French counterparts.

Indeed, after the accession of Ferdinand and Isabella, the Spanish towns and the representative assemblies (*Cortes*) of Spain's constituent states lost many of the powers and privileges which they had acquired in the late medieval period. During the sixteenth century, military and economic needs fostered a degree of centralization of power in the Crown and of central administrative direction of economic activities unequaled even in England under the Tudor monarchy. The increasing power of the Crown and the development of an elaborate bureaucracy for administering Spain's domestic provinces and its European and overseas

---

[2] While during the sixteenth century Spanish merchants had both a legal and an actual monopoly of trade between Spain and its new overseas possessions, they were never able to supersede first the Italians and later the Dutch and the English in the much larger and more rapidly growing trade between the Iberian peninsula and the rest of Europe. Moreover, at the beginning of the seventeenth century, they lost their monopoly of trade with the New World as Dutch and English smuggling increased and important Spanish mercantile houses became "fronts" for Dutch and English firms.

possessions were probably the most significant changes of the period. In effect, the social structure and the political system evolved in Spain during the medieval period in large part to meet the needs of the Reconquest also proved capable of supporting the much greater Spanish imperial effort of the sixteenth century because the limited efficiency of these institutions was maximized by the centralization of political power and economic decision making in the Crown. The cost, however, was the eventual stifling of economic innovation and administrative initiative and their replacement by a detailed legal formalism—the more stultifying for its minute conscientiousness—that pervaded every aspect, public and private, of Spanish life (*vide* the importance of the notary).

In the light of Spain's gradual economic and social stagnation in the course of the late sixteenth and the seventeenth centuries, we may look for the sources of its earlier dynamism and will to power less in its institutions per se than in the dramatic design of its culture. Under the spur of its conquest by, and long centuries of war against, the Moslems, Iberian society had become more profoundly and overtly religious and the Catholic Church more powerful and dedicated than in any other European country. The spirit of the medieval Crusades—fanatical, devout, intolerant and resolved to convert or exterminate the infidel—was deeply embedded in the Spanish consciousness. In consequence, Spain had a sense of Christian identity and mission substantially stronger and more pervasive than did other European countries. It was expressed in such diverse manifestations as the enforced conversion or expulsion from Spain of the Jews and the Moors; in the work of the Inquisition in uncovering and extirpating Protestant and other heresies both in Spain and in Spanish-dominated Europe; and in the gigantic effort of the missionary orders to convert the Indians of the New World and protect them from the rapacity of the conquistadores.

The overt and pervasive role that religion played in Spanish society of the sixteenth century was medieval in character, reflecting the peninsula's distinctive experiences during the preceding centuries. This characteristic can be seen in the effort devoted to analyzing the nature and discharging the responsibility of the "cure of souls," which expressed itself in part in a new interest in theological studies and in the development of canon law—in effect, the last creative phase of medieval scholasticism.[3] Nor was it an accident that the Jesuit Order was founded in Spain during this century and that it embodied par excellence the chief characteristics of Spanish Christianity—Catholic militancy, missionary zeal, theological preoccupation and political astuteness. Another major characteristic of Spain's highly religious society was its propensity to eschatological, messianic and millennial expectations. They took many diverse forms, depending upon their particular sources in medieval theology and mysticism, and contributed a key element to the dramatic design of Spanish culture in the sixteenth century.

The Significance of the New World and the Process of Settlement

It is against this background of Spain's institutions, values and beliefs that the significance for Iberian society of the discovery and settlement of America can be understood. We need to be concerned with the significance of this experience for sixteenth-century Spaniards because their ideas, motivations and expectations regarding it constituted the initial formulations of the conceptions about the nature and destiny of their own society that Latin Americans have further developed over the intervening centuries. Fortunately for our purpose, Spaniards of the period were unusually conscious of and wrote much about the role that their country was playing not only in contemporary European politics and overseas expansion but also on the cosmic stage where the

[3] This theological concern was strongly oriented toward the problems of the moral life, as may be seen, for example, in the practice—widespread at all levels of Spanish society, including the Crown—of consulting theologians and canonists with respect to every kind of political and personal decision. Indeed, as Francisco de Vitoria, the greatest Spanish theologian of the sixteenth century, declared, "the duties and functions [of the theologians] extend over a field so vast that no argument and no discussion seem alien to the practice and purpose of theology." This theologizing of everyday life was also fostered by the work of the great Spanish canonists, particularly in their attention to casuistry—an indispensable technique for reconciling the abstract demands of conscience with the actual complexities of social existence. This interpretation of the function and importance of casuistry is derived from Benjamin Nelson, "Casuistry," *Encyclopaedia Britannica* (Chicago, 1965).

drama of human destiny was being performed. As explained in Chapter 2, this self-consciousness and sense of historical destiny have been distinctive characteristics of Western civilization. They were particularly pronounced in sixteenth-century Spain owing to its intense religious consciousness and to the strong will to power that emerged from the centuries of the Reconquest and was validated by the European hegemony established under Charles V.

Spaniards of the sixteenth century were well aware that the discovery of the New World was a major achievement in the unprecedented process of planetary exploration begun under Portuguese auspices early in the fifteenth century, and they fully appreciated the political and economic importance for the growing Spanish empire of the conquest of the rich and populous territories of the Indies. But, to the elite groups of the period, these developments were not merely fortunate historical accidents, nor the inevitable results of economic and political processes, nor the justified consequences of deliberate and farsighted policies. Pervading and transforming all such naturalistic and rationalistic explanations of the discovery and settlement of the New World was a preponderant sense of their cosmic significance—an interpretation that expressed in their fullest and most operationally powerful forms the eschatological and millennial expectations of sixteenth-century Spanish society.

Thus, toward the end of the period, Francisco López de Gómara, a historian of the conquest of the Indies, hailed the discovery of America as the greatest event in human history since the Creation except for the Incarnation of Christ. While many Spaniards—and other Europeans as well—were convinced that the discovery and settlement of the New World were apocalyptic events, there was a wide range of specific interpretations of their precise nature and implications for the future. To the more worldly minded, the extraordinary ease with which a few dozen conquistadores had seized the populous and rich empires of the Aztecs and the Incas was fulfillment of the belief that the Spaniards were the new "chosen people" destined under their Emperor-Messiah to rule the world during the final age of mankind. To many others, particularly Dominican theologians and missionaries, the discovery of America opened the way for the destined mission of Spain and her kings—the conversion of the heathen, now possible on a planetary scale. To more eschatologically minded Spaniards, however, especially the missionaries and dignitaries of the Spiritual branch of the Franciscan Order—who played a major role in the establishment of the Church in the New World—the discovery of America confirmed the prophecies of the twelfth-century Cistercian mystic, Joachim of Fiore, whose apocalyptic writings and those of his followers contained the most influential formulations of messianic and millennial expectations in the late medieval and early modern periods.

Joachim postulated three historical ages denominated by the three persons of the Trinity; in the final age, presided over by the Holy Ghost, the conversion of the heathen would mark the coming of Antichrist, whose defeat and destruction by the Messiah would usher in Christ's millennial rule—the thousand years of universal peace and plenty—after which human history would be terminated by the Resurrection of the Dead, the Last Judgment, and the dispatching of all souls either to heaven or hell for eternity. To the Spiritual Franciscans and others influenced by Joachimite prophecies, the American Indians—initially believed to be the inhabitants of Eastern Asia—constituted the largest body of infidels in the known world; therefore, their conversion would be the decisive development that would soon be followed by the earthly millennium. Columbus himself—who had close connections with the Franciscans and wore the habit of their lay branch on his deathbed—believed that the main significance of his voyages was the "opening of the door of the Western sea" through which the missionaries would rush to convert the heathen and thereby initiate the final age of the Holy Ghost.[4]

Millennial expectations were also expressed in more worldly forms. Ponce de León's search for the Fountain of Youth in Florida, Coronado's quest for the City of Gold in the southwestern part of the United States, and the many efforts to find El Dorado —the Golden Prince—in the northern mountains of South America are only the best-known manifestations of the widespread

[4] These expectations have been analyzed in detail by John Leddy Phelan in *The Millennial Kingdom of the Franciscans in the New World* (Berkeley and Los Angeles: University of California Press, 1956).

belief that the millennial kingdom, free from all the ills of the flesh, already existed somewhere in America.

Interpretations of the significance of the discovery and settlement of the New World were not limited to expressions in theological writings and missionary efforts. More important, they exercised a powerful influence over the motivations and activities of the Spaniards who went to America in the sixteenth century and over the policies followed by the Crown in administering the new settlements. Evidence of this influence on conquistadores and royal officials can be seen in their efforts to explain and justify their activities and policies, particularly as they affected the Indian population of the New World. This concern was unique in Western history until the analogous mid-nineteenth-century debate in England over the advantages and the morality of colonial empire. Throughout the sixteenth century, dispute was continuous both in Spain and in America over the right of the Spanish Crown to conquer and rule the Indies, over the reciprocal obligations of Indians and Spaniards, and over the methods to be used for converting the former and for restraining the rapacity of the latter.

A detailed analysis of this extraordinary self-examination and of its actual effects on activities and policies in the New World is beyond our scope.[5] The disparate motivations of the conquistadores have been summarized in the famous statement of Bernal Díaz del Castillo—one of Cortés' foot soldiers who wrote the best eyewitness account of the conquest of Mexico: "We came here to serve God, and also to get rich." According to Gómara, Cortés himself said that "The main reason for our coming to these parts is to extol and preach the faith of Christ, although at the same time honor and profit, which can seldom be contained in one sack, follow in our path." Other conquistadores, however, must have shared the simpler motivations of Pizarro, the conqueror of Peru, who apparently felt neither a sense of mission nor a sense of guilt and desired only to obtain wealth and lead a life of ease in the New World.

Although the motivations of the great majority of Spaniards

---

[5] For a detailed history, see Lewis Hanke, *The Spanish Struggle for Justice in the Conquest of America* (London: Geoffrey Cumberlege, Oxford University Press, 1949).

were mixed, neither conquistadores nor royal officials were left free to resolve their conflicting feelings in favor of material self-interest. The vigilance and the pressure of Spaniards, clerical and lay, concerned for Spain's missionary and messianic obligations were unremitting throughout the sixteenth century and exercised an extraordinary degree of influence over the policies of the Crown. The lifework of the Dominican Bartolemé de Las Casas— "the Apostle to the Indians"—exemplifies in fullest degree the unique combination of missionary activity among the Indians in the New World, learned disputations among the theologians and humanists in Spain, and what today would be called "lobbying" in the inner chambers of the King and the Council of the Indies that also characterized the efforts of many other Spaniards who sought to make their country's policies conform to the values and expectations of sixteenth-century Iberian society.

The extent to which the Crown and the senior royal officials of the Council of the Indies—the highest administrative body responsible for governing Spain's overseas empire—solicited and were responsive to the arguments and proposals of Las Casas and the many other Spaniards who shared his concern for the morality and the eschatological significance of Spanish behavior in the New World has not generally been appreciated by historians within the Protestant tradition. Throughout the sixteenth century, the Crown issued a series of decrees and laws designed to define narrowly and unambiguously the circumstances under which an armed attack by conquistadores upon independent Indian communities would be morally and legally justified; to protect the personal freedom and property rights of Indians already under Spanish rule; and, in the famous New Laws of 1542, to abolish the serfdom entailed by the *encomienda* system (see below) and to forbid further grants of *encomiendas*. There can be no doubt that the Crown sincerely intended these measures to be operative, particularly since they coincided with the royal interest in preventing the development of an autonomous feudal aristocracy in Spanish America. In consequence, these efforts exercised a significant restraint over the behavior of the settlers, although their results fell far short of their objectives with respect to the welfare of the Indians. The patterns of behavior possible in the New World were rather narrowly limited by the nature of the existing Indian societies, the capabilities of the Spanish settlers, and the character of their political and economic relationships with Spain and the rest of the world.

The most advanced indigenous societies of the New World were those of the Aztecs on the central plateau of Mexico, the Mayas in Guatemala and Yucatán, and the Incas of the Andean altiplano from Ecuador southward to northern Chile and Argentina. These communities conformed in their main outlines to the characteristics of the traditional subsistence societies of Asia and Africa as described in Chapter 3, although their technology was significantly different. On the basis of a communal agriculture predominantly for subsistence purposes, they generated an output large enough to support ruling elites of warriors and priests, monumental construction for religious and ceremonial purposes, and a limited trade in local agricultural and mineral specialties, cult objects and materials, and luxury goods. Franciscan, Dominican and Jesuit missionaries, impressed by the absence of acquisitive and contentious behavior on the part of many Indian tribes and predisposed by their own millennial expectations, saw the indigenous inhabitants as innocent children of nature in grave danger of being corrupted and eternally damned by contact with the greedy and pugnacious Spaniards. However, the proponents of this religious antecedent of Rousseau's romantic primitivism overlooked the fact that among the Indians of the New World human sacrifice and ceremonial cannibalism were practiced on a larger and more organized scale than in any other society known to have existed on the planet.

The Spanish conquistadores and settlers substituted themselves for the indigenous elites through seizure of power and intermarriage. It is not generally recognized how small was the total number of Spaniards who settled permanently in the New World—an estimated 150,000 during the more than three centuries of colonial rule—as compared with well over double that number of Portuguese who settled in Brazil, mainly during the eighteenth century, and with the considerably larger number of people from the British Isles who came to the thirteen English colonies during their much shorter colonial period. In consequence, the Europeanization of Latin America was biologically accomplished by intra- and extramarital relations between a comparatively small number of Iberian males and a presumably much larger number of Indian women. The exceptions were regions such as Costa Rica, which had been largely abandoned by the Indians due to natural calamities prior to the coming of the Spaniards, and Chile and Argentina, to which there was substantial additional European immigration during the nineteenth and early twentieth centuries. Also, in Brazil and along the coasts and on the islands of the Caribbean, there was a large —and in some places a predominant—Negro element in consequence of the prevalence of African slavery.

Since the settlers had been reared in the feudalistic society of sixteenth-century Spain, it was only natural that they sought to establish its familiar institutions, values and interpersonal relationships in the New World. The great bulk of the Spanish settlers came from the lesser—often impoverished—Iberian nobility, and were imbued with the expectations and behavioral norms of this group. Hence, as soon as the possibilities for plunder were exhausted in each newly conquered territory, the settlers were impelled to create a system of landed estates that would be worked for them by others. The few attempts made in the early years to encourage Iberian peasants to emigrate to the New World were soon frustrated by the refusal of the landowners at home to lose their own tenants and day laborers. In consequence, the conquistadores were forced to rely upon the indigenous inhabitants to provide the necessary labor supply.

As each newly conquered territory was pacified, the best lands were divided among the conquistadores, but subsequent settlers generally had little difficulty in obtaining land grants of their own. Often, these estates included one or more Indian communities whose inhabitants were "commended," or entrusted, by the Crown to the protection of the new Spanish landowner. Under this arrangement, known as the *encomienda* system, the landowner was responsible for civilizing the Indians and converting them to Christianity, while they had to work a specified number of days each week and to perform other services on the estate. A similar arrangement was used to provide labor for Spaniards to whom mining and pearling concessions were granted. In effect, the *encomienda* system was a form of serfdom; although in theory the landowner and the Indians each had specified rights and obligations, in practice, the latter were usually at the mercy of the former.

For this reason, the *encomienda* system was the chief target during the sixteenth century of Las Casas and other Spaniards who endeavored to protect the freedom and rights of the Indians. While, despite the provisions of the New Laws of 1542, the system was not abolished outright, the Crown did succeed eventually in limiting the duration of *encomiendas* to not more than three generations of owners. Thus, the surviving Indians were sooner or later freed from their servile state, although the land generally continued to be owned by the settlers. As this process occurred, somewhat less onerous systems of forced labor were introduced to provide the necessary work force.[6]

The Structure and Personality Types of Latin American Society

The society established in the New World during the sixteenth century soon came to be composed of three main groups arranged in a hierarchy that in broad outline has persisted into the twentieth century. At the bottom of the social pyramid were—and still are —the indigenous Indian inhabitants, numerically much the largest portion of the population at the beginning but steadily declining in relative numbers ever since. Until the contemporary period, they consisted of two intercommunicating groups: the free Indians living on their communal lands in traditional subsistence ways, and the Indian communities continuously or intermittently compelled to provide the labor force for the estates and mines of the elite groups. Except in central and northern Mexico, where the Indians were largely Europeanized through missionary efforts in the sixteenth century, most members of both groups of Indians have to the present day sought to "live on their own," independent of the European econ-

[6] In the West Indies and the low coastal plains bordering the Caribbean Sea and the Atlantic Ocean, the enslaved Indians soon succumbed to European diseases and the unaccustomed discipline and cruelty of the *encomienda* system. Accordingly, it was in these areas that Negro slavery was introduced, and the African slave trade—called the *asiento*—became a profitable monopoly for Spanish and Portuguese merchants until it was assigned to the English in 1715 by the Treaty of Utrecht.

omy and culture. The major respects in which they did not resist
Europeanization were religion—owing to the presumed superior
efficacy of the conquerors' faith and to the efforts of the missionaries—and technology, where the Indians adopted certain
European products and techniques that fitted harmoniously into
their own subsistence activities and social values. Although the
African slaves must also be considered as belonging to this lowest
social group, they differed from it in two important respects. Economically, they immediately became integral parts of the plantation system, and they absorbed European culture readily in consequence of their complete loss of contact with their original
societies in Africa.

Next in the social hierarchy are the groups of mixed Indian,
Negro and European ancestry who wish to and do follow a largely
Europeanized way of life. Called mestizos, ladinos, mamelucos or
by other names in different parts of Latin America, they have been
numerically the fastest-growing portion of the population as a result both of biological increase and of the adoption of Europeanized ways of living by numbers of Indians. Today, mestizos
predominate in all but a few countries, such as Bolivia, Ecuador,
Guatemala and Peru, where Indians still constitute half or more of
the population. Sharing the prejudice against manual labor held by
the members of the elite group, who constitute their social and cultural paradigms, the mestizos have sought to rise in the social hierarchy by becoming small landowners, retail and wholesale merchants, proprietors of artisan workshops and service-trade establishments, and petty officials of the government. However, economic necessity has compelled most of them to do manual labor
for wages in the enterprises and estates of the ruling elites and of
the more successful mestizos. Nonetheless, in consequence of their
Europeanized way of life, they have regarded themselves, and have
been regarded by the rest of the society, as members of the intermediate social group.

At the top of the social pyramid have been the small elite
groups of landowners, mining concessionaires, large merchants engaged in foreign trade, and higher government officials, augmented
in the late nineteenth and twentieth centuries by industrialists, professionals and technicians. Over the centuries, they have come to

be predominantly of European ancestry, as the initially high percentage of Indian genes has been progressively diluted by continued European immigration—largely of males of similar social status—and by the preference for intragroup marriages.[7] Mestizos and mulattos of more marked interracial backgrounds have, however, always been able to gain admission to the elite groups if they achieved socially acceptable forms of property and magnitudes of incomes; in such cases during the colonial centuries, they could purchase certificates which designated them as "whites."

At all levels of the social structure, the primary social unit was—and continues to be—the family. Although from the beginning essentially nuclear in type, the Latin American family has some resemblance to the extended family of the traditional society described in Chapter 3. This has been particularly true among the landowning elite, whose households have often included several generations with their respective wives and children, as well as cousins, nephews and other collateral relatives, all under the absolute authority of the male head of the family—the patriarch. Among the non-elite groups, family households have tended to be smaller and somewhat less cohesive. While primary loyalty was and continues to be felt for the family as a social unit, the members of both elite and non-elite families have always thought of themselves as individuals with identities and interests of their own. Thus, the Latin American family has been Western in nature and has not been characterized by the kind or degree of identification of the individual with the social group which has been typical of the traditional societies of Asia and Africa.

In keeping with the organization and policies of the royal administrations of Spain and Portugal, the system of government established for the colonies was centralized, authoritarian and bureaucratic, and these characteristics have persisted into the twentieth century. All power emanated by divine right from the King, and was in practice vested in the Council of the Indies,

---

[7] During the colonial period, the top elite consisted of two parts. The largest and fastest growing were the *criollos*—those born in the New World. The remainder were the *peninsulares*—those who came as adults from the Iberian peninsula to fill the top posts in the government and the Church. Throughout the colonial period, there were conflicting interests between these two groups which constituted a major cause of the independence movement early in the nineteenth century.

which exercised full jurisdiction over all aspects of colonial life—political, social, economic, ecclesiastical and cultural. The Crown was represented in the New World by viceroys, and under them were the governors of settled provinces and the captains general —with considerably greater freedom of action—of the frontier areas. These top royal officials presided over the *audiencias*—councils appointed by the Crown to exercise both judicial and administrative responsibilities. In addition, there were large numbers of royal officials at local, provincial and viceregal levels responsible for collecting the revenues owed to the Crown, auditing the official accounts, regulating trade and industry, administering the royal monopolies, and organizing and protecting the annual treasure fleet to Spain.

Throughout the colonial period, the Council of the Indies endeavored—and was to a considerable extent able—to control in detail the activities of this elaborate administrative hierarchy. In consequence, an enormous volume of orders, instructions, requests and appeals passed between the Council and the colonial officials. Responses often took years and sometimes were never forthcoming. The system was saved from complete immobilization only by the unique Spanish legal principle of *obedezco pero no cumplo* (I obey but I do not comply) under which colonial officials acknowledged the obligation to obey the law but suspended its enforcement, pending an appeal to the Council of the Indies, if they judged it inapplicable to their local conditions.

The second structure of authority throughout the Spanish and Portuguese colonies was that of the Catholic Church. Under a bull of Pope Alexander VI, the kings of Spain and Portugal were granted the *patronato,* the right both to appoint all ecclesiastical officials in the New World, and to collect and dispense all tithes and other ecclesiastical revenues. Thus, the Church in the New World was even more fully intertwined with the state than it was in Europe, and it was as dependent upon the central authority of the Crown as was the civil administration. Both the secular and the regular clergy received large grants of land—and even *encomiendas*—from the Crown, as well as subsidies and other benefits.

The upper ranks of the hierarchy were filled largely by

peninsulares until the mid-nineteenth century, and even a portion of the parish clergy continued to be of European origin. The degree of learning, piety and apocalyptic fervor steadily declined among the secular clergy after the early seventeenth century, as among the regular clergy after the early nineteenth century. Only in recent decades has the Church in Latin America begun to reverse this process under the influence of contemporary changes in Latin American society and of the encouragement and assistance of the Vatican and of North American Catholics.

The system of royal absolutism, with power emanating from the Crown and delegated sparingly to lower levels of administration, was mirrored in all relationships of authority and subordination throughout the society. In accordance with the values and behavioral norms of sixteenth-century Spain and Portugal, the colonial landowner was supreme on his estate or ranch, exercising even the power of life and death over the Indians commended to him and the African slaves owned by him. Mestizos working for or living near the estate were also subject to the landowner's social and economic authority, as well as to his political power, since the large landowners have dominated local administration even into the present period. Indeed, except for the free Indians, most members of the non-elite groups were not only subject to the authority but were also in need of the protection of a powerful local *patrón*.

This patronal relationship has been an essential element in Latin America's basic social institutional pattern, which was originally established by the method of European settlement, in turn copied from the practice followed in Spain during the Reconquest of the peninsula from the Moors. As New-World territory was conquered or occupied by the original settlers, it was divided into rural townships, each with a municipal center—often located at the largest or best-situated Indian village in the region. Following Iberian custom, the landowners of the rural township maintained residences both on their estates and in the municipal center, with the latter generally preferred. Thus, town and countryside were linked—socially, politically and economically—through the local elite families, with their groups of mestizo and Indian dependents both at their estates and in the municipal centers. This basic institutional pattern of rural estates and municipal center joined and dominated by a small elite of landowning patronal families was repeated continuously over the centuries as European settlements spread more and more widely from the areas originally colonized. Even today, it still constitutes the predominant pattern of inter-group relationships in the countryside of Latin America.

This institutional pattern is of fundamental importance because three of Latin America's most significant characteristics—its particularism, its personalism and its paternalism—have been rooted in and sustained by it for the past four and a half centuries. Until Latin American society began to be differentiated by industrialization in the late nineteenth century, particularistic conflicts mainly reflected the personal feuds, factional rivalries and clashes of economic interest among the patronal families locally and, after independence was achieved, nationally. The social units engaged in these particularistic conflicts have all been similar: a landowning elite family, or group of related or affiliated families, locally based, with the loyalty of its mestizo and Indian dependents focused upon the patriarch as their *patrón*. Thus, Latin American particularism reflects "segmentation"—to use another term of Talcott Parsons —the division of the society into increasing numbers of social units differing in size but not in nature. In contrast, the contending particularistic groups in the transitional societies of Asia and Africa have been very diverse, consisting of many different kinds of social organizations and affiliations, further divided into traditional and modern. In other words, it is the particularism of a differentiated society. For this reason, also, Asian and African particularism has been much more intense, expressing a "life-or-death" quality characteristic of the transitional society, as explained in Chapter 3. Latin American particularism has not been so intense, even though particularistic conflicts have from time to time led to bloodshed and internal disorder.

The fact that, until recent decades, the particularism of Latin American society expressed primarily segmentation rather than differentiation was a contributing factor to social stability. Despite diversities of interest among the three main social groups, the high degree of homogeneity within the society as a whole helped to inhibit the emergence of conflicts severe and persistent enough to threaten the continuance of the relationship of elite-group dominance and mestizo and Indian subordination and passivity.

This stability was also reinforced by the markedly personalistic and paternalistic character of the intergroup relationships embodied in the basic institutional pattern. The members of the quasi-extended elite-group families have been subject, socially and legally, to the absolute authority of the patriarchal head. The subordinate social groups have also been bound by strong ties of personal loyalty to him as their *patrón,* and their welfare has depended upon his paternalistic direction of their activities and his gracious protection of their interests. In a society that has continued to be characterized by an elaborate legal formalism, detailed governmental regulation of many aspects of economic and social life, and disproportionate privileges and obligations reflecting the wide disparities in status and power, the non-elite groups have always been under the necessity of relying upon their *patrón* to influence the outcome of legal proceedings in their favor, to protect them from the rapacity of officials, and to help them in coping with economic and personal misfortunes. The Iberian practice of the *patrón* serving as co-godfather (*compadre*) to the children of non-elite families dependent on him was widely established in the colonies and has persisted in the rural areas into the present period. It has invested the patronal relationship with a religious sanction and the durability of a quasi-kinship bond. Throughout Latin American history, the patronal relationship has increased the sense of dependence and inferiority of the great bulk of the population and enhanced the power and self-confidence of the elites.

The attitudes and relationships comprising the basic social pattern have also been expressed in and maintained by the paradigmatic personality types and sets of behavioral norms regarded as appropriate for each of the three main social groups.

From the beginning of Latin American society, the model personality type for the elite group has been the benevolent despot, absolute master within his own economic and social domain, subject only to obligations of political loyalty to the Crown (and later to the nation) and of moral obedience to the Church, and conducting his relationship with his peers with acute sensitivity to his own privileges and prestige and with meticulous regard for the formalities of social intercourse. Under the influence of this model, the ruling elites of Latin America have tended to be individualistic, authoritarian, self-indulgent, arbitrarily benevolent, touchy and formalistic. Their paternalistic concern for the welfare of their dependents has usually been manifested in impulsive acts of largesse and personal protection rather than in sustained and organized efforts at social and economic improvement. Like their actual or adoptive forebears, the conquistadores, the members of the ruling elite have generally been callous toward social injustice and economic hardship and have often exhibited a detached and impersonal cruelty in the suppression of insubordination and rebellion.

During the colonial period, members of the elite group were willing to acknowledge and obey the authority of the Crown, which was sanctioned by the theological concept of divine right and buttressed by the habit of centuries. However, after independence was achieved and the integrating and centralizing authority of the Crown was removed, they were unable to engage among themselves in cooperative ways of exercising power through compromise and consensus in part because their self-respect depended upon enjoying unrestrained domination over their subordinates and upon jealously maintaining their privileges and prestige vis-à-vis their peers. These psychological needs and limitations have also been expressed in the behavioral norm called *machismo*—the anxiety allaying assertion of masculinity through sexual prowess and through domination over other males. Combined with the particularistic nature of the society, these psychological characteristics help to account for the ruling elite's inability to establish stable and orderly oligarchical regimes after independence.

There have been two general behavioral patterns among the non-elite groups—one for the Indians and the other for the mestizos.

A substantial part of the Indian population has always clung tenaciously to an attenuated version of its indigenous culture, supplemented by elements adopted from Catholic Christianity. For the Indians, the expected norm has for centuries been to have as little as possible to do with Europeanized society and culture, within whose interstices they lived and which depended largely upon their labor. As a conquered people, whose efforts at emancipation had been cruelly and bloodily suppressed, the Indians tended to be passive, awaiting a miraculous redemption that would restore the dimly remembered and idealized society believed to have existed prior to the coming of the Europeans. Only in recent decades has this passive and withdrawn attitude begun to change under the influence of slowly spreading educational facilities and of programs aimed specifically at raising Indian productivity and living standards.

The mestizos have shared to some extent the characteristics of both the ruling elite and the Indians, as well as possessing certain traits of their own. Like the Indians, from whom they were in part descended and with whom many of them lived in close contact, the mestizos have tended to accept passively the superiority and authority of the ruling elite. In addition, they have been prone to imitate certain elite-group characteristics. For the mestizos also, *machismo* has constituted a prestigious behavioral norm; moreover, they shared in the prepotent *macho* of their *patrón* or political leader, with whom they identified through extravagant adulation and unquestioned obedience. This identification has been a major component in the strongly personalistic relationships between the ruling elite and the great mass of the population.

One of Latin America's leading sociologists, the Jesuit father Roger E. Vekemans, has pointed out that the passivity of Latin American subordinate groups, who expect benefits to be bestowed upon them by their social superiors as an act of grace, has been matched by a tendency to evade or disobey laws and regulations which, by their nature, are impersonal norms. These seemingly contradictory traits are the opposite aspects of the domination-dependency relationship as it is manifested in the highly personalistic Latin American society. As Vekemans explains, in Latin America "all norms are ethical, rather than existing to fulfill a functional purpose. . . . [and] in the face of norms, the Latin American [believes that he can appeal to authority to] cancel the rule and establish the exception, or grant forgiveness in his specific case." [8] Among the ruling elites, this characteristic was expressed in the *obedezco pero no cumplo* principle, and in the individualistic touchiness and punctiliousness of their relations with one an-

[8] Roger E. Vekemans, "Economic Development, Social Change, and Cultural Mutation in Latin America," in William V. D'Antonio and Fredrick B. Pike, eds., *Religion, Revolution and Reform* (New York and Washington: Frederick A. Praeger, 1964), pp. 138–139.

other. It has continued to characterize Latin American society at all levels and helps to explain the persistent difficulty of establishing functioning democracies and a consensus regarding national goals.

Inherited Political Characteristics

The countries of Latin America achieved their independence during the period from 1808 to 1825, peacefully in the case of Brazil, and only after protracted though intermittent warfare in the case of the Spanish colonies. The decade and a half of revolutionary struggle in Latin America found expression in and was in turn sustained by a burgeoning of new ideas and expectations, in large part inspired by those of the Enlightenment and the American and French Revolutions. They supplied much of the rationale and many of the political slogans for the independence movement, and were a major influence in reviving in secularized form the millennial expectations that had been characteristic of the early colonial society.

Despite the defeats and continuous hardships of the wars of independence, colonial morale was sustained by the belief that liberation from Spanish rule would initiate an era of rapid progress in eliminating the irrational conflicts, superstitions and injustices of the existing society. Freed from the dead hand of European rule, the new nations of Latin America would quickly achieve the greatness, the harmony and the prosperity for which their location in the uncontaminated New World destined them. These expectations and their inevitable frustration constituted a nineteenth-century parallel to the sixteenth-century belief—and its similar disappointment—in the early coming of the millennial kingdom. The later experience was secular and rationalistic, and pervaded both elite-group and popular attitudes much more broadly. But, like the earlier experience, it expressed perfectionistic aspirations unrelated to the real possibilities and needs for social progress, and the tendency to regard the achievement of such noble and humanitarian goals as dependent essentially upon proclamatory rather than programmatic activities.

The most widespread manifestation of these early nineteenth-century expectations was the importance attached by the new regimes during and after the wars of liberation to embodying in their written constitutions the ideals of the French Revolution: liberty, equality and fraternity. In some cases, these constitutions contained definitions and legal guarantees of individual rights and liberties that went beyond those envisaged by even the most idealistic Jacobins. In political form, however, most of the new Latin American governments followed that of the United States, which served as the model of a democratic, presidential and federal system. But, nowhere in Latin America did it prove possible either to enforce these ambitious expressions of the rights of man or to establish functioning democratic systems. Instead, the new political regimes reflected the characteristics and limitations of Latin American society inherited from the three centuries of colonial rule.

As the Great Liberator, Simón Bolívar, recognized, the new national regimes were of necessity oligarchical in nature, regardless of whether they proclaimed themselves to be conservative or liberal. The great mass of the people—mestizos, Indians and slaves—possessed neither the experience nor the sense of solidarity required to enable them to play an independent role in Latin American politics; nor was the necessary leadership and organizing ability provided to them by disaffected members of the ruling elite. Although the social ferment and the political disintegration of the decade and a half of revolutionary warfare stimulated some outbreaks of popular discontent, the non-elite groups in Latin America were neither willing nor able to sustain independent political initiatives.

In consequence, until the rise of middle-class and populist movements in the twentieth century, Latin American politics were largely a matter of elite-group initiative and concern—and still are today in some countries. But, though oligarchical rule was never basically threatened, the oligarchical regimes were characterized by chronic instability. During the early post-independence decades, virtually every Latin American country suffered one or more civil wars generated by conflicts within the ruling elite. Dictatorship immediately became the rule and, though national legislatures continued to exist, they possessed only nominal authority except during brief interregnums between the dictators (*caudillos*). Administrations succeeded one another not in accordance with orderly procedures specified in the constitutions but usually by the *golpe de estado*—the actual or threatened use of force.

While there have been significant differences in political orientation and philosophy within the ruling elites, such doctrinal disagreements have been only one of the factors responsible for the chronic instability of Latin America's oligarchical regimes. Basically, this instability—as well as the fact that continuously functioning democracies have not yet taken root in Latin America—has stemmed from the particularistic character of Latin American society, which in turn has reflected its familial and local loyalties and its personalistic and affective norms. As noted above, since the colonial period, the paradigms and norms governing the behavior of the ruling elites have operated against consensus and compromise in their social relationships with one another. The strong family loyalties within the elite groups and the devotion of mestizo dependents to prepotent local and provincial leaders have provided them with the followers, financial support and, when necessary, armed men required to exercise political power.

In the course of the nineteenth century, the homogeneity that had characterized the ruling elites during the colonial period was gradually differentiated by the emergence of new groups and their acquisition of the economic resources and the social influence necessary for political power. As explained in the next chapter, growing demand in Western Europe and North America for primary products stimulated rapidly increasing production of certain export crops in Latin America during the second half of the nineteenth century. This expansion provided new economic opportunities not only for the long-established owners of estates, plantations, ranches and mines, but also for comparatively large numbers of ambitious mestizos who acquired land by various means and, to a lesser extent, engaged in foreign trade and wholesale distribution in the domestic market. As self-made men, these new landowners and businessmen tended to be aggressive and ruthless, impatient of customary elite-group privileges and elaborate bureaucratic procedures inherited from the colonial period, and exploitative in their relationships with the Indians and poor mestizos. They provided a large part of the impetus for the introduction of new forced-labor devices and for the large-scale preemption of the public domains and communal Indian lands which occurred in many countries during the second half of the nineteenth century. However, owing to converging interests and the prestige of the values and self-images of the older elite groups, the new landowners and businessmen—or rather their sons and grandsons—eventually acquired many of the older attitudes and behavioral norms.

In the twentieth century, the ruling elites of Latin America have been further differentiated by the affiliation of additional groups who have achieved influence and prestige directly or indirectly as a result of the process of industrialization and of the attendant expansion of governmental and educational systems. These newest elites consist of the owners and managers of industrial and related enterprises, and of the professionals and technicians needed for modern industrial management and public administration, as well as for the educational system. Included among the new elites are also the officers of Latin America's military establishments, which have grown substantially in size, equipment and technical training during the twentieth century, particularly since World War II. Until recent decades, however, this differentiation of the ruling elites did not result in a significant structural weakening of the oligarchical nature of Latin America's political system.

In consequence of these characteristics, Latin American political systems have differed from those of North America and Western Europe. The main structural units of Latin American politics have not consisted of individual voters and national political parties, as in North America and Western Europe, but of an intermediate level of elite-group families, factions, cliques, clubs, and groups of affiliated provincial and local interests, supported by those of their mestizo dependents who were qualified to vote under the restricted franchises that were initially universal, and still persist in some countries. Since independence, Latin American politics has largely been the history of shifting alliances and alignments among these elite groups and local interests. A minimum degree of stability has been imparted to the system by the existence of national political parties to which specific families, factions and local interests have been customarily affiliated. However, national party loyalty has generally been much weaker than particularistic commitments. For this reason, Latin American political parties have been comparatively undisciplined, and have been characterized by internal factionalism and periodic schisms resulting from rivalries among individual political leaders. This factionalism has expressed not only conflicts of interest and doctrinal differences but also the anarchic and affective behavioral norms of the ruling elite groups.

The particularism of Latin American society has largely determined not only the nature of its political life, but also the character of its nationalism. Loyalties expressing both family and other interpersonal relationships and economic and political interests have tended to be local in character, identified with a particular rural region or urban center. Beyond these local identifications, the sense of loyalty to larger and more extensive political entities becomes progressively weaker. Among the geographically larger political entities, those that had a continuing power to evoke individual and group identifications during the independence period proved to be the major administrative subdivisions of the colonial regime—not the four great viceroyalties of the late eighteenth century, but the smaller and older provinces and captains-generalcies into which the viceroyalties had been subdivided.[9]

Although Latin America's sense of cultural identity has continued to be a strong bond throughout the region, political identity

[9] During and immediately after the revolutionary period, efforts were made to promote the concept of hemispheric unity and, when this ideal proved illusory, to establish federal or confederal unions which followed in the main the boundaries of the four colonial viceroyalties. However, within a few years, the United Provinces of Central America, which had previously severed its tie with Mexico, split further into the original captains-generalcies which now constitute the five small countries of the region; Gran Colombia separated into Ecuador, Colombia and Venezuela; Bolivia and Chile broke away from Peru; and Paraguay refused to join Argentina, while Uruguay was made independent of the latter as the price of Brazil's renunciation of claims to its territory. Only Brazil, despite the distance and the divergent interests between north and south, preserved its unity in consequence of its sense of Portuguese identity vis-à-vis Spanish America and the special circumstances (e.g., common loyalty to the locally based monarchy directly derived from the Portuguese dynasty) which made possible the peaceful achievement of independence without a break in the continuity or effectiveness of the central administration.

has never gone beyond these national boundaries established during the post-independence period. In effect, these boundaries have represented the perimeters at which the sense of political identity and of common loyalty has seemed equal to the sense of otherness, of difference. Thus, until the mid-twentieth century, Latin American nationalism has been a broader and more attenuated form of Latin American particularism. This characteristic may be seen in the post-independence struggles between centralism and federalism in all of the larger Latin American nations. More fundamentally, the particularistic nature of Latin American nationalism accounts for its failure to become, until the mid-twentieth century, a transcending nexus of social identification and loyalty capable of integrating and orienting the competing parochial groups and localities of which the national societies have been composed.

Since the beginning of the independence movement, there have been two main political groupings among the elites of Latin American countries expressing—and often named—conservative and liberal political orientations. They have continued into the twentieth century, although their composition, party names and platforms have been changing. Each time liberal regimes came to power in the nineteenth century and their equivalent left-of-center parties in the twentieth century, they have sought to institute political and economic changes usually in forms derived from European and North American conceptions.

For example, liberal regimes during the nineteenth century were interested in stimulating industrialization but their efforts to follow *laissez-faire* economic doctrines, particularly in foreign trade and monetary policies, helped to inhibit the establishment and growth of manufacturing. The political and legal principles of English utilitarianism were important influences on many outstanding liberal statesmen during the mid-nineteenth century and contributed to their willingness to abolish Indian communal land tenures and to divide these lands into individual private properties. While they hoped that the Indians would thereby be converted into progressive farmers, the result more often was that existing landowners and ambitious mestizos acquired title to the most desirable communal lands, and many of the Indians among whom the remainder were divided were eventually forced to sell their farms because of debts, fractionization of the property through division among heirs, and other causes.

Although the effort to apply European liberal concepts to Latin America during the nineteenth century often miscarried or produced unintended results, many desirable reforms were nevertheless accomplished. Legal slavery was abolished, although not forced labor or debtor servitude (peonage); the beginnings of public-education systems were established; suffrage was gradually widened; codes of civil and criminal law were modernized; and government assistance was provided for the construction of railroads, port facilities, municipal improvements and, toward the end of the century, public utilities and urban transportation.

Increasingly during the second half of the nineteenth century, the major European influence was that of positivism. Indeed, nowhere in Western society have the specific social and political doctrines of Auguste Comte been as widely and as literally accepted as in Latin America or have such deliberate efforts been made to embody positivistic prescriptions in legislation and in administrative arrangements. The significance of Comtean positivism's influence on Latin American thought and attitudes will be discussed in the next section of this chapter. Here, it may only be noted that, under the influence of positivistic concepts and expectations, Latin American *científicos*—as the politicians and intellectuals of this persuasion were called in the late nineteenth century —envisaged grandiose schemes of social engineering which would enable their countries rapidly to catch up with and to surpass the economic progress achieved by Western Europe and North America and which would renovate their societies under the authoritarian but benevolent direction of a scientifically trained elite. Efforts to implement such promises and plans were of necessity on a much more modest scale and, during the late nineteenth and early twentieth centuries, usually amounted to stimulating industrialization largely through the encouragement of private foreign investment from Europe and North America. The earlier *laissez-faire* policies were gradually abandoned, and—with positivism reviving and reinforcing the traditional Iberian practice of detailed administration of the economy by a paternalistic central authority —the role of the state in economic life was steadily enlarged.

From positivism it was not a long step for some members of Latin America's new elite groups to socialism in Marxian and other forms. To many Latin Americans, the most appealing aspect of socialism has been its utopian promise—the millennial kingdom in secular form. To others, however, the Marxist-Leninist concepts of the class struggle, of "the expropriation of the expropriators," and of the inevitable world-wide victory of communism have provided, as in other parts of the world, both a plausible explanation of the reasons for the lack of social progress by their countries and a means for expressing and satisfying their resentment. Nonetheless, in Latin America, the various types of socialism have not superseded positivism; rather, they have themselves become permeated by its faith in the miraculous efficacy of social science and technology in the hands of a benevolent trained elite. Moreover, a residue of nineteenth-century liberalism has persisted among the elites, even among the technocrats and socialists, reinforcing their inherited individualism with the ideals of personal freedom and civil liberties.

During the early decades of the twentieth century, and particularly during the great depression of the 1930s, the old liberal parties tended to merge with the conservatives, and their place was taken by new radical and labor parties led by members of the new industrial and commercial groups. These parties arose in response to the needs created in both town and countryside by population growth, increased industrialization, urban unemployment, and other economic and social changes. Despite the intellectual influence of Marxism, there was little political interest in or popular support for revolutionary socialist remedies for these problems. Instead, the continuing strength of positivist convictions among the elite groups, combined with the populist aspects of contemporary Latin American politics discussed in the next chapter, have generally led to technocratic and bureaucratic responses to these problems.

Once again, the model used by the new radical and labor parties was derived from Western Europe and the United States, specifically their social-welfare legislation—social-security measures covering unemployment, illness and old-age retirement, legal guarantees of trade-union rights and workers' job security, etc.—

as well as reliance upon state enterprises. However, resources have generally been inadequate to carry out these extensive social-welfare schemes and, in many countries, the value of such benefits as have been provided has been steadily diminished by inflation. Labor's freedom to organize in support of its own interests has often been dissipated in political ambitions and doctrinal squabbles reflecting the preference of many trade-union leaders for political over economic goals, the rivalries of different Socialist and Communist factions, and personalistic and individualistic behavioral norms. In addition, the danger that economic growth might be stunted by excessive increases in consumption has led both conservative and left-of-center administrations to conclude that trade-union activity should be carefully controlled and supervised by the government. Thus, social-welfare and trade-union policies have also had the effect of enlarging the role of the government in economic life.

The benevolent authoritarianism of Latin America's newer elites and the expansion of government bureaucracy have found their most recent expression in the efforts to achieve accelerated economic growth and social reform in the period since World War II. All political parties in Latin America today profess devotion to these objectives. They are, however, especially congenial to the newest elites of professionals and intellectuals, nationalistic businessmen resentful of the more competitive foreign-owned companies, trade-union and other leaders of popular movements, and the growing group of modernizers within the Church. These elements comprise the main left-of-center parties in Latin America today, variously designated as social democratic, social Christian, people's progressive, labor, etc. The characteristics of these contemporary political movements, as well as the problems and prospects of achieving accelerated economic growth and significant social reform, will be discussed in the next chapter.

The Dramatic Design of Latin American Culture

From the foregoing sketch of the establishment and evolution of Latin American society during the past four and a half centuries, certain major characteristics may be selected and discussed again in their relationships with one another because together they have constituted throughout the region's history the main elements of the dramatic design of its culture.

As established during the sixteenth century, the dramatic design of Latin American culture reflected the general Christian ethos of Western society in its late medieval form, and the more specific social motivations, ethical concerns and eschatological expectations that characterized Spanish discovery and settlement of the New World. From the beginning, the main theme of Latin American culture has been redemption and perfectibility—the search for deliverance from the ills of the flesh primarily *in* this world rather than *from* this world. During the early colonial period, expectations were focused mainly on the coming of the millennial kingdom, with its harmonious personal relationships and material plenty for all, rather than on the final translation to the unknown bliss of eternity. In the course of the eighteenth century, these expectations were increasingly secularized, resulting in even greater emphasis upon social perfection. Yet, in both its religious and its secular forms, Latin America has expected to achieve this largely mundane destiny less by worldly efforts than by faith in a miraculous act of grace from above.

Within this general conception of the nature and destiny of Latin American society, there have been differences of content and emphasis between the elites and the dependent social groups reflecting their different roles and interests.

The ruling elites found justification for their social roles and privileged status in the perpetuation and transformation of the sense of mission which had permeated the original Spanish effort of discovery and conquest. Through the exercise of authoritarian and paternalistic rule, the members of the elite group during the colonial period validated their conviction that they were discharging their obligation to convert the heathen, civilize the barbarian, and guide the behavior of their social dependents so as to maintain the stability and effective functioning of the society. Among the *criollo* portion of the ruling elite, the original messianic and millennial interpretations of the significance of the New World were gradually transformed into the belief that only in unspoiled America could there develop a new society, more virtuous and more vigorous than that of Europe. Thus, America also contained a prefigurement of the millennial kingdom in the orderly hierarchical, secular, colonial society as well as in the model Indian communities established by the missionary orders.[10]

This elite-group notion of the unique perfectionist possibilities of unspoiled America free of the corrupting influence of Europe played a significant role during the independence movement in the early decades of the nineteenth century. Equally important was the secularization and rationalization of Latin America's millennial expectations under the influence of the ideas of Enlightenment and of the American and French Revolutions. During the early nineteenth century, as we have seen, the landowning elite envisaged the achievement of social perfection through national independence and the continuation of its own benevolent rule. With the emergence of the newer elite groups of businessmen, professionals and technicians in the late nineteenth century and increasingly in the twentieth century, the major influences on such renovative expectations have been positivism, Marxism and modern science. In particular, as already noted, Comtean positivism—including during the late nineteenth century even Comte's now forgotten religious doctrines and rituals—has had strong and continuing appeal to the newer elite groups in Latin America in large part because certain of its key principles coincided with their attitudes and beliefs.

Positivism has a pronounced elitist bias, with little faith in the capacity of the people to elect competent leaders and to support socially responsible and economically feasible policies owing to

[10] As distinct from the secular clergy, which soon lost its millennial expectations, the regular orders of Dominicans, Franciscans and Jesuits never abandoned the missionary zeal and apocalyptic hopes that initially motivated their interest in the New World. The missionary orders represented the Church on the advancing frontiers of settlement, and they established hundreds of missions throughout the predominantly Indian areas to convert the inhabitants and to educate them in more productive agricultural and handicraft techniques. In particular, the Franciscans and Jesuits repeatedly established and supervised model Indian communities which were intended to be prefigurements of the millennial kingdom. Deliberately isolated by their spiritual directors from corrupting contact with the European settlers, these millennial communities flourished in remoter parts of the New World, notably under Franciscan auspices in Mexico and the southwest of the United States and under Jesuit auspices in Paraguay, Uruguay, northern Argentina, southern Brazil and the Amazon region. The Jesuit communities and Dominican missions were terminated by the expulsion of these orders from the New World in the mid-eighteenth century; the Franciscan communities and missions persisted until the struggles for independence and the rise of anti-clericalism in the nineteenth century.

popular lack of the required scientific training and knowledge. In consequence, a ruling elite choosing its own successors on the basis of executive ability and scientific knowledge was preferred by Comte and many other positivists, who tended also to assume that the policies and activities of such an elite would naturally conduce to the common good. For the newer elite groups in Latin America, this positivistic conception of the role of the elite represented a modern scientific version of the authoritarian, paternalistic and quasi-messianic role which the older Latin American elites had hitherto played. Hence, today, the newer elites of businessmen, professionals and technicians are inclined to take a very limited view of the capacity of the people to make wise political choices; they tend to regard themselves as the natural and unquestioned managers of social reform and economic growth; and they assume that their decisions are automatically for the good of all.

A second characteristic of positivism that has been congenial to the newer Latin American elite groups has been the central importance attached by Comte in the mid-nineteenth century to the then new concept of the social sciences as the indispensable means for governing society in the unprecedented conditions created by the industrial revolution. However, unlike Comte, who was addicted to grandiose general principles, subsequent European and North American positivists have stressed the need for continued empirical research and rigorous theoretical analysis so as to improve the capabilities of sociologists, economists, political scientists, administrative experts and engineers. In contrast, in Latin America, the tendency has been to assume that the social sciences and the engineering disciplines already possessed the understanding of social and technological processes necessary for the government of society and the management of the economy. Hence, the approach to the study of the social sciences in Latin America has largely been dominated by the weight of authorities—European in the nineteenth century and North American in the twentieth century—and by a deductive and formalistic application of their insights and techniques to Latin American conditions, to which they have not always been relevant.[11]

[11] In a sense, Latin American social science has, until very recently, been pre-Baconian, owing in large part to the continuing strength of scholastic concepts and methods in Latin American universities and to the central position occupied

This characteristic has been the intellectual counterpart of the political tendency, noted in the preceding section, of Latin American liberal elites to legislate European and North American prescriptions for social reform and economic welfare long before Latin American institutions and resources were capable of realizing them. It has also reflected the tendency to attach primary importance to the word rather than to the action, as explained below. In effect, the original religious expectation of a miraculous act of divine grace redeeming mankind was secularized by Latin American positivism into the miraculous power of an authoritative and omnipotent science to eliminate the ills of society.

Millennial expectations have also been strong among the subordinate social groups, both mestizo and Indian, with those of the former focused upon the coming of a promised future and of the latter upon a return to an idealized past. Beginning in the colonial period, both groups have tended to expect their salvation, in this world as in the next, to come through a personal act of grace by a political leader or patron saint and not from efforts or actions of their own. This attitude of looking upward in the social or heavenly hierarchy for salvation has been of major significance throughout the history of Latin American society. Not only has it reflected and reinforced Latin America's authoritarianism, paternalism and personalism, but it also has been embodied in many other aspects of the culture as well.

A major locus of this characteristic attitude has been the particular form of Catholic Christianity prevailing among the great majority of mestizos and Indians. For both groups, Catholicism has consisted largely of prayers and offerings to the saints and the Virgin—often equated in the minds of the Indians with pre-Columbian deities—as well as in pilgrimages to their shrines and elaborate and often expensive celebrations of their feast days. The performance of most of the sacraments has been comparatively

---

by legal studies in their curricula. Only in the past two decades has Latin America begun to apply the lessons of that "battle between the old and the new learning"—between textual research in the works of recognized authorities and deductive application of their principles and prescriptions, on the one hand, and free inquiry, empirical research, and inductive analysis relevant to particular situations, on the other hand—which had been fought and won in Western Europe by Francis Bacon and many others in the sixteenth and seventeenth centuries.

neglected, except by the elite groups. Among the mestizos and Indians, although baptism has been widely practiced, the marriage ceremony has not; the mass has generally been poorly attended; and confession and communion have been relatively rare. Thus, the religious behavior of the subordinate groups has reflected and reinforced their paternalistic and personalistic attitudes and their expectations of forgiveness and salvation granted by a benevolent ruler of heaven or of earth.

The Catholicism of the Latin American elite groups has been much more sacramental in character. But, they, too, have tended toward a non-activistic conception of the redemptive role which the subordinate groups expected them to play. Perhaps the best-known manifestation of this attitude has been the proneness of Latin American elites, present as well as past, to regard the promulgation of the word as equivalent to the performance of the deed. Just as the word of God is efficacious per se, so a proclamation of his intentions by the ruler or the political reformer is, by virtue of his status and the compelling power of his personality, sufficient to ensure that his will shall be done without the need to provide for the implementation of his prescription. This attitude has been buttressed by the legal formalism of the society, with its insistence on proper documentation and its propensity to regard the use of the correct verbal formulas as the operational factor in administrative and legal transactions.

Faith in the power of the word has also been expressed in the nonprogrammatic character of prescriptions for salvation in this world. Whether the expectation is for the coming of the millennial kingdom of Christ or for the establishment of the utopia promised by scientific positivists and socialists, the process has been conceived as essentially miraculous and not pragmatic. If the word expresses with sufficient fullness the absolute values to which the society aspires and if personalistic faith in the power of the leader is sufficiently strong, then there is correspondingly little need for empirical investigation of the limits of the possible, for the prudent balancing of goals and resources, and for the practical planning and careful execution of programs. Only in the past two decades have these technical requirements for effective policies of social reform and economic growth begun to be systematically met in Latin America.

A final aspect of Latin American personalism that may be noted is the intentionalist ethic derived from the medieval character of Iberian Catholicism. Concerned for the salvation of the individual soul and convinced that the redemption of society could be effected only by an act of grace from above, Latin American Catholicism has stressed the intentions motivating a person rather than the social consequences of his actions. Attention was focused upon determining whether or not the individual intended to conform to ethical norms and standards and was impelled by feelings considered praiseworthy. Whether the actions following from such intentions produced social benefit rather than injustice or exploitation was regarded as of derivative importance.

This intentionalist preoccupation helps to explain the indifference of the Church in Latin America to social reform and economic growth—an attitude that has only recently begun to change. The intentionalist ethic has also been perpetuated by and in turn has helped to reinforce the personalistic devotion of followers to prepotent leaders—psychologically by magnifying the affective element in the relationship, and socially by minimizing the importance of the leader's actual accomplishments as compared with his proclaimed intentions and manifest feelings. Moreover, the significance attached to an action related largely to its interpersonal, rather than to its social, aspect. For example, impulsive and intermittent acts of generosity and charity by leaders to followers and of loyalty and self-sacrifice by the latter for the former were more often noticed and more highly valued than were organized, sustained and impersonal efforts at social amelioration and institutional improvement.

Thus, the dramatic design of Latin American society has embodied a combination—unique in Western civilization—*of this-worldly goals and other-worldly means.*[12] Latin America has aspired to social perfectibility in this world, as this goal has gradu-

[12] There are many examples in the history of Western civilization of the reverse—of other-worldly goals sought by this-worldly means—of those who have tried "to take the Kingdom of Heaven by force" (Matthew XI, 12).

ally evolved from the millennial kingdom of the sixteenth century to the secular utopia of the twentieth century. But, it has sought to achieve this end through the power of the word proclaimed by an authoritarian leader whose potency derives from the force of his *macho* and the nobility of his feelings. In the course of the nineteenth and twentieth centuries, other elements—liberalism, positivism, Marxism and modern science—have crystallized around and modified these central characteristics. But, their influence continues to be powerful and may be discerned even in the newer personality types and attitudes directly involved in the modernization process in Latin America.

Today, Latin America's prospects for economic growth and social reform depend not only upon the availability of resources and the relative power of competing particularistic groups but also upon the attitudes, expectations and behavioral norms of the people participating in the modernization process. The paradigmatic personality types and the attitudes and expectations inherited from the past have not been strongly conducive to the kind of behavior required to use available resources effectively and to reform existing institutions and relationships. Past failures to realize aspirations for social reform and economic welfare inspired by progress elsewhere in the West have generated a sense that present efforts, too, may be foredoomed to failure and have helped to keep alive the yearning for other-worldly means to ensure the achievement of this-worldly goals.

Even among the newer elites—the more dynamic businessmen, politicians, professionals, technicians and intellectuals—whose interests and expectations impel them to press for modernizing changes in institutional relationships and resource use, many still tend to be influenced by inherited values, attitudes and norms. These weaken the modern types of motivations and behavioral patterns which are inculcated into the newer elites by their scientific, professional and managerial training and by the nature of their modern occupational activities and interests. The next chapter explores more specifically such interactions between the old and the new as they affect the modernization process in Latin America's political and economic systems.

CHAPTER SEVEN

Political and Economic Modernization in Latin America

Not since the great transformation of the sixteenth century has the Latin American region known a period of such profound changes in long-established institutions, values and norms as are occurring today. But, although the second half of the twentieth century resembles the first half of the sixteenth century in this respect, it would be a mistake to conclude that the social transformation now under way in much of Latin America has been, or is likely to be, as rapid and drastic as that imposed by the conquistadores upon the indigenous societies of the New World. Nor is it even remotely as bloody.

That the current transformation is not so rapid and profound as that of the sixteenth century is owed largely to the nature of the social institutions and cultural values established during the earlier period. Their stability over the past four centuries has been unusual within Western civilization, whose other great subcultures (i.e., Western Europe, Eastern Europe, and North America) have experienced far-reaching transformations during the intervening centuries. Until the contemporary period, the kinds of changes that have occurred in Latin American society have been comparatively superficial and limited. Even the new political activities instituted after independence and the unprecedented growth of the export sector during the late nineteenth and early twentieth centuries did not fundamentally transform the society. Rather, these and other significant developments in the past involved only those changes in

211

and additions to Latin America's inherited institutions and values necessary to enable them to preserve their essential characteristics in the midst of the new ideas and expectations originating in other parts of the West and the new economic pressures and opportunities generated in the world economy. Not until the contemporary period have changes of a more pervasive and fundamental kind begun to occur in Latin America.

Today, in essence, the countries of Latin America are engaged in a process of modernization. This term is much more relevant to the transformation now being experienced by Latin America than it is to the transition under way in Asia and Africa. There is a relevant value judgment implicit in the concept of modernization: the capabilities and achievements of North America and Western Europe—the most dynamic subcultures of Western civilization—are assumed to be the standard by which the modernization performance of other regions is to be judged. As we have seen in Chapters 3 and 4, such a standard is only partially relevant to Asia and Africa because their inherited institutions and attitudes differ essentially from those of the West. This consideration does not apply to Latin America. Its inherited institutions and values are derived from the same antecedents as are those of the other parts of Western society, and its most probable evolutionary direction is toward increasing similarity to the other great subcultures of the West.

In effect, therefore, the process of modernization in Latin America consists of trying to catch up with the more dynamic parts of Western society. Latin America's need is to hasten the changes in institutions and attitudes and the increase in resources required to make it better able to realize the goals and aspirations that it has tried and failed to achieve on several occasions in the past century and a half. This chapter explains in broad outline the ways in which Latin America's inherited institutions and values have been impeding political and economic modernization and the manner in which these obstacles are today gradually being overcome.

The Process of Political Modernization in Latin America

Political modernization in Latin America means essentially the achievement of changes in attitudes, norms and relationships that can reduce or offset the importance of particularism, paternalism and personalism so that these inherited characteristics no longer exercise the decisive influence on political institutions and procedures. In Latin America today, there are three universalistic values that are rooted in its cultural heritage and past aspirations and are capable of expressing its current needs and expectations. These universalistic values—which may be more usefully discussed in their less abstract forms as national goals—are improved welfare through economic growth, greater justice through social reform, and increased freedom through political democratization. In one or another specific formulation, these national goals have been articulated by the newer elites and have been supported by growing numbers of politically conscious members of the non-elite groups, particularly in the expanding urban centers.

However, both the goals themselves and the means by which they can be achieved are to a significant degree competitive with one another, and their effective harmonization requires a national consensus, explicit or implicit, regarding their relative importance and priority. With the possible exceptions of Mexico and Costa Rica, there appears to be no Latin American country in which such a national consensus has definitively emerged. Particularistic interests and loyalties are still powerful and the groups concerned are unwilling to sacrifice the privileges and status that they believe are essential for maintaining their wealth and influence. The great majority of the people in the countryside are still largely passive, and even those in the urban areas, where they are becoming politically conscious, are not yet structured and organized into continuously active political forces. The members of the newer elites, who are endeavoring to provide leadership and a sense of direction to the inchoate mass of the people, are not sharply separated from the older elites by competing interests, and they are seriously divided among themselves over the means of achieving national goals and the relative priorities to be assigned to them. Their own conception of their leadership role still manifests strong elements of paternalism and personalism, thereby fulfilling and helping to maintain the inherited popular expectation that welfare and justice will be obtained as an act of grace conferred from above by prepotent authorities.

In pursuit of these national goals, a new pattern of politics under the leadership of the newer elites has been emerging in all of the larger or economically more advanced Latin American countries during the past three decades. Its prototypes were the two Vargas regimes in Brazil during the period from 1930 to 1954 and the Perón regime in Argentina during the late 1940s and early fifties. Today, in Argentina, Brazil, Chile, Colombia, Mexico, Peru, Uruguay and Venezuela, the inherited pattern of Latin American politics, by which contending factions and cliques within the ruling oligarchy alternated in office, usually by extra-constitutional means, is being or has been superseded by a new populist politics.

The characteristics of the new populist pattern may be briefly summarized. As the franchise has been extended to the rapidly increasing urban population in these countries, election to the presidency has depended more and more upon winning the support of the urban voters and less and less upon the mobilization by the older landowning elite of its rural voting dependents. To win popular support so that they can achieve political power, the newer elites are prepared to make extravagantly unrealistic promises of large and immediate increases in economic welfare and social justice to the mass of poor and still mainly illiterate urban voters. Once in executive office, the efforts of the newer elites to fulfill these election promises are frustrated not only by the scarcity of resources but also by the active opposition or passive resistance of the national legislatures. The latter continue to be dominated by the older landowning elite in consequence of its control over most local and many provincial administrations through limiting the franchise outside the urban areas largely to its rural dependents. The resulting executive-legislative impasse may be broken by a dictatorship established by a prepotent political leader, such as Vargas or Perón. Alternatively or subsequently, the military intervenes either when a persistent impasse paralyzes political administration and economic activity, or when the efforts of the populist dictatorship to fulfill its promises threaten national bankruptcy or social turmoil.

Thus, the emerging new pattern of Latin American politics differs significantly from the pattern inherited from the past. First, the issues at stake are no longer comparatively superficial differences and rivalries within the ruling oligarchy, but affect the basic institutions and relationships of the society. Second, with the extension of the franchise to the urban areas and the greater concentration and accessibility of the voters in the cities, a substantial and growing portion of the population is no longer politically passive, and the attitudes and expectations of these people are becoming increasingly significant factors in the political process. Third, the military no longer merely provides armed forces to rival leaders and factions within the ruling oligarchy, but tends now to play a more independent and active role in national politics.

The nature and future development of this emerging new pattern depend essentially upon the characteristics of the groups actively involved in it and on the distribution of power among them.

The politically conscious and enfranchised urban population is still largely an atomized mass of illiterate, poorly paid and, in many cases, underemployed or unemployed individuals, many of whom are recent arrivals from the countryside. In other words, the great concentration of urban voters is not yet structured into differentiated groups with specific common interests based upon occupation, economic and social status, or local residence. Except for the comparatively small minority who belong to trade-unions or to the evangelical and neopagan religious sects—the latter a characteristic symptom of periods of social atomization and rapid change in Western society—they are still largely without organization and leaders developed from their own ranks. In consequence, while they have become more and more politically conscious and active, their participation in the political process is generally intermittent and impulsive, and they do not constitute a permanently independent political force.

Moreover, their political attitudes and expectations continue to be dominated by paternalism and personalism. Many have replaced their former rural *patrones* by their new urban employers, political leaders, or economically successful relatives or migrants from the same village; and all expect the bureaucratic state also to play a paternalistic role. Their political loyalties are quickly focused upon any political leader with a prepotent personality who promises to provide the greatest economic and social benefits. Lacking education and without experience in judging political promises by realistic and socially responsible standards, they are attracted by utopian slogans and xenophobic panaceas, which they believe can be quickly realized through the will and sincerity of an authoritarian political leader. Frustration and provocative incidents lead to outbreaks of lawlessness and of mob violence, expressing the persistence of the impulse to disobey norms and regulations that has accompanied their inherited behavior pattern of passive subordination.

The characteristics of the elite groups provide the other end of the relationship in the new pattern of Latin American politics. Although a distinction has been made between the older and the newer types of elite groups, differentiation between them is by no means sharp and complete. Particularly in the larger and more advanced countries, where the populist pattern is emerging most clearly, both types of elite groups continue to have overlapping economic and social interests, as well as to share common attitudes and behavioral norms rooted in Latin America's heritage. With respect to economic interests, many landowners have invested in manufacturing industry in recent decades, and even more of the successful industrial entrepreneurs have bought rural estates, which they farm directly through resident managers or rent to sharecroppers and tenants. Thus, the elite groups constitute a continuum rather than two sharply differentiated and mutually contending classes of landed interests and manufacturing interests, respectively. This situation differs from that of nineteenth-century England, for example, where the landed and the manufacturing interests were more sharply differentiated and pursued opposing economic policies. In Latin America today, the two types of elites are often in agreement regarding broad areas of national economic policy.

While the professional and technical elite can be distinguished on educational and occupational grounds from both the newer businessmen and the older landowners, it, too, shares certain important characteristics with these other groups. On the basis of West European and North American experience, it has generally been assumed that the technical, intellectual and professional elite group, along with the new businessmen, would be the equivalent of a middle class, and hence would be by nature democratic, providing the support for political regimes characterized by universal suffrage, functioning representative institutions, orderly changes of administration consequent upon free elections, and effective civil rights. And, this view is bolstered by the fact that Latin America's newer elites customarily profess devotion to democratic institutions and procedures and verbally condemn authoritarianism and dictatorship. There can be no question of their deep concern with improved economic welfare and social justice for the people. But, they, too, act on the implicit expectation that these benefits will be bestowed by a qualified, authoritarian elite—i.e., by themselves—rather than being achieved by entrusting the people with continuing responsibility for significant participation in national decision making. Thus, in practice, the difference between the older and the newer elites in Latin America is, with some exceptions, that between a traditional feudalistic paternalism and a modern technocratic paternalism. Despite the contrast between the aristocratic superiority and conservative opposition to change of the former and the positivistic faith and liberal democratic slogans of the latter, both tend to be authoritarian and convinced of their own benevolent and ordained redemptive role.

This substantial degree of common interests and characteristics between the older and newer elite groups helps to blur the real issues now involved in national politics, and weakens the willingness and ability of the new populist leaders and technocrats to press strongly and consistently for their political programs. Their political effectiveness is also—and more seriously—restricted by the nature of their political power. In contrast to the older landowners and even to the newer businessmen, the professional, technical and intellectual members of the newer elites—who have been playing the major role in articulating national goals and popular political objectives—possess little, if any, political power based either upon wealth or upon social position. Instead, their political influence depends upon their capacity to reach and mobilize the inchoate mass of urban voters and upon their predominance within the government bureaucracy. However, neither of these two sources of political power is as certain and as continuously reliable as are the sources of political power of the older landed oligarchy and the newer businessmen.

The uncertain and sporadic nature of popular support is implicit in the characteristics of the urban population noted above and needs no further elaboration. However, a word may be said about the relationship between the new technocratic elite and the bureaucratic state in Latin America today. As we have seen in the preceding chapter, the bureaucratic state was inherited from Latin America's Iberian and colonial past. In recent decades, the size and the scope of governmental functions have expanded substantially in consequence of efforts to achieve greater social justice and accelerated economic growth. Yet, large as they may be, and pervasively as their influence may penetrate economic and social life, the numerous departments and agencies of government in each country are by no means unified and coordinated organizations nor are they effectively controlled by the technocratic elite, although its members usually staff their upper ranks.

The great majority of personnel in the departments and agencies of Latin American governments—not only at local and provincial levels but also in the national administrations—have not been trained in modern administrative skills and do not constitute a career civil service graded according to qualification and appointed and promoted on merit. Instead, most owe their jobs to patronage and divide their loyalties among their *patrones,* their personal and family interests, and the responsibilities of the agencies in which they serve. Latin American bureaucracies operate in a highly formalistic manner, with long-established and elaborate procedures for handling government business, both important and trivial, and with recognized methods of circumventing the resulting cumbersomeness and delay through personal influence, bribery and mutual favors.[1] In such organizations, the small group of trained and competent top-level technocrats carry a superhuman burden not

[1] One of Brazil's leading economists has pointedly stressed the inhibiting effects on the modernization process of "the crippling tradition of the notarial state, the complicated bureaucratic machinery based on distrust of citizen and civil servant alike, where every absurdity is possible provided the required documents can be produced, and where the most reasonable thing is impossible without them." Alexander Kafka, "The Theoretical Interpretation of Latin American Economic Development," in Howard S. Ellis, ed., *Economic Development for Latin America,* Proceedings of a conference held by the International Economic Association (New York: St. Martin's Press, 1961), p. 8.

only of policy making but also of routine program execution. Their capacity to mobilize bureaucratic energies and direct them toward the achievement of national goals is dissipated in trying to keep up with their disproportionate work load, and their efforts are also frustrated by the lack of necessary skills, the divided loyalties, and the inherited formalism of the great majority of subordinate personnel. For these reasons, the bureaucratic state does not constitute an effective power base for the newer technocratic elites.

An alternative possibility for them would in theory be an alliance with the military, but arrangements of this kind have hitherto been only *ad hoc* and temporary. The professional and intellectual members of the technocratic elite tend to be highly suspicious of the military on ideological grounds, and the latter reciprocate this suspicion. As already noted, the newer elite considers itself devoted to democratic principles and deplores the military resort to the *golpe* and dictatorship. In turn, the military elite tends to regard the technocrats, often without justification, as Marxists and Communists.

In most countries, members of the military elite have been drawn from the wealthier business and landed groups, although in recent years opportunities for military careers have increasingly been open to young men from non-elite backgrounds as a result of the spread of education and the expansion of the armed forces. However, despite mutual suspicions and differences in backgrounds, there are certain common interests and attitudes between the professional and technical elite and the military. During the past two decades, the proportion of officers who are "gentlemen soldiers" has rapidly declined as Latin American armed forces have increased in size and have been trained and equipped—to a substantial extent through U. S. military-aid programs—for modern types of warfare. In consequence, the great majority of younger officers are themselves technically oriented and many have had periods of training in the United States. This has provided the basis for the intermittent collaboration between civilian and military technocrats that has been occurring in recent years, and it may lead to a more deliberate and permanent alliance in the future.

Because of these characteristics of the groups involved in it, Latin America's emerging pattern of populist politics is inherently

fluid and unstable. Essentially, it represents a transition between the
inherited oligarchical regime and, hopefully, an eventual democratic
system. Experience to date indicates that the transition will be
neither rapid nor easy. It has already lasted for three decades in
Brazil and for two decades in Argentina with no signs yet in either
country of the emergence of a new set of political relationships and
procedures expressing an effective consensus on national goals and
a willingness to subordinate particularistic interests and loyalties to
their achievement. Colombia and Peru are even further behind; in
these countries, the transitional pattern of populist politics has not
yet clearly emerged from the older pattern of oligarchical rule.
Conversely, Uruguay has in a sense gone too fast, having established
earlier in the century an extreme form of popular democracy that
has virtually paralyzed its political life in recent years. Only in
Chile and Mexico—and perhaps also in Venezuela—is it possible
to discern developments that may foreshadow an eventual constructive outcome for transitional populist politics.

In Chile, for the first time, a left-of-center populist party succeeded in electing both a president in 1964 and a majority of the
lower house of the national legislature in 1965. Although increasing
its representation in the upper house, the new Christian Democratic party did not obtain a majority there. The upper house still
has the power to prevent, delay or emasculate reform legislation,
but the new regime has hitherto been able to obtain sufficient additional support to pass workable compromises. The party itself is
more unified and its social and economic objectives are more specific, consistent and congruent with reality than has been customary in Latin America. Although not under clerical control, it
has a religious commitment that appears to generate a type of
disciplined enthusiasm so far rare in Latin American politics.
Moreover, its unprecedented electoral victories were not won by
making the most unrealistic promises to the voters. This role was
played by two coalitions of political parties opposing the Christian
Democrats—one to its right and the other to its left. Nonetheless, a
substantial majority of Chilean voters had a sufficient sense of responsibility and maturity of judgment to resist these blandish-
ments. Whether this experience is a unique event in Chilean politics or the beginning of a new phase in political modernization

cannot yet be determined. Admittedly, formidable obstacles must be overcome to attain the economic and social objectives of the Christian Democratic regime, and there is no assurance that it will achieve sufficient success to establish itself permanently. But, even if the period of transitional populist politics is prolonged in Chile, the Christian Democratic party may foreshadow one type of evolution toward more democratic and effective political systems in Latin America.

A second type of political modernization is represented by the Mexican experience of the past three decades. In contrast to Chile's multi-party system, Mexico has been ruled by the Revolutionary Institutional party (PRI) which has controlled all levels of the political system. Although several small opposition parties have been permitted to exist, they have been closely controlled and none has ever been able to win a significant percentage of the votes. The PRI is itself a coalition of different interest groups, political factions and personal cliques but, despite the persistence of these inherited characteristics, it has been able to achieve and preserve an effective consensus regarding national goals and specific political objectives, as well as agreement on the choice of candidates and the distribution of patronage. The PRI has been supported by the great mass of urban and rural voters and by the newer elites of prosperous commercial farmers and industrial entrepreneurs, even though the latter also finance the small right-wing opposition party. Since the 1930s, the military has been effectively subordinated to the civil government and, in marked contrast to its previous history, Mexico has enjoyed an orderly succession of presidents and legislatures in accordance with its constitutional procedures. While the PRI is authoritarian, particularly in its control of elections and its inhibition of meaningful dissent and public criticism, the Mexican political system has demonstrated not only a stability unprecedented since the colonial period but also a significant concern for and responsiveness to the needs and expectations of diverse social groups, whose interests it has succeeded in harmonizing with considerable skill. Thus, despite its authoritarian features, it has already evolved, and could continue to evolve further, toward an increasingly more democratic regime. But, whether it will do so is by no means certain.

So far, the other countries now engaged in or entering upon the phase of populist politics have not yet foreshadowed the nature of their possible future evolutions, although Venezuela may be following the Chilean model. The process of political modernization in Latin America is bound to be highly uncertain. Countries may retrogress as well as progress, or they may stagnate politically for indefinite periods, as Argentina and Brazil appear to be doing. The heritage of four and a half centuries of particularism, paternalism and personalism cannot be easily or quickly overcome. The formulation of realistic national goals and the willingness and ability to implement them by practicable measures are still inhibited by the inherited tendency to equate the word with the deed. While demagogues certainly exist in Latin American political life, most populist politicians and technocrats are sincerely convinced of the practicability of utopian prescriptions. Such attitudes and expectations are more deeply rooted and difficult obstacles to rapid political modernization than the mere cynicism of the demagogue.

Nonetheless, the experiences—successful and unsuccessful, satisfying and frustrating—of the groups actively involved in the contemporary pattern of populist politics are among the most powerful influences working toward modernization in Latin America. As educational facilities become increasingly available to the great mass of urban voters, and as they become more differentiated and structured occupationally and by other types of modern social affiliations, their personalistic loyalties and paternalistic and redemptive expectations are likely to be lessened and offset by a more realistic understanding of the nature of their own interests and of the impersonal means by which they might be advanced. In addition, the quality of the leadership provided to them by the elite groups is a crucial factor in hastening or delaying such political maturity.

Members of the newer elite groups engaged in politics and in public administration similarly benefit from their contemporary political experiences, acquiring a more realistic understanding of the responsibilities of leadership and of the limitations of political power. Already, there is evidence that they are learning to maneuver with increasing skill among contending political factions and to manipulate the cumbersome bureaucratic machinery with growing effectiveness—not to obtain or preserve personal benefits and privileges, but to carry out the policies and programs that they believe are in the national interest.[2] The experiences of politics and administration can temper their predilection for ideological abstractions, particularly of the Marxist variety, and their positivistic faith in the miraculous efficacy of science to perfect society. In time, there can be a more pragmatic understanding of the complexities and uncertainties of social change and more realistic policies and programs that take adequate account of resource availabilities and of the power structure in their countries.

Evidence of this process may be seen in Mexico where, since the 1930s, pragmatism has increasingly prevailed over ideology, and utopian expectations have been giving way to practicable prescriptions for maintaining a satisfactory rate of economic growth. The converse has been true in Cuba in recent years, reflecting not only its lack of Mexico's long and sobering experience but also the more important role played in the post-revolutionary years by intellectuals and ideologues. Elsewhere in Latin America, current indications are that the professionals and technicians—as distinct from the literary and academic intellectuals—are tending toward emerging Mexican pragmatism rather than Cuban dogmatism.

For their part, members of the older type of elite, despite their inherited sense of superiority and conviction that their privileges and property are divinely ordained, are beginning to recognize that preservation of their wealth and status is no longer assured by the passivity of the subordinate groups and the absence of alternative political leadership. With the contrasting examples before them of the destruction of the older elites in the French, Russian and Cuban Revolutions and of the preservation of the corresponding elite groups in England and the United States, it is possible that sufficient numbers of Latin America's older elites may recognize that their future depends upon their willingness to emulate the latter in developing more socially responsible attitudes and sacrificing obsolete privileges and short-term economic benefits for modern forms of political influence and longer-term economic gains. This possi-

[2] Examples of their successes and failures may be found in Albert O. Hirschman, *Journeys Toward Progress: Studies of Economic Policy-Making in Latin America* (New York: The Twentieth Century Fund, 1963).

bility is enhanced by the fact that the education of the older elites in social responsibility is today a deliberate and conscious process. They have an advantage over their counterparts in nineteenth-century England, and even in early twentieth-century North America, in being subjected to an intensive educational process, both within their own countries and from the United States, designed to induce them to recognize and behave in accordance with their own long-term interests.

Of more fundamental importance is the fact that, in recent years, the elite groups and the people generally have been increasingly influenced by the universalistic values of economic welfare, social justice and political freedom. In consequence of the pressures noted above, there is beginning to be some acceptance of these values and their implications for national policies even among the traditional elites. As this process advances, a corresponding weakening—and eventual atrophying—will occur of their inherited notion that the oligarchical, paternalistic agrarian society that predominated in previous centuries constituted the prefigurement of the millennial kingdom and, as such, was divinely ordained. The new orientation and activities of the Catholic Church in Latin America are also powerfully fostering this change in the attitudes of the traditional elites as well as in those of the people generally, and it is likely that this influence will be strengthened in consequence of Vatican II.[3] The increasing importance of universalistic values and of a sense of social responsibility among all groups in many Latin American countries can be the decisive factor in accelerating both political and economic modernization.

However, it must also be recognized that, unlike the societies of Western Europe and North America, Latin American society has not been accustomed to rapid and profound social change since its establishment in the sixteenth century. Hence, there is

[3] To the extent that the Church was interested in social and economic reform, it tended in past decades to prescribe a hierarchical contractual system of fixed classes with specified mutual responsibilities and privileges modeled on an idealized version of medieval society. For example, this was the program advanced by the Church in Mexico during the 1920s as an alternative to the revolution, and vigorous promotion of it was a major cause of the suppression of Church activities by the government. Today, in contrast, the Church is supporting pluralistic democratic reforms appropriate for a modern industralized society in a growing number of Latin American countries.

reason to question the assumption—widespread today both in the United States and in Latin America—that such complex and ambivalent processes as democratic political modernization, accelerated economic growth, and more equitable distribution of incomes can be accomplished simultaneously within a decade or so and without encountering serious difficulties or risking grave disorder. These three processes are both mutually supporting and mutually competitive. An overriding effort to accomplish them quickly, as in a social revolution, inevitably means that two of them must be sacrificed to the third. In Bolivia and Cuba, which have both experienced social revolutions in recent years, democratization and economic growth have been sacrificed to retributive and distributive justice. In Mexico, after more than a decade of violent revolution, there was gradual recognition that significant progress, although in varying degrees, in all three processes required difficult and complex compromises among goals and means. But, this change has taken a generation to accomplish and its results are only now becoming evident.

Thus, for different reasons, Latin America's goals of economic welfare, social justice and political democratization cannot be achieved simultaneously through social revolution nor can they be accomplished rapidly through social evolution. But, the fact that social revolution is not a panacea for Latin America's aspirations does not mean that it cannot occur in one or more countries in consequence of frustration and impatience on the part of the people and inflexibility, shortsightedness and incompetence on the part of the ruling elites. Indeed, Latin America is today more susceptible to violent social revolution than are most of the countries of Asia and Africa for two main reasons.

First, social revolution—i.e., involving the violent overthrow of the existing ruling elite and the rapid replacement of a significant part of the society's inherited institutions, values and norms —is a phenomenon that can occur in societies experiencing strong pressures for rapid social change frustrated by major political and economic rigidities. Such situations are beginning to develop in several Latin American countries and if this process continues, they will become increasingly susceptible to social revolution. Second, as Alexis de Tocqueville discerned more than a century ago in his analysis of the French Revolution, the likelihood of violent social upheavals is greatest not when exploitation and repression are greatest but when, following such a period, the condition of the subordinate groups begins to improve. The gains already achieved heighten the sense of frustration and of impatience at the slowness and difficulty of further progress. At the same time, the reforms already conceded, voluntarily or perforce, by the ruling elite weaken its privileged position, political power and self-confidence. If it lacks the understanding or the skill to control the nature and timing of further changes, its folly or incompetence provides opportunities for its own disaffected members or for educated members of the non-elite groups to organize sporadic popular unrest into sustained social revolution.

Thus, social revolution is a possible—though by no means a certain—outcome of the existing situation in Latin America. However, whether such revolutions in Latin America would be organized and controlled by the Communists is another question. Two of Latin America's three social revolutions—the Mexican and the Bolivian—have been of the indigenous nationalist type. Even the Cuban Revolution contains important indigenous features, and neither in origin nor in subsequent development has it conformed to the patterns of other Communist revolutions. It was not initially organized and led by the Communist party nor is it as yet under its complete and unquestioned control. From the beginning, Fidel Castro has played the typical Latin American personalist role of prepotent leader; although he is a self-proclaimed Marxist and Communist, his impulsive and egoistic personality exercises at least as much influence upon the policies and actions of the regime as do Communist doctrine, party discipline and Soviet pressures.

Despite the prevalence of Marxist rationales and prescriptions among Latin America's intellectuals, and particularly among its students, there is today less likelihood of social revolutions organized and controlled by Communist parties tied either to Moscow or Peking than there was at the beginning of the 1960s. Cuba's economic difficulties and mistakes, its dependence upon large-scale Soviet aid and consequent susceptibility to Soviet influence, and Castro's efforts to subvert other Latin American countries with money, arms and men have disillusioned many would-be imitators of the Cuban Revolution and have aroused nationalistic fears of foreign domination. Rivalry between Moscow-oriented and Peking-oriented factions has weakened many Latin American Communist parties. But, there is no guarantee that current Communist prospects in Latin America may not change. Supported by Moscow or Peking, organized and disciplined Communist groups continue to be active, openly or covertly, in all Latin American countries and, as elsewhere in the world, they are capable of leading peasant outbreaks, conducting guerrilla operations, and capturing control of trade-unions and other workers' and students' organizations. The extent and seriousness of such activities and the possibility that they might lead to revolutionary situations which the Communists could dominate depend not only upon their efforts but, more importantly, upon the ability of Latin America's non-Communist elites to tackle in a realistic manner the difficult tasks of accelerating economic growth, mitigating social injustice, and fostering democratic political modernization.

The Historical Export-Subsistence Economies of Latin America

Latin America's economic history from its settlement by the Spaniards and Portuguese in the sixteenth century until the middle decades of the twentieth century has exhibited a pattern of alternating periods of expansion and contraction determined essentially by the supply capabilities of the region's export sector and the demand for its products in Europe and North America. However, neither the expansion and contraction of the volume of its exports nor changes in their composition has altered in any significant way the characteristic features of Latin America's economic system for over 400 years. Only in the mid-twentieth century have fundamental economic changes been occurring on a substantial scale, and even now they have not yet become significant in the smaller and more thinly populated countries.

From the earliest settlements in the sixteenth century, the economies of the Latin American countries have consisted of an export sector and a subsistence sector, each in turn divided into two parts. Until the start of major industrialization in the twentieth century, the basic pattern of expansion and contraction manifested itself in the relationships among the different parts of these two broad sectors. To understand the particular course of Latin America's economic history and its implications for contemporary problems and future prospects, it is necessary to examine these sectors and their interrelationships.

Latin America's exports have always consisted predominantly of primary products. Depending upon their climatic and soil characteristics and their mineral deposits, Latin American countries have at one time or another produced—or collected—for export certain agricultural and animal products (sugar cane, tobacco, timber, coffee, cocoa, cotton, wheat, corn, rubber, chicle, wool, hides and skins, meat, etc.) and various metals and minerals (gold, silver, pearls, diamonds and other precious stones during the colonial period; copper, tin, other nonferrous metals, and nitrates in the nineteenth century; and, additionally, petroleum and iron ore in the twentieth century). Because the farming and ranching activities have differed from the mining operations in their organization and techniques, as well as in the nature of their output, these two types of production for export can be considered as different parts of the export sector. However, before sketching the characteristics and history of the export sector, it would be helpful to outline first the nature of the two parts of the subsistence sector, each of which—in somewhat different ways—has supplied the labor and the land required by the export sector.

The oldest of the two types of subsistence economy in Latin America resembled in all of its essentials the traditional subsistence activities of Asia and Africa described in Chapter 3. This traditional subsistence economy was universal prior to the coming of the Europeans, and even today persists in those parts of Latin America inhabited by Indians clinging to their indigenous languages and cultures. Although in the course of the sixteenth century, a substantial majority of the Indian population was forced into *encomiendas,* there continued to be communities of free Indians whose numbers increased slowly after their drastic decline during the first hundred years of colonial rule. Spreading gradually into the less desirable mountainous, semi-arid and jungle lands, these Indian communities preserved the main features of their traditional subsistence economy. This portion of the subsistence economy is significant for the economic and social history of Latin America only in one major respect. It provided a reservoir of both labor and land which was drawn upon by the export sector during periods when it was profitable to expand production of agricultural, animal and mineral products in response to increased demand in the world market. Until the twentieth century, people from the traditional subsistence economy were incorporated into the export sector by absorption into the second type of subsistence activity, which was either physically part of or closely tied to export production.

This second—and much more significant—type of subsistence activity was established by the Europeans during the sixteenth century to serve the needs of the two parts of the export sector.[4] Each of the latter had its characteristic form of economic organization: medium and large estates and ranches in the case of agricultural and animal products, and mining camps in the case of metals and minerals. Both types of export activities used predominantly—though not exclusively—either slaves or forced labor. On the estates, this labor generally raised all or most of its own food; thus, it was simultaneously engaged in exporting and subsistence activities. Food for the workers at the mines usually came from nearby estates specialized in supplying this need and also worked mainly by forced labor. Draft animals for the estates and mining camps, as well as dried meat and leather—then an indispensable material for many purposes now largely met by metals, glass and plastics—were provided by ranches also using mainly forced labor and located in the grasslands and semi-arid regions which exist throughout Latin America.

Whenever demand for an export product slackened or disappeared or mineral deposits were exhausted, the slaves and other workers on the export-producing estates, as well as on those supplying food and animal products to them and to the mining camps,

---

[4] This relationship—crucial to Latin America's economic and social history— has been analyzed in detail by the Brazilian economist Celso Furtado in *The Economic Growth of Brazil* (Berkeley and Los Angeles: University of California Press, 1963). While Brazil's economic history differs in certain important respects from that of Spanish America, Furtado's analysis of the basic relationships and interactions is valid for the latter as well.

could be maintained by the landowners at very little cost because virtually all of their necessities of life were being, or could be, produced on the estates and ranches. Thus, the estates and ranches could, and periodically did, revert to subsistence activities, thereby enabling their owners to preserve their labor force at little or no expense until demand in export or domestic markets for their particular product once again revived.

On the farming estates, there was generally no decline in the technical level during the periods of increased autarchy. In contrast, the ranches, particularly those in the remoter interior areas, often reverted to much lower technological levels, and thereafter sometimes persisted as largely subsistence operations resembling the traditional subsistence economy. Many of Latin America's very small farms—the *minifundia*—originated through this process. Usually, the landowners continued to hold and cultivate the more level and fertile lands, while the hillsides and narrow mountain valleys were occupied by mestizo squatters. Share tenants and day laborers might also cultivate a few unoccupied acres and might eventually be given title to them by their *patrones*.[5]

In the case of Brazil, Celso Furtado distinguishes three periods of expansion, each involving a new export product: sugar production by slaves in the northeast during the sixteenth century; gold and diamond production on the central plateau in substantial part by slaves during the eighteenth century; and coffee production in the south initially by slaves and later in part by contract immigrant labor during the second half of the nineteenth century. In contrast, the seventeenth century and the late eighteenth and first half of the nineteenth centuries were periods of comparative economic stagnation, with considerable reversion to subsistence activities and formation of *minifundia*.

The same basic pattern of relationships can be found in the economic history of Spanish-speaking America, although these

---

[5] Two other significant sources of the *minifundia* were the dissolution of Indian communal tenures in the nineteenth century, and the migration to unoccupied regions of self-reliant mestizos seeking economic and social independence. The latter process is analogous to the westward movement of small farmers in the history of the United States. In Latin America, it occurred on a much smaller scale and had a negligible effect on the region's cultural characteristics because of the passive and dependent behavioral norms of the great majority of mestizos.

countries had much slower rates of economic growth until the late nineteenth century and their export sectors were, in consequence, much smaller in relative terms than in Brazil. Thus, the economies of Spanish-speaking America were much more autarchic than that of Brazil until the twentieth century. Initially in the sixteenth century, silk was exported from Mexico and olive oil from Peru until this trade was prohibited owing to competition with Spanish products. Thereafter, the colonies exported sugar, tobacco, vanilla, cochineal, indigo, cotton, cinchona bark, and mahogany and other tropical hardwoods. In most cases, however, the overseas markets for these primary products were limited and many were eventually lost by competition from more efficient producers elsewhere in the world or by the development of substitutes. As the rural population increased during the colonial period and until the mid-nineteenth century, subsistence activities expanded geographically both on existing estates and by the formation of new estates and *minifundia* in hitherto uncultivated regions. Moreover, except in alluvial river plains and other naturally favored areas, this subsistence agriculture was shifting in character, since the lack of incentive and the means to maintain soil fertility necessitated periodic movement to fresh acreage.

In Latin America, the largest export development in the late nineteenth century was that of coffee in Brazil. Among the Spanish-speaking countries, Argentina took the lead in developing the export of wheat, corn and meat in consequence of the growth of European demand for those commodities during the last two decades of the nineteenth century. Even earlier, other countries were turning to the production of coffee, cocoa, bananas, vegetable oils, wheat, corn and animal products where climate and soils were suitable. Existing and new deposits of nitrates, copper and other nonferrous metals, and petroleum were worked on a growing scale for export as well as for local consumption.[6]

Throughout Latin America, the expansion of the export sector during the second half of the nineteenth century required both addi-

[6] This account of the expansion of the export economy after the mid-nineteenth century is in part based on Sanford A. Mosk, "Latin America and the World Economy, 1850–1914." *Inter-American Economic Affairs,* Vol. II, No. 3. Winter 1948, pp. 53–82; and Sanford A. Mosk, "Latin America Versus the United States," *American Economic Review,* Vol. XLI, No. 2, May 1951, pp. 367–383.

tional land and additional labor. This need provided a major incentive in Mexico, Central America and the Andean countries for the dissolution of Indian communal tenures and the conversion of their lands into individual private properties—changes that, as we have seen, liberal regimes undertook in accordance with utilitarian legal principles and *laissez-faire* prescriptions. This development made possible the sale of desirable Indian lands to existing estate owners and enterprising mestizos, who were also often able to claim for themselves the best portions of the communal lands on various pretexts and to obtain possession of them without compensation through political influence. In addition, much of the remaining accessible and usable portions of the public domains—the former Crown lands—in all Latin American countries were rapidly sold to or legally preempted by the existing landowners. By these means, large additional acreages were made available for increased production of the new export crops.

Other legislation passed in most countries by liberal regimes in the late nineteenth and twentieth centuries abolished the *repartimiento,* the *mandamiento,* and other forced-labor systems that had replaced the *encomienda* in the late colonial period and the early nineteenth century. The rural population was thereafter free to work for money wages or under various share-tenancy arrangements. However, lacking adequate land of its own or alternative employment opportunities elsewhere in the economy, the rural working population was soon forced to accept wage rates and tenancy arrangements which left it at minimum levels of living, in many cases worse off than when it had been engaged in subsistence activities. Moreover, as many Indians and poor mestizos fell into debt to the landowners, they once again lost their recently acquired economic freedom, and peonage—debtor servitude—spread among them, particularly in Mexico, Ecuador, Peru and Bolivia. In Central America, Indian families and communities lacking adequate land of their own were forced to sign disadvantageous wage contracts with coffee and banana estate owners; as debts to the latter increased, these contracts became self-perpetuating. When these devices proved inadequate for obtaining sufficient labor, vagrancy laws were passed under which local officials could assign Indians to nearby estates for a specified number of days each year.

Thus, as the export sectors of the Latin American countries began to grow substantially during the later decades of the nineteenth and the early decades of the twentieth centuries, the condition of much of the rural population steadily worsened. This deterioration was particularly acute in Mexico and was responsible for the widespread peasant support of the Mexican Revolution during its radical agrarian phase in the second and third decades of the twentieth century. A similar development happened in Bolivia during the Revolution of the early 1950s and was on the verge of occurring in Guatemala during the same years. Sporadic rural outbreaks have taken place in parts of Colombia since the 1920s and, more recently in Peru and Venezuela but, owing to the persistence of inherited behavioral norms and in the absence of organizational competence provided by educated or trained revolutionaries from other social groups, these peasant revolts have not developed into effective nationwide revolutionary movements.

Moreover, under left-of-center regimes since World War II, many of the worst abuses of the contemporary forced-labor systems have been mitigated. Today, debtor servitude is no longer legally enforceable; exploitative and self-perpetuating wage contracts have been declared illegal; and vagrancy laws have been liberalized or repealed. Nonetheless, these and other forced-labor arrangements persist in practice in many rural areas owing to the illiteracy and passivity of the tenants and day laborers and to the inertia of customary relationships.

It must, however, be recognized that in Argentina, Brazil, Chile, Uruguay and even in large parts of Colombia and Venezuela —the countries in which during the nineteenth century the Indians and former Negro slaves had been almost completely absorbed into mestizo culture and considerable interbreeding had occurred —the relationships between landlords and permanent tenants have often involved social and psychological benefits which both offset and mitigated the worsening economic condition of the non-elite groups in the countryside. Even today, the patronal relationship inherited from the colonial period persists in these countries as part of the basic institutional pattern in the countryside, described in Chapter 6. Tenant families are assured of the landowner's protection against the local officialdom, his help in times of sickness, personal difficulties and economic distress, and—increasingly today—his assistance in obtaining some education and broader economic opportunities for their sons. For his part, the landowner uses these benefits to attract to and keep on his estate or ranch the most loyal and cooperative tenant families at a minimum cost, and he is also assured of their votes to maintain his influence in the local government and party organizations.

However, this still mutually advantageous patronal relationship is not available to the owners of *minifundia* and to increasing numbers of short-term tenants and agricultural wage laborers, although the possibility of achieving it still acts as an incentive to them. Nor even for permanent tenants does this relationship have the same significance in the Central American and Andean countries, with their large unassimilated Indian populations, since it does not usually involve a strong sense of mutual commitment and obligation owing to the racial and cultural differences that continue to be stressed by both parties.

Problems of Modernizing Latin American Agriculture

In sum, the basic pattern characteristic of Latin America's economic history during its first four centuries consisted of interrelated exporting and subsistence sectors organized into large estates and mining camps using slave or forced labor and served by subsidiary ranching and farming activities. Moreover, this system still predominates today in the smaller Latin American countries. Only in Argentina, Brazil, Mexico and, to a lesser extent, Chile, Colombia and Venezuela has a more articulated and market-oriented economic system of industrial production to meet urbanized domestic demand begun to make substantial inroads upon Latin America's historical export-subsistence economy. And, contrary to much popular and official opinion in the United States and even in Latin America, the export-subsistence system is not moribund even in the most industrialized countries. Inefficient as many of them may be by the agricultural standards of North America and Western Europe, the great bulk of Latin America's estates, plantations and ranches are still profitable operations for their owners in terms of their characteristic set of values and expectations. The system as a whole has a built-in stability that has enabled it to survive without essential change since the sixteenth century.

The system continues to be profitable, despite the competition of more efficient producers of the same products elsewhere in the world, for several reasons. First, as Sanford A. Mosk pointed out, the smallness of the investment in modern machinery and equipment, fertilizers, insecticides and irrigation, as well as in the development of improved plant and animal varieties, has been at least partly offset by reasonably efficient use of the labor force. Second, the continued increase in rural population, the lack of alternative employment even in the cities, and the generally passive attitudes of the rural people have continued to keep agricultural wages and share-tenancy arrangements at levels advantageous to the landowners.

Finally, Latin American governments have followed economic policies that have had the effect of buttressing incomes derived from the production of export commodities. Continued currency depreciation and periodic devaluations over the past hundred years have made possible the maintenance of relatively high prices in terms of national currencies for the commodities exported by estate and mineowners despite declining prices for these products in world markets. In the twentieth century, this advantage has been supplemented by direct methods of supporting the domestic prices of export commodities, such as government purchases, subsidies and other devices. These policies have led inevitably to overproduction of export crops, and to large and growing budgetary deficits, with consequent inflationary effects. But, set at a level high enough to enable the less efficient producers to remain in operation, these subsidies have *ipso facto* guaranteed extra profits to the more efficient estate owners. Only in recent years have some countries begun to change such policies.

In consequence of these factors, the great bulk of Latin America's estates and ranches still yield reasonably satisfactory incomes. In addition, the system tends to be self-perpetuating. In past centuries, as we have seen, the most important mechanism for maintaining it was the expansion of subsistence activities whenever export markets stagnated or declined. Although this device has become much less important in the twentieth century, other factors help to perpetuate the system. The values and norms inherited from the Iberian background and the colonial period, and the desire to maintain political power and party influence at the local level reinforce the effects of inflation in preserving elite-group preference for investment in real property even though other activities might yield a greater or more assured economic return. The presence of unused arable land—still available even today in many parts of Latin America—and the abundance of cheap labor provided the additional factors of production needed for expanding the system during periods of increased demand for Latin America's exports.

More fundamentally, in the course of its normal cycle of expansion and stagnation, the export-subsistence economy does not directly generate any intrinsic economic or social process that could basically transform its pattern of relationships. Accumulations of profits beyond the amounts needed by the landowners for reinvestment in the system itself and for conspicuous consumption have since the mid-nineteenth century tended to be invested in Western Europe and North America. This process of foreign investment—or capital flight, as it is called today—has been facilitated by the fact that the proceeds of export sales have usually been initially realized in the more stable currencies of Western Europe and North America. Hence, Latin American producers of these exports have had the option of converting their foreign-exchange earnings into domestic currencies, generally at advantageous rates as noted above, or of using them abroad for investment or for financing travel, education and luxury purchases in the great cosmopolitan centers of Western society.

For their part, the rural day laborers, tenant farmers and owners of *minifundia* have rarely, if ever, earned sufficient incomes above bare subsistence requirements to embark upon more dynamic activities of their own in agriculture, commerce or industry. Moreover, the persistence of the patronal relationship in the countryside deters a still substantial portion of the rural population from exercising new forms of initiative either individually for self-betterment or collectively for fundamental social and economic changes.

Thus, the historical pattern of social and economic relationships in rural Latin America has not directly produced the incentives and the means for its own self-transformation. This is one of the fundamental problems confronting Latin America, and its resolution is not likely to be accomplished by attempts at agrarian reform, however well intentioned, which do not take into account the realities of political power and the momentum of existing economic and social institutions in the countryside, as well as the dependent and passive values and norms which continue to govern the behavior of a large part of the rural population. So far, such reform efforts have aroused expectations without being able to satisfy them. The constructive alternative to violent revolutions of the Mexican and Cuban types lies in accelerating the operation of certain long-term trends which are gradually having the effect of modernizing the agricultural sector and, in addition, of adopting and implementing certain measures of policy which could also foster this process.

The long-term trends are the influences of industrialization and the growth of integrated national—and, hopefully, regional—markets in Latin America. Such economic developments can, in the course of time, help to impart to the agricultural sector the more dynamic attitudes and the rationalized capital-intensive methods characteristic of the industrial type of production. This process has already occurred in North American agriculture and is now well under way in that of Western Europe. However, industrialization has not yet advanced far enough in Latin America to produce an interaction sufficiently powerful to stimulate, and to provide the resources required for, the modernization of agricultural production through diversification and the adoption of more capital-intensive and efficient techniques.

Among the deliberate measures of policy proposed for accelerating agricultural modernization, land reform is much the most ambitious and difficult. There are two types of problems involved. The first are sociopolitical. In all Latin American countries except Mexico, Bolivia and Cuba, the landowners are still politically powerful, controlling—as we have seen—the rural vote and also retaining considerable influence in the armed forces. In these circumstances, left-of-center and populist regimes have lacked the power to institute land-reform programs rapidly and on a large scale.

Even where reasonably effective legislation has been passed—usually after many years of pressure and compromise—its implementation has fallen far short of expectations. A ruling elite whose incomes and power have for 450 years depended upon its ownership of the land is not likely to acquiesce in a program for distributing to others the bulk of its property and the source of its influence unless it has strong incentives for doing so.

Such incentives would have to be predominantly economic in nature, involving adequate compensation, or price relationships and tax rates which would make it profitable for landowners to concentrate their resources on more intensive cultivation of a limited acreage with a corresponding diminution of their reluctance to dispose of the rest, or a combination of both. Latin American governments have lacked the financial resources to offer adequate compensation, and landowners have lacked faith in the value of bonds and other types of deferred payment owing to the long history of Latin American inflations and currency devaluations. Therefore, more will have to—and could—be done with respect to price and tax incentives. Although their effects take time to manifest themselves, such mechanisms are self-reinforcing, as the knowledge of a profitable response to incentives by one landowner spreads to others in the locality.

Another economic problem relates to the lack of capital and of skills on the part of the owners of *minifundia* and the tenants and day laborers who would receive land under agrarian reform programs. Credit for various purposes and technical assistance covering all aspects of operating a modern type of farm would be needed by most of these people. Such financial and technical assistance programs are expensive owing to the scale required for them to be effective, and they are difficult to administer because qualified personnel is scarce and much of the necessary sociological and technological knowledge has not yet been obtained through research and experimentation.

Nonetheless, these are the directions in which agricultural modernization will have to be pursued in Latin America. Above all, much greater stress needs to be placed upon price incentives and other market factors which can substitute for the deficiencies of administered programs and which have a more powerful influence on attitudes and motivations. Policies of this type are especially important with respect not only to the prospects for effective land reform but also to the emerging problem of food production in Latin America. In recent decades, many Latin American countries, including the largest and most populous, have either been increasing their imports of food or, as in the case of Argentina, have been increasing their domestic consumption of indigenously produced foodstuffs at the expense of their exports of such products. In both situations, balances of payments have been adversely affected; retail food prices have been extremely volatile during periods of inflation; and temporary food shortages have occurred in the urban areas.

In the countries where economically feasible food production has lagged behind the growth of population and urban incomes, the fault lies mainly in the rigidities of the prevailing agricultural system and in the absence of adequate incentives for overcoming them. These rigidities reflect the inherited attitudes and expectations of the landowners, both large and small; the composition of the existing capital invested in agriculture; the customary techniques and methods of cultivation; inadequate transportation and marketing arrangements; and the unfavorable price relationships between food crops and the historical export staples. While physical conditions of soil and rainfall do not always permit replacement of tree crops (e.g., coffee, cocoa) by field crops (e.g., wheat, corn, rice), such shifts can be encouraged, wherever feasible, through price and tax incentives, improvements in transportation and marketing, and provision of the necessary credit and technical assistance, particularly to small farmers. Effective encouragement of increased food production is one of the most urgently required aspects of agricultural modernization in Latin America. However, efforts of these kinds have hitherto been inadequate owing to the resistance to change in the countryside and to misconceptions on the part of governments as to the nature, extent, and duration of the incentives and assistance required.

Characteristics of Latin American Industrialization

While economic modernization in Latin America does not require abandonment or drastic reduction of primary production for export, it does mean that the resources devoted to this activity have to be used more efficiently, particularly in agriculture, where diversification, technical innovation, and improved methods are required. In addition, the increased resources made available by rising agricultural productivity and in other ways (e.g., growth of other sectors, capital inflows) need to be devoted to new forms of economic activity, notably industrialization, which can yield higher and faster growing returns. The two processes of industrialization and agricultural modernization are closely interrelated. Industrialization in Latin America has indirectly been stimulated by developments in the historical export economy and, in turn, the modernization of raw material production, particularly in agriculture, can be accelerated and facilitated by the growth and dynamism of the industrial sector.

Increasing internal market demand, the availability of indigenous capital earned from export activities, and price relationships favorable to domestic products as compared with imports have provided general economic conditions conducive to industrialization in the larger Latin American countries. However, the process of industrialization has not yet occurred on a large enough scale or in ways that encourage the kinds of changes in attitudes and opportunities required to accelerate the growth of modern industry, as well as to stimulate modernization of the agricultural sector. Even in the most rapidly industrializing countries, there is a need to transform certain of the attitudes and norms which have hitherto predominated within the industrial sector. A brief sketch of the main characteristics of the entrepreneurs and enterprises that have been involved in Latin American industrialization may help to illuminate the nature of these inhibiting factors.

With the abolition after independence of mercantilist trade restrictions, many of the handicraft industries developed in Latin America during the colonial period were unable to compete with imported manufactured goods from England. In consequence, while foreign trade increased, the early post-independence decades witnessed the decline—and in many cases the extinction—of centuries-old handicraft activities. By the mid-nineteenth century, merchants and others in the seaports became interested in trying to establish modern types of factories to produce textiles, light construction materials, clay and ceramic products, beverages, furniture, and other household consumer goods. Until the turn of the century, however, their efforts were on a small scale and often failed after a few years in consequence of the competition of imports and the deficiencies in management skills and methods. In general, during the nineteenth century, Latin Americans were more successful in establishing commercial and financial operations than they were in industry. It was not until the twentieth century that substantial numbers of Latin Americans began to move into industrial production. Today, most of the small and medium and some of the large industrial enterprises in Latin America are under indigenous ownership and management.

The second type of industrial enterprise has been of foreign origin. During the late nineteenth and twentieth centuries, manufacturing and related activities on a larger scale began to be established by West European and North American investors, usually in the form of subsidiaries or branches of parent companies based in those regions. Initially, these private investments from abroad went predominantly into the production of primary products for export, in most cases metals and minerals, but also including some agricultural commodities, such as bananas in Central America and sugar in the West Indies. Foreign investment was also attracted into the development of railroads and of urban transportation and power systems because of the need to move large and increasing quantities of primary products from the interior to the seaports and of imports to the growing inland urban centers. During the early decades of the twentieth century, foreign investors began to establish manufacturing operations in the larger countries to process primary products (e.g., meat packing and canning in Argentina) and then to make an increasing variety of consumer goods. Briefly during the boom of the 1920s and on a much larger scale since World War II, North American and West European companies have taken the lead in Argentina, Brazil, Chile, Colombia, Mexico, Venezuela and other Latin American countries in initiating manufacturing activities in the newer industrial fields: consumer durable goods, electrical and electronic equipment, machinery and vehicles, chemicals and plastics, metal fabricating, and the parts, components, operating supplies and containers which they require.

The third group of entrepreneurs who have played an important role in the development of industry and related activities in Latin America have been late nineteenth- and twentieth-century immigrants, and their descendants, from Italy, Germany, England, France, Eastern Europe and the United States, as well as the so-called Turcos from the countries of the Levant. Enterprises owned and managed by this group have proliferated, particularly since World War II, both in the newer industrial fields noted above and in the older industries, such as construction materials, textiles, processed foods and beverages, household furnishings and other light consumer goods. In addition, entrepreneurs in this group have been active in starting wholesaling, retailing and banking operations.

The fourth type of enterprise has been the government corporation. In many countries, the governments have reserved for themselves the establishment of all or some of the facilities producing iron and steel and other basic industrial products. This practice has reflected both the bureaucratic and socialistic bias of the newer technocratic elites in favor of state ownership and management and the fact that Latin American entrepreneurs have generally lacked the large amounts of capital and the advanced technical skills required to establish factories of this type. In addition since World War II, railroads, public utilities, urban transport systems, and, in some countries, petroleum production and refining have been nationalized and are now owned and managed by government corporations.

It is important to recognize that the second and third types of enterprise—that is, the subsidiaries and branches of North American and West European companies, and the firms established by the newer immigrants from those regions and the Levant—have played an unusually important role in the process of Latin American industrialization. Besides the necessary attitudes and skills, they brought with them, or accumulated within the region, much of the capital required for Latin America's transportation systems and public utilities as well as for virtually all of its facilities in the newer fields of industry. Not only did these foreign companies and immigrant entrepreneurs supply the capital and technical knowledge, but they also organized and managed the enterprises involved. In the United States during the nineteenth century, a significant—though much smaller—proportion of the capital required for its railroads and manufacturing industry was also provided by European, primarily British, investors. But, the U.S. import of capital largely took the form of portfolio investment; that is, European investors purchased the stocks and bonds of railroad companies and industrial corporations which were organized and managed by U.S. entrepreneurs. In contrast, Latin America's import of industrial capital has largely taken the form of direct investment; that is, the foreign companies and the newer non-Iberian immigrants have themselves organized and managed the enterprises involved.

The foreign companies and the newer immigrants have played this distinctive role in Latin America's industrialization largely because of the inherited characteristics of Latin American society. For more than four and a half centuries, landowning has been the most prestigious form of property and source of income. Even today, neither investment in industry nor active management of an industrial enterprise has as yet achieved comparable status except in a few industrial centers, such as São Paulo in Brazil, Monterrey in Mexico, and Medellín in Colombia, where dynamic indigenous entrepreneurs have emerged. In general, the older landowning elite still does not regard active management of industrial, commercial and financial enterprises as the most desirable form of career, although it has been willing to invest some of its capital in these activities. Even so, it continues to regard investment in rural properties and urban real estate as the most economically secure and socially stabilizing form of wealth.

In addition, the many small- and medium-size enterprises owned and managed by Latin Americans have been predominantly family-type firms. In effect, they have been industrial, commercial or financial analogues of the agricultural estate, plantation or ranch. The main purpose of these enterprises has been to provide income to maintain and increase the status, influence and living standards of the family owning the business. Large and immediate profits have generally been preferred to reinvestment of earnings in the improvement and expansion of the enterprise over the longer term. Managerial positions and responsibilities have usually been reserved for members of the family, who have qualified for them by learning the business from within and not by obtaining managerial and technical training at modern universities or professional schools. Little, if any, effort has been made to train and promote nonfamily employees to managerial levels within the enterprise and, in cases where outsiders have had to be hired for such supervisory positions, they have not generally been entrusted with much responsibility.

Such family-type enterprises still predominate in Latin America and are able to survive, despite their largely static management philosophy, because they are concentrated in the older, less competitive industrial and commercial fields, in which technology has been comparatively simple and has been changing relatively slowly. The growth of market demand during recent decades for the products of these older industries has been met mainly through the proliferation of small- and medium-size firms, rather than through amalgamation into larger units enjoying economies of scale. This has been owed to the still limited integration among the separate local markets within many national economies, each served by one or two enterprises occupying monopolistic positions, and to the persistence of long-standing ties between small manufacturers and retailers. Thus, as in the case of the estates engaged in the production of the historical export crops, the attitudes and expectations of the owners of these family-type firms have been generally consistent with the conditions for carrying on their economic activities, and their need to modernize has hitherto not been pressing.[7]

The older family-oriented type of enterprise is, however, not suitable for the newer economic fields. These industries are by nature dependent upon a complex and rapidly changing technology, upon extensive inter-industry relations, and upon a relatively

[7] Family firms have played a role in the development of Latin American industry analogous in certain respects to that of peasant farms in the development of Asian and African commercial agriculture (see Chapter 3). Although it has been the main form of Latin American participation in industrialization during the initial decades, the family firm tends to stagnate after the founding generation owing largely to the non-entrepreneurial values it serves and the restrictive behavioral norms of its owners. Thus, for industrialization to be accelerated, the older family-type enterprise needs to be transformed into or replaced by more dynamic kinds of economic organizations.

large and integrated market demand; and they are affected by a wide variety of economic and political factors operating both within the country and in the international environment. Hence, if they are to survive, much less to prosper, such enterprises need managers with technological and administrative training, who are willing and able to plan operations over comparatively long periods of time, and who have the education required to base business decisions on a broad and complex range of factors, many of which have indirect and delayed effects. The owners and managers of such enterprises must in consequence regard the organization as having an existence and interests of its own, independent of those of the family. In particular, the improvement and expansion of the enterprise through the planned reinvestment of earnings over the long term take precedence over paying out the largest amount of profits in the short term. Members of the owning family must qualify through managerial and technical training for supervisory positions, which must also be increasingly open to promising employees and outsiders because this type of enterprise generally requires more managerial personnel and a broader and more complex range of skills than the owning family can supply. Because many entrepreneurs of Iberian and mestizo descent lack the attitudes and qualifications for meeting these requirements, the establishment of enterprises in the newer fields of industry has largely been undertaken by North American and West European companies, by the newer immigrants from these regions and their descendants, and by Latin American governments themselves.

However, the activities of these newer types of enterprise are already disseminating a more dynamic standard of industrial performance to the older kind of family firm. Largely for this reason, a trend is now under way among Latin American family enterprises to change their attitudes and management philosophy in accordance with the requirements for efficient and dynamic industrialization. Moreover, increasing numbers of Latin American firms are entering the newer industrial fields and are naturally behaving in accordance with their more rigorous managerial and technical requirements. This process of adaptation and expansion has been most noticeable in the larger and more industrialized countries—especially Brazil and Mexico—where national markets have become bigger, more integrated and more competitive and where the rewards of emulating the methods of the newer type of enterprise have been most evident. In addition, many of the larger foreign companies have been following deliberate policies of assisting indigenous enterprises to become suppliers of the materials, parts, subassemblies and operating supplies required for their own manufacturing activities, as well as to become wholesale and retail distributors of their products. These two processes have helped importantly to stimulate Latin American industrialization by generating pressures on the older type of enterprises to modernize their attitudes and methods and by providing them with new opportunities and often with the financial and technical assistance required to take advantage of them.

Development Strategy in Latin America

As we have seen in the preceding chapter, Latin American governments have been concerned for the past hundred years with policies to accelerate the growth of their economies. Reflecting the influence of successive European and North American political and economic concepts, these Latin American efforts were first characterized by *laissez-faire* policies; then by positivistic "social engineering," which in practice amounted largely to encouragement of private foreign investment; next by attempts to adopt European social-welfare measures; and finally by the current commitment to economic development through comprehensive national planning, the expansion of state enterprise, and the active direction and often detailed regulation of the private sector by the government. Regardless of their differences, these successive development strategies have all been pluralistic in nature. Even the current phase of development strategy, despite the major role assigned in it to the government and the socialistic bias of some members of the newer technocratic elite, nevertheless relies mainly upon private activities in agriculture, industry, commerce and finance.

Such decentralized economic decision making within a market system exists on a much greater scale in Latin America than in Asia and Africa. Private commercial agriculture and manufacturing industry are much more extensive and constitute a larger proportion of Latin American economies than in Asia and Africa. In addition, wholesale and retail distribution, importing and exporting, banking and finance, and the service trades are much more developed in all of the larger Latin American countries than in Asia and Africa. Conversely, the authoritarianism of Latin American governments—as of Latin American society as a whole—is not so great as that of Asia and Africa and, as we have seen, is offset by individualistic values and voluntaristic behavioral norms particularly among the elite groups. Hence, because the economies of Latin America have such large and comparatively diversified private sectors, they fall within the pluralistic portion of our scale of development strategies, although not so close to the pluralistic end as do the economies of Western Europe and North America.

Space does not permit a discussion of the major economic policy issues confronting Latin American countries seeking to hasten their economic modernization. In purely economic terms, they are similar to those outlined in Chapter 5 with respect to Asian and African development strategy. However, the foregoing discussion of the problems of agricultural modernization and industrialization in Latin America indicates that the social, political, and cultural context within which people actually deal with these issues is significantly different. Latin America's problem in economic modernization may be characterized as a serious lag between economic aspirations and the institutions and attitudes available for realizing them. As in Asia and Africa, these noneconomic factors, rather than the scarcity of capital and skills per se, constitute the effective limits on the rate and nature of economic modernization. But in Latin America, the kinds of changes needed in institutions and attitudes are less profound than in Asia and Africa. The gap to be bridged is between inherited and modern values and norms that are parts of the same cultural heritage; indeed, as can be seen in the other subcultures of Western civilization, the latter evolve organically from the former. In Asia and Africa, the gap is much broader between traditional and Western values and norms, and their relationship is often one of radical conflict rather than of organic evolutionary connection.

While this and the preceding chapter have dealt at some length with the institutional and attitudinal obstacles to more rapid political and economic modernization in Latin America, we may look more particularly at some of the main ways in which they manifest themselves in the governmental activities and relationships directly important for development strategy. Because of the pluralistic nature of this strategy, the attitudes of Latin American governments toward the private sector and vice versa are of central importance. These attitudes are complex and ambivalent, reflecting inherited paternalism as well as contemporary socialistic preferences and bureaucratic interests.

The professionally and technically trained civil servants and experts—who tend to be much more influential in the populist regimes than in those of the inherited oligarchical type—are well aware of the deficiencies of the older family enterprises and they have little, if any, confidence that Latin American entrepreneurs can be transformed into more dynamic and efficient managers within a reasonable period of time. The positivistic convictions of the technocrats also predispose them to the view that the acceleration of economic growth requires investment decisions to be made and production priorities to be fixed by the central government authorities rather than by market processes. Those influenced by Marxism are opposed *a priori* to private ownership of the means of production, which they believe to be the cause of exploitation and the source of the political power of the ruling elites, whom they wish to supersede. Finally, while populist politicians and technocratic civil servants are generally inclined to be contemptuous of Latin American private enterprise, their attitude toward the foreign companies tends to be even more negative, owing to their belief that it is harmful to the national interest for foreigners—particularly North Americans—to own and manage any significant portion of the economy regardless of whether or not they are efficient and dynamic.

In recent years, even conservative oligarchical regimes have evidenced—although not nearly to the same degree—a nationalistic attitude toward foreign private enterprise. In addition to nationalism, however, their suspicion of, or objection to, the foreign companies reflects the attitude of their supporters among Latin American entrepreneurs. Although some family-type firms are beginning to adopt the competitive and dynamic attitudes of the foreign companies, both they and the more numerous entrepreneurs who still cling to older methods resent the necessity for such changes and are aware of their own handicaps vis-à-vis the foreign subsidiaries, which can draw freely upon the capital, technology, product diversity, and research of their much bigger and more experienced parent companies in North America and Western Europe. However, conservative politicians generally recognize the important role that foreign private investment has been playing in Latin American economic growth. Although they may share the resentment of their indigenous business supporters, their aim has usually been to assert the government's sovereignty over the foreign companies rather than to restrict their activities unduly or to discourage foreign investment altogether.

For their part, Latin American entrepreneurs have had ambivalent attitudes toward their governments. On the one hand, they are generally opposed to extensive and active government involvement in the economy, particularly the spread of state enterprises, the practice of comprehensive development planning in which representatives of the private sector are not permitted to participate, and the multiplicity of specific administrative decisions and licenses they must obtain from public officials in order to carry on their own operations. Nor can there be much question that these governmental practices help to impair the efficiency and dynamism of the private sector. But, on the other hand, Latin American entrepreneurs also expect their governments to assist them in a wide variety of ways, many of which can be accomplished only through such detailed and direct administrative procedures. In addition to financial and technical assistance, Latin American entrepreneurs expect their governments to rescue them from the consequences of their own inefficiency or of unfavorable developments beyond their control by granting them monopoly privileges of various kinds and by subsidizing them in various ways.

Reflecting the persistence of inherited characteristics, Latin American industrial workers are not yet fully committed to industrialization, and they, too, expect paternalistic assistance not only from their governments but also from their employers. It is natural that, in the early decades of industrialization, there should be shortages of the kinds of labor skills required by modern technology. By and large, the more industrialized Latin American countries have made good progress in alleviating such shortages by providing the necessary training both on the job and in technical schools and apprenticeship programs. Nonetheless, there are other problems involved in labor commitment to industrial employment that cannot be so directly and readily overcome. Many workers are newcomers from the countryside and are unaccustomed either to the tensions and difficulties of urban living or to the pressures of industrial work disciplines. In consequence, rates of labor turnover and absenteeism tend to be high; and inadequate housing, sanitation and local transportation further impair the efficiency of the labor force.

Labor organizations are often rigidly controlled by paternalistic government ministries, or by authoritarian leaders more interested in doctrinaire political objectives or personal aggrandizement than in practicable economic benefits for the members. Moreover, even where trade-unions do obtain real economic gains for their members, paternalistic relationships with employers often continue to be an important source of worker benefits. Paternalistic relationships in industry are not necessarily harmful, as the case of Japan proves. But, when the industrial *patrón* is excessively authoritarian and capricious, paternalism can impair labor motivation and initiative. Finally, populist regimes have aroused expectations of social-welfare benefits and improved housing for which, in most countries, the necessary resources and administrative competence are lacking. All of these factors operate in various ways to inhibit the modernization of labor attitudes and the increase of labor productivity.

Concern by governments for the welfare of private groups and a sense of social responsibility by the owners and managers of private enterprises are essential prerequisites for a progressive society. However, in Latin America, the paternalistic quality of these necessary relationships often militates against their effectiveness, inhibiting initiative and self-reliance, and thereby impairing the dynamism and efficiency of the economic system.

In addition to the attitudes toward one another of the government and the different groups in the private sector, contemporary bureaucratic practices significantly affect the nature and extent of economic modernization. As already noted, oligarchical and populist regimes have differed only in degree in their active and continuous intervention and involvement in many aspects of national economic life. However, government administrators are often no better equipped in terms of attitudes, skills and experience for the specific economic tasks they believe that governments must perform than are most of the older type of entrepreneurs in the private sector. This deficiency is particularly conspicuous in the case of the many state enterprises requiring heavy subsidies, and is evident also in other official economic activities involving direct and detailed administration. It reflects not only lack of the necessary education and training on the part of civil servants but, more important, the effects of the inherited legal formalism and elaborate bureaucratic procedures of Latin American governments.

The inefficiency and lack of dynamism in the managerial and administrative activities of Latin American governments have retarded economic growth, just as have the similar deficiencies of many private entrepreneurs. Moreover, the comparatively small group of experienced and capable government administrators is forced to divide its efforts among so many diverse functions that it cannot operate with high efficiency. Roberto de Oliveira Campos, one of Latin America's best-known economists and currently Minister of Economic Planning in Brazil, has written that

. . . this problem of the scope and limits of government intervention . . . is at the very core of the problem of public administration in Latin America. A comparatively small number of skilled administrators must undertake quite impossible tasks not only of conducting the normal operations of the government but also of supervising and managing a proliferation of government enterprises and entities. In most of these fields, the necessary objectives could best be accomplished by a simple regulatory control. . . . While recognizing that a regulatory agency requires fewer personnel and, therefore, could be more adequately staffed than a host of public enterprises, many people somehow still prefer to load civil servants with the overwhelming responsibility of direct administration. . . .

. . . the regulatory powers of the state should be in principle preferred to direct managerial control by the government, and the latter in turn to full ownership by the government. This principle is based on two considerations: that the government's financial and managerial resources are inadequate in Latin America even for those conventional tasks which are beyond the capacity of private enterprise; and that socially desirable regulations can in most cases—though not, of course, in all—be enforced without either managerial control or full state ownership.[8]

As we have seen, the willingness and ability of many entrepreneurs and enterprises to use the factors of production efficiently, to improve living standards through competitive prices, and to save and reinvest an adequate share of earnings are still limited by their inherited attitudes and norms and by the institutional characteristics and limitations of their governments. Insofar as these inhibiting factors are susceptible to correction by deliberate policy measures, the greatest and most rapid impact is likely to be achieved through appropriate price and tax incentives and the fostering of more integrated and competitive market conditions. Measures of these kinds can improve the dynamism and efficiency of existing industrial enterprises; encourage increases in the capital invested in further industrialization; and hasten the shift of resources by the marginal producers of export staples into food production and the adoption of the industrial-type methods necessary for agricultural modernization.

It is for this reason, among others, that free-trade arrangements in Latin America constitute one of the major elements in the development strategy of Latin American countries. Two efforts of this type have been under way in recent years. The more successful is the Central American Common Market (CACM), embracing Costa Rica, El Salvador, Guatemala, Honduras and Nicaragua. In form a customs union, CACM is rapidly creating a single-market area of these five countries, and it has already markedly accelerated the process of industrialization in their hitherto overwhelmingly agrarian economies. Paradoxically, CACM's success is mainly owed to the previously rudimentary industrialization of its member countries—to the virtual absence of entrenched industrial interests which might have been unwilling to face competition or unable to survive if a still fairly narrow market had to be shared

---

[8] Roberto de Oliveira Campos, "Public Administration in Latin America," in Burton A. Baker, ed., *Public Administration—A Key to Development* (Washington, D.C.: The Graduate School, U. S. Department of Agriculture, 1963), pp. 50, 48.

among additional producers. Such considerations are, in contrast, among the main reasons why the larger arrangement, the Latin American Free Trade Association (LAFTA)—embracing Argentina, Brazil, Chile, Colombia, Ecuador, Mexico, Paraguay, Peru, Uruguay and Venezuela—has been making very slow progress toward free trade among its member countries. Nonetheless, despite its frustrations and disappointments, LAFTA continues to exist and its importance is still widely conceded among Latin America's new elites. Their continued support for it and periodic efforts to make it more effective provide hope that Latin America will eventually achieve an integrated market area for the region as a whole.

In assessing the longer-term prospects for Latin America's modernization, it is important to give proper weight to the negative and positive factors involved. On the one hand, as we have seen, inherited particularism, personalism and paternalism still tend to inhibit the development of attitudes, expectations and behavioral norms which can foster the evolution of responsible democratic political institutions, stimulate an increasingly productive use of resources in agriculture and industry, and make possible improvements in the living conditions of the people in town and countryside. Utopian expectations and unrealistic methods, along with the enervating memories of past failures, still impede the choice of rational goals and effective means and weaken the motivation to pursue them.

On the other hand, the significant degree of industrialization already achieved in many of the larger countries, the increasing recognition of the need for more effective policies for agricultural modernization, and the pluralistic development strategy followed by Latin American governments mean that more dynamic attitudes and more productive methods are being inculcated through the operation of market incentives and pressures, and their effectiveness could be increased through more appropriate fiscal, monetary and price policies. Of fundamental significance is the fact that, in contrast to Asia and Africa, the dramatic design of Latin American culture has always been redemptive and perfectionistic, aiming to overcome personal deficiencies and to eliminate social ills, however unrealistic the methods by which such changes were expected to occur in the past. Today, the influence of the universalistic values of economic welfare, social justice and political freedom, and the sense of social responsibility to behave in ways conducive to them, are becoming increasingly powerful in Latin American society. Each year, too—however reluctantly—more of the older elites come to recognize that preservation of their property and influence requires them to adapt to the new economic requirements and political and social expectations.

These and other positive factors cannot, of course, guarantee that Latin American progress will be rapid, steady and smooth. Indeed, the foregoing review of the obstacles to political and economic modernization indicates that the process will continue to be slow, interrupted and difficult. Progress itself will generate new pressures and tensions, all the more difficult to handle without violence and bloodshed as the restraining influence of inherited attitudes and behavioral norms is relaxed by the spread of new conceptions and activities. Nonetheless, Latin America should make increasingly substantial progress over the longer term as its people acquire a clearer sense of direction and a greater measure of agreement on the realistic methods needed to achieve relevant and practicable goals.

CHAPTER EIGHT

Implications for Policy

The foregoing chapters have sketched in broad outline the nature and prospects of the transitional process under way in Asia and Africa, and of the efforts of Latin American countries to modernize their political and economic systems in order to catch up with the more dynamic parts of Western society. The analysis of these processes and prospects is at variance in important respects with the assumptions and expectations, implicit and explicit, on which the customary conceptions regarding them have been based. This chapter is concerned with certain implications for American policy of these differences.

As noted in the Preface, however, specific prescriptions will not be proposed for the existing problems in U.S. relations with Asia, Africa and Latin America. My concern is rather with a more fundamental and continuous aspect of the policy process: the way in which Americans—particularly policy makers and opinion leaders—think about these countries and the conceptions they have of the role that the United States could and should play toward them. Specific U.S. policy measures and action programs in large part reflect American ways of thinking and the self-image of America's role. Changes in this perceptual and conceptual framework sooner or later translate themselves into changes in particular policies and programs. In the following pages, specific suggestions are discussed more for the purpose of illustrating the implications of changes in ways of thinking about the U.S. relationship with Asia, Africa and Latin America than to offer immediate policy and program prescriptions.

Relations with Asia and Africa

The countries of Asia and Africa have a complex relationship with the West comprised of economic and political interests and cultural and social factors. For their part, Asia and Africa sell most of their exports to and buy most of their imports from the West, which is also the source of most of their imported investment capital. Both on a bilateral basis and multilaterally through international agencies, the West supplies the largest part of the financial aid and technical assistance that Asian and African countries have been obtaining. France in Africa, and the United Kingdom and the United States in Asia and Africa have been providing military aid of various kinds. The American conviction that the United States must contain Soviet and Chinese communism within its existing boundaries has hitherto given Asian and African countries a virtual guarantee against Communist invasion and internal subversion, however reluctant most of them are to acknowledge it and however fervently they hope that it will not have to be invoked.

Permeating, transforming and infusing with strong emotions these considerations of economic and political interest are the cultural and social factors discussed in Chapter 4. On the one hand, these interests are reinforced by the positive aspects of Western society's paradigmatic role vis-à-vis Asia and Africa—their admiration for and desire to emulate the model it sets of achievement in economic productivity, political effectiveness, military prowess, scientific and technological advancement, and artistic and intellectual creativity. On the other hand, the conflicts between Asian and African interests and those of the West are exacerbated by the negative aspects of the relationship—the need of Asian and African countries to assert their own identity against the West through intensified nationalism, rejection of Western influence, and resentment of the alien standards to which they are expected to conform. Rooted in their continuing encounter with the West, this deeply ambivalent relationship has survived the end of colonialism and is an essential aspect of the transitional process through which the countries of Asia and Africa are slowly passing. When and as individual Asian and African countries develop their new senses of cultural and national identity—the new dramatic designs of their cultures—the conflicted character of their relationship with the West will gradually be resolved, although not necessarily in ways consistent with Western security and welfare. As this resolution is not likely to occur soon, Asian and African countries will, for the foreseeable future, continue to have strongly ambivalent attitudes toward the West, which will limit and warp their capacity to benefit to the fullest extent from their common interests with the West and to obtain mutually satisfactory compromises of the divergent interests between them and the West.

For their part also, the nations of the West have economic and political interests vis-à-vis Asia and Africa but, in terms of such interests, the relationship is significantly less important to the West. Trade with Asian and African countries constitutes a substantial but much smaller proportion of the West's total exports and imports than does Asian and African trade with it. Moreover, there are few imports from Asian and African countries for which the West could not find other sources of supply or substitute or synthetic materials, although their cost would be greater. Beyond these immediate and specific interests, the West has a more fundamental concern that the external initiatives and domestic problems of these countries neither upset the precarious peace of the world political system nor impair the effective functioning of the international economic system.

Finally, the West has a major long-term interest in the eventual outcome of the transitional process in Asia and Africa—in the kinds of societies that will emerge in these regions. Although their cultures and institutions will differ significantly from those of the West, they can either be compatible with continued Western security and welfare or constitute a threat to them. If the outcome is favorable to this long-term Western interest, it will be expressed —among other manifestations—in the gradual constructive resolution of the conflicted character of the West's relationship with Asian and African countries. The basic policy problem of the West is how to effectuate this long-term interest in its day-to-day relations with Asia and Africa which, by their nature, must be primarily concerned with existing and imminent interests and issues.

Moreover, Western ability to advance its long-term and current interests is both reinforced and offset, as well as charged with emotional content, through the operation of the cultural and social factors discussed in Chapter 2. In these respects, the motivations and expectations of the United States play the crucial role. Cultural factors exaggerate the valid Western security interest in Asia and Africa to produce the moralistic belief that any Communist advance in these continents must be prevented even if the armed forces of the United States have to be used for this purpose. The senses of mission and guilt, strengthened by America's positivistic convictions, distort the valid U.S. interest in the outcome of the transitional process by generating the expectation that Western society—or the American way of life—must be the goal to which Asian and African countries aspire. These factors motivate the desire to provide economic aid and the need for vocational expression through active participation in formulating and carrying out the development strategies of Asian and African countries. They validate the assumption that the West can have a major influence over both the process of social change within these countries and their behavior in international affairs.

However, as we have seen, these cultural factors are in part contradicted by the failure of reality to conform to expectations, resulting in deep ambiguities in Western—and particularly American—attitudes regarding Asia and Africa. On the one hand, Americans—especially within the elite groups—tend to feel that the lack of progress in Asian and African countries is the result of the inadequate size of the U.S. foreign-aid program and of the inadequate scale of their own participation in development work. On the other hand, other cultural factors in Western society foster the conviction that the failure to achieve progress is owed to the moral deficiencies and lack of competence of Asians and Africans. In both reactions, attention is diverted from the true nature of the transitional process and from a realistic assessment of the extent to which and the ways in which it can be influenced either by Asians and Africans themselves or by Westerners. Nor is there adequate recognition of the conflicted nature of Asian and African attitudes toward the West and of its implications for their behavior both domestically and in international affairs. The desires and expectations that express the value system and the dramatic design of Western culture are to a significant extent substituted for accurate perception and understanding of the realities of Asian and African countries and of their relationship with the West.

An obvious implication is that the United States needs to distinguish more clearly than it has hitherto been able to do between the requirements of U.S. and Western interests, on the one hand, and the expression of its characteristic values and dramatic design, on the other hand. The principal elements of such a re-examination have been sketched in earlier chapters; here their main outlines are briefly recapitulated.

Although Asian and African countries vary widely in their economic and political capabilities, they are all transitional societies, characteristically divided by deep conflicts of particularistic interests and loyalties and held together as nation-states by more or less authoritarian regimes. Accelerated economic growth and increased political effectiveness are among the goals they seek, but other national objectives compete with them for resources and attention, as do particularistic and individual interests. In large part, their patterns of order and of motivation are still those of the traditional society which, however, continues to be eroded and disorganized by the influence of dynamic Western institutions, values and norms. Nonetheless, out of the traditional culture, informed and transformed in various ways by Western concepts and expectations, will eventually emerge the new dramatic designs of these societies and their definitive senses of national identity. Thus, they are not in process of becoming replicas of Western society; they do not behave like Western nations; nor do their people react to problems and strains like Westerners.

In consequence of these characteristics, most Asian and African countries should not be expected to make rapid and substantial progress in raising productivity and living standards or in achieving greater political effectiveness. The obstacles are not simply, or even mainly, the scarcity of economic resources and technical skills. They are the characteristics of the transitional society itself, and the most important of them are not susceptible to rapid removal through deliberate policy measures. For most Asian and African countries, significant and conspicuous changes in economic capabilities and in the effectiveness and stability of political regimes will take generations to accomplish—not a decade or two. Meantime, their internal problems and external initiatives and ambitions are bound to generate dangers and difficulties for the world political and economic systems. The West, particularly the United States, will have to live with and find ways of offsetting the adverse consequences for its own interests of such developments. They cannot be prevented through the exercise of the American will to action; nor, for all of America's faith in technocratic positivism and its wealth and power, can it provide panaceas for the internal and external problems of Asian and African countries.

This way of thinking about the future of Asia and Africa has certain implications for existing American policies regarding these regions. While, as already indicated, it is neither necessary nor even desirable to spell out such implications in detail, a number of generalizations may illustrate their main characteristics.

The most important implication is the need for much greater understanding of the nature of these societies and cultures and of the ways in which their characteristics have to be taken into account in improving the effectiveness of U.S. policies. The considerations of rational economic and political interest involved in the domestic and international activities of Asian and African countries must, of course, continue to be given their appropriate weight in the formulation of American policies. However, as this analysis has attempted to show, these factors are not sufficient by themselves to explain the behavior of Asian and African countries nor can they constitute the only significant considerations determining U.S. objectives and tactics. It is also essential to understand the particular ways in which Asians and Africans conceive their own interests and the distinctive manner in which they perceive and interpret Western motivations and actions. It is necessary to know and appreciate the significance of the characteristic sets of values and norms governing the expectations and actions of individual Asian and African countries. It is important to grasp the main elements of their histories if realistic estimates are to be made of the possible patterns and limits of their future development. New training techniques will have to be devised for transmitting this knowledge not only to regional specialists but also to those concerned more generally with making U.S. foreign policy and influencing public understanding of its problems and possibilities.

The implications of a more realistic way of thinking about Asian and African countries may be further illustrated by a brief discussion of U.S. conceptions of the threat of communism in these regions. Hitherto, the United States has tended to assume that, if sufficient military aid were supplied, any Asian or African country would be able to resist Communist subversion and aggression except for a direct assault by the Soviet Union or China. The view of these countries explained here would have precluded acceptance of this unqualified assumption. Such Western help is likely to be effective in an Asian or African country only if its people have a sufficient sense of national identity to support actively the national effort to resist aggression and if its elite groups are willing and able to subordinate their particularistic interests and personalistic rivalries to providing unified and effective leadership. Conversely, if the United States must commit its own armed forces to the defense of the country and if it must endeavor to supply leadership and a sense of national purpose to an apathetic population and elites whose morale has been deeply impaired by their own particularism, self-seeking and sense of failure, then the costs are likely to be many times greater for the United States, quite apart from the danger of escalation involving China or the Soviet Union. Moreover, such a substantial—and inevitably growing— degree of direct U.S. involvement in resisting a Communist advance means increasing U.S. control over the country's internal affairs. Although conducted in the cause of freedom, such actions by the United States paradoxically undermine the self-determination of the people it is trying to defend.

It is, of course, difficult to determine before the situation arises whether an Asian or African country has the will and ability to make the minimum essential effort in its own defense. But, the difficulties of reaching such decisions are compounded by the failure to distinguish between objective realities and the motivational biases of American culture. Not only does this confusion impair judgment, but it also precludes the effective use by the United States of many subtle and sophisticated means of policy short of the direct commitment of its armed forces.

With respect to the long-term interest of the West in the nature of the societies likely to evolve in Asia and Africa in the course of the transitional process, the considerations involved are even more problematical. In a long-term perspective, communism is only one of the possible social systems which could characterize an Asian or African country and not necessarily the most probable or even the most dangerous to the security and welfare of the West. Growing disparities in population and wealth on opposite sides of the longest land frontier on the planet, and increasing divergences of interests and objectives between the Soviet Union and China, as well as among other Communist states, make it less and less probable with each passing decade that we or our children will witness the fulfillment of the eschatological Marxist prophecy of the forces of "socialism" united in a final victorious assault upon the beleaguered camp of Western "capitalism." Moreover, as we have seen, the search for national identity is so fundamental a characteristic of the transitional process that few, if any, Asian and African countries will be likely to adopt communism voluntarily and to submit to either Soviet or Chinese direction. Indeed, over the long term, the possibility is greater that—owing in part to the influence of Western messianism and redemptive activism—nativistic religious or political movements in Asia and Africa will generate the will and the ability to undertake sustained common actions expressing racial antagonisms and cultural and economic resentments against the West. In such a contingency, the Soviet Union—as also a rich, white, Western society—would be under assault along with the nations of North America and Western Europe.

These long-term possibilities do not make the problem of communism unimportant in Asia and Africa, particularly in the shorter term. Folly or ineptitude on the part of the ruling elites could open the way for Communist take-overs. Moreover, there would be few better ways of fostering the spread of communism in Asia and Africa—or, for that matter, anywhere in the world—than for the West to act in the shorter term as though the longer-term eventuality of deepening Soviet-Chinese antagonism had already come to pass. Regardless of present Sino-Soviet conflicts, Communist conceptions of the nature of world politics and traditional Russian ambitions are still sufficiently powerful among the ruling Soviet elite to prevent significant—much less overt—cooperation between the Soviet Union and the United States against China.

For this reason, among others, exploitation by the West of Soviet-Chinese differences in the shorter term has to be very skillful or else it will be counterproductive. Unfortunately, U.S. policy in Southeast Asia and the Far East has been hampered by inadequate American understanding of Asian cultures, particularly China's, and by doctrinaire American attitudes compounded of unrealistic expectations and neurotic rigidities. In these circumstances, it has been the Soviet Union rather than the United States that has been able to exploit the hostility between the other two protagonists to its own advantage.

Thus, even though major Western interests are at stake in the longer-term future of Asia and Africa, the extent to which the United States can influence the external behavior and internal development of these countries is limited not only by the realities of their transitional societies and cultures but also by the nature of American capabilities. In the next few years, it is probable that events themselves will force changes in U.S. attitudes and policies toward Asia and Africa that will make them both more realistic and more relevant to longer-term Western interests. But, the United States may well be too moralistic to be willing and too unskilled to be able to pursue such realistic policy objectives in Asia and Africa by the only kinds of tactics that could be effective without excessive cost: the sophisticated use of diplomacy; the skillful dispensing and withholding of support and subsidies; the subtle promotion and exploitation of emerging differences between its two major opponents; and the maintenance of an efficient armed force for use only when a vital interest is at stake and all other means of policy have failed. Should the United States become capable of such tactics, much could be done to increase the effectiveness of U.S. influence in Asia and Africa while avoiding a disproportionate commitment of America's own men and resources. Two of the essential preconditions for such an improvement are better understanding of the nature of Asian and African societies and greater awareness of the sociocultural elements in America's attitudes and motivations regarding them.

Relations with Latin America

A reassessment is also necessary of the influence of sociocultural factors on U.S. expectations and policies regarding Latin America. The most important policy implications of the analysis presented in the two preceding chapters flow from recognition of the fact that there are very few purposes for which it is intellectually significant and operationally useful to continue to treat the nations of Latin America as though they were similar in all essential respects to Asian and African countries. The major conceptual and attitudinal changes needed by both the United States and Western Europe are explicit acceptance of the fact that Latin America is part of Western civilization, and the consequent willingness to behave accordingly toward Latin America.

There would be nothing essentially novel in such a change in the Western, especially the North American, way of thinking about Latin America. In effect, it would mean reverting to the conception of Latin American society that prevailed until the end of World War II; since then, preoccupation with "development" has obscured the significance of sociocultural similarities and differences. Reversion to the older way of thinking would contribute more than any other possible change toward making the relationship between these different parts of Western civilization less conflicted and more beneficial to all concerned.

However, the difficulties should not be minimized, particularly as they affect the most important strand of the relationship—that between the United States and Latin America. In the main, these difficulties arise from the asymmetrical character of the relationship inherent in the fact that the countries of Latin America occupy the same hemisphere with a neighbor whose wealth and power exceed by several times the total of theirs and whose society is the most restless and dynamic on the planet. This basic asymmetry is also reflected at the level of specific interests in the closer and more dependent economic and political relationship that Latin America has with the United States as compared with any other part of the West. The United States is by far the biggest market for Latin America's exports and the largest source of its imports both of goods and of capital; and U.S. military protection is vital for Latin America's continued freedom. However, the converse of this dependency does not exist. Latin America is not the largest trading partner of the United States nor is it the biggest field for U.S. overseas investment, although it is nonetheless of great importance to the United States in both respects.

This asymmetrical relationship has been the source of two types of difficulties for Latin Americans. First, they have understandably resented the extent and depth of their dependence on the United States and the fact that the latter does not focus comparable attention and concern on them. This resentment is heightened by the specific conflicts of interests and attitudes involved in the relationship. Among such conflicts are disagreements over the responsibilities and the freedom of action of the United States with respect to Western Hemisphere defense and to security arrangements against Communist subversion; over the composition of and the barriers to trade between Latin America and the United States; over the relationship between U.S. economic aid and the policies of Latin American countries affecting their economic growth, fiscal and monetary conditions, and balance-of-payments difficulties; over the issue of state versus private enterprise; over alleged U.S. support for Latin American dictatorships opposed to social reform; and over other political and economic problems.

Second, the asymmetrical relationship contributes to Latin America's sense of cultural and social inferiority vis-à-vis the United States. As in the case of Asia and Africa, the United States sets the standards of achievement in most of the fields—economic productivity, social welfare, political democratization, military capability, scientific and technological advancement—considered important by the newer elites in Latin America. In all of these respects, Latin Americans look to the United States not simply as a model to be emulated but also as the source of the ideas, techniques and financial resources which they believe necessary to improve their own performance. For their part, North Americans have borrowed from Latin American culture only in limited respects, principally in the arts.

To relieve the anxieties of its dependence and its feeling of inadequacy, Latin America's self-examination during the twentieth century has included a search for a satisfying explanation of why its performance has lagged so far behind that of the United States despite geographical propinquity, a common cultural and historical background, parallel colonial origins, and the achievement of nationhood through analogous wars of independence against European powers. Regardless of their empirical justifications, the explanations that Latin Americans have found for these disparities have naturally reflected their inherited social and cultural characteristics. Of particular relevance in this connection has been the tendency to transfer to authoritative figures the blame for and the obligation to correct Latin America's inadequacies. Just as redemption from or in this world has been expected as an act of grace from a divine savior or a prepotent political leader, so, too, have the deficiencies and evils that plague Latin American society been regarded as the result of divine punishment or human maliciousness against which Latin Americans have been powerless to protect themselves.

With considerable justice, as we have seen in earlier chapters, some Latin Americans blame their contemporary inadequacies on certain aspects of their Iberian heritage, although it has also been a major source of their evolving sense of identity and self-respect. A more popular and less ambiguous villain held responsible for Latin America's lag has been the United States which, even by non-Communists, has long been denounced as the capitalist exploiter whose investments have kept Latin Americans in economic bondage, and the imperialist tyrant whose political and military interventions have supported dictators and restored oligarchical regimes.[1] Con-

---

[1] Today, the explanation of Latin America's deficiencies most popular among the newer professional, technical and intellectual elite groups is the more sophisticated rationale developed by the Secretariat of the United Nations Economic Commission for Latin America (ECLA). According to the ECLA doctrine, since the mid-nineteenth century, the countries of Latin America have been seduced by growing market demand in Western Europe and the United States—just as Asia and Africa were compelled by European colonial rule—into specializing in the production of primary products, both agricultural and mineral, while Western Europe and the United States have thereby been enabled to specialize in the production of manufactured goods. This international specialization has benefited the industrialized countries much more than the raw-material producers because world trade in primary products has grown more slowly than in manufactured goods largely in consequence of the development of synthetic substitutes and technological improvements which have made possible progressive savings in the

sistent with the conviction that the United States is the villain responsible for Latin America's current inadequacies is the long-established image of North Americans as robber barons, dollar diplomats, military interventionists and insensitive gringo tourists. Consistent with the conviction that the United Sates has the obligation of remedying Latin America's difficulties is the expectation that it will act as the easy-going and benevolent *patrón,* placing its wealth and power at Latin America's disposal for the achievement of economic growth, social justice and political democratization. These conflicting images of the United States also reflect Latin America's intentionalistic ethic—its preoccupation with the good or bad motives believed to be involved in the actions of North Americans, official and private.

U.S. actions, especially during the first three decades of the twentieth century, provided a basis for Latin America's continuing fears of intervention and exploitation by the United States. These actions reflected in part U.S. political and economic interests, however narrowly conceived, and in part the U.S. will to make its power paramount in the Western Hemisphere. Unfortunately, despite the "Good Neighbor" policy instituted in the 1930s and the various pledges of nonintervention signed by the United States in the 1940s and fifties, the exigencies of the cold war have made U.S. policy highly sensitive to real and imagined threats of Communist penetration in Latin America, particularly since the Cuban Revolution. To many members of Latin America's newer elite

---

amounts of raw materials required per unit of manufactured goods. The ECLA doctrine further asserts that the consequence of these disparate rates of growth has been that such technological improvements as have occurred in primary production have been reflected in falling world prices for these commodities, while the much greater and more numerous technological improvements in the production of manufactured goods have been reflected in rising incomes and living standards in the industrialized countries. Thus, the ECLA doctrine maintains, the industrialized countries have been able to enjoy the benefits not only of their own increased productivity but also of that of Latin America, which has thereby been compelled to subsidize their rising incomes and living standards. It follows from the ECLA doctrine that the industrialized countries—particularly the United States as the most industrialized and the largest importer of primary products—are responsible for the lag in Latin America's economic growth and thus have the obligation to provide the resources necessary to overcome it. The ECLA doctrine is congenial to many Latin Americans because it absolves them of responsibility both for their present predicament and for their future salvation.

groups, resentful of past U.S. actions, U.S. intervention seems today a more dangerous possibility—and certainly a more humiliating prospect—than subversion by their own Communist countrymen. The traditional elites would favor U.S. intervention against any movement, Communist or otherwise, which threatened their property and privileges. But, even they have been sufficiently nationalistic to resent such dependence on foreign support and sufficiently realistic to recognize that it eventually weakens their own power.

For its part, the United States has had conflicted feelings about its policies and actions in Latin America, as well as about the performance and problems of Latin American countries. On the one hand, the processes of social change now under way in Latin America have made these countries more susceptible to internal social revolution than are most Asian and African nations. The U.S. concern that such protest movements may fall under strong Communist influence, if not complete control, was justified by the Cuban Revolution, and the danger of such developments for the security of the United States was demonstrated by the Cuban missile crisis. North American security would be much more directly and powerfully threatened by the spread of Communist regimes in Latin America than in Asia and Africa. In consequence, the United States has legitimate grounds for believing that compelling reasons of national interest—and not simply moralistic convictions—may require it to intervene in Latin America whenever there is a clear and present danger of Communist take-overs.

The problem has been, of course, to determine when a clear and present danger exists. The difficulty of making a valid judgment is compounded by the perceptual and conceptual biases of the United States and the tendency to ignore social and cultural factors. At the same time, even the valid expression of American national interest has been felt, particularly among the elite groups in the United States, to conflict with such deeply rooted Western values as respect for national independence, the right of democratic choice, and the restraint that the strong should exercise toward the weak.

North Americans generally know very little about Latin America's history and consequently they fail to understand that it is not possible to overcome in a few short decades the effects of the late medieval Iberian heritage and of four centuries of comparative stagnation. Most members of U.S. elite groups are as impatient as are the newer elites in Latin America with the slowness of economic growth, social reform and political democratization in that region. They optimistically expected that the expenditure of U.S. aid funds under the Alliance for Progress would provide both the resources to and the "leverage" on Latin American governments needed for them to achieve these objectives within a decade or less. When, after a year or two, substantial progress was not made, they swung to the opposite extreme of pessimism and disillusionment concerning Latin America. This disappointment is not attributed to the unrealism of their expectations but rather to the irrational perversity of Latin Americans. Nor is the remedy sought in more profound comprehension of the nature and prospects of social change in Latin America but rather in demands for large increases in U.S. aid and for more vigorous exhortations to Latin American governments. Nonetheless, despite these fluctuations in U.S. attitudes and policy prescriptions, significant progress is being made under the Alliance for Progress by a number of Latin American countries, although it is neither so rapid nor so widespread as North American and Latin American positivists expect.

As explained in Chapter 7, Latin America's progress will be slow, interrupted and difficult in achieving its goals of improved welfare through economic growth, greater justice through social reform, and increased freedom through political democratization. In seeking to realize these objectives, Latin America depends fundamentally upon the power inherent in the dramatic design of its culture as a part of Western civilization. Until the mid-twentieth century, the expression of these Western characteristics was blocked or diverted into unrealistic expectations by certain characteristics of the cultural and social systems inherited from the Iberian background. In recent decades, however, Latin America's redemptive yearnings, its sense of the worthiness of this world and of the possibilities of individual and social improvement within it, and its growing commitment to universalistic humanitarian values have been increasingly powerful factors inducing a greater dynamism, a more unified sense of purpose, and a more realistic conception of the requisite means.

Today, this growing Latin American dynamism is both an indispensable asset and a major danger. It generates the conception of goals that correct existing deficiencies and the motivation necessary to achieve them. At the same time, it produces social disintegration, alienation and the resulting possibility of social revolution. Thus, the fact that, after four centuries of comparative stagnation, Latin America is today responding to the dynamism derived from its Western cultural heritage constitutes both the greatest hope for and the greatest danger to its future welfare and security.

The constructive possibilities can be enhanced and the destructive potentialities inhibited through closer association of Latin America with the more progressive and stable parts of Western civilization—that is, with North America and Western Europe. Latin America has for many decades been associated with the United States in the complex of organizations and treaties comprising the Inter-American system. In turn, the United States has been bound to Western Europe in a military alliance and organization, the North Atlantic Treaty Organization (NATO), and in the Organization for Economic Cooperation and Development (OECD), whose functions include coordinating national economic policies, tackling common economic problems, and fostering development assistance to Asia, Africa and Latin America. Our analysis suggests the desirability of relating these two systems much more closely and continuously. It may not be practicable or even desirable at present to merge the military aspects of the North Atlantic and Inter-American systems, although prospective fundamental changes in NATO resulting from other causes may eventually make it so. There would, however, be important symbolic and material benefits from a more direct and permanent association of the economic parts of the two systems.[2] In the next few years, a variety of ways could undoubtedly be found for associating Latin

---

[2] Such ties could take the form, for example, of collective representation of Latin America in the OECD by means of a permanent delegate in Paris of the Inter-American Committee for the Alliance for Progress (CIAP), the intergovernmental agency coordinating economic affairs within the Western Hemisphere.

America much more substantively with North America and Western Europe at both governmental and private levels. The essential precondition is for North Americans and Europeans to think of Latin America as part of the West; then, the actions appropriate for expressing this conception will increasingly suggest themselves.

Foreign Aid and Social Change

The conflicted character of the attitudes on both sides of the relationship between the United States and the countries of Asia, Africa and Latin America, as well as the former's misconceptions, are most conspicuous with respect to the effort to accelerate and influence the so-called "development" process through financial aid and technical assistance. The reason is that sociocultural factors play so large a part, magnifying the ambiguities that permeate the aid relationship and producing frustration and dissatisfaction on both sides.

However, since the United States began in the early 1950s to provide financial aid and technical assistance on an increasing scale to Asia, Africa and Latin America, the significance of sociocultural factors on both sides has generally been ignored by the policy makers and opinion leaders responsible for the U.S. foreign-aid program and for interpreting its purposes and results to the American people. In consequence, their prescriptive analysis and rhetorical argumentation have tended unconsciously to express the sociocultural factors entering into the formation of American motives and expectations instead of being based deliberately on an understanding of the processes operating in the recipient countries. Only in the last few years has the growing frustration resulting from these misconceptions begun to generate doubts about the assumptions and operations of the U.S. foreign-aid program. While there have always been opponents of foreign aid, the significance of current disillusionment is that it is coming increasingly from government officials, members of Congress, development technicians and scholars who are—or have been until recently—strong proponents of the foreign-aid effort. Implicit in this situation is the danger that the growing criticism from friend and foe alike will lead to drastic curtailment of foreign aid. But, this dissatisfaction with the existing foreign-aid program also opens the way for substantive improvements in its concepts and methods. It is not possible to analyze here the problems of the U.S. foreign-aid program and to explain the changes in assumptions, objectives and techniques that could significantly ease them.[3] However, certain general observations may be made that reflect the changes in ways of thinking implied by the analysis in preceding chapters.

First, however, it is important to emphasize that there is nothing wrong per se in the fact that a major role in American motivation to provide aid is played by the urge to express the values and achieve the expectations inherent in the dramatic design of American culture. As the opinion polls noted in Chapter 2 indicate, the national-interest arguments for foreign aid are not compelling enough by themselves to enlist adequate public support for it.[4] In consequence, the United States would not be providing foreign aid on a meaningful scale if this activity did not also constitute a major way of expressing the American will to action, positivistic conviction of mastery over nature and society, and senses of mission and guilt. The problem arises not because of our humanitarian and positivistic concerns—which, indeed, constitute the major justification for providing aid—but because we have allowed these cultural factors to obscure our perception and understanding of the realities of social processes in Asia, Africa and Latin America. The result has been to aggravate the ambiguities of the relationship between the United States and these regions and to intensify certain elements in the American behavioral pattern that inhibit realization of the other legitimate purposes which both donors and recipients have in mind in giving and obtaining foreign aid.

One important example of such harmful effects may be seen in the rhetoric of foreign aid—the combination of pseudo-diagnosis and unattainable promises by which many opinion leaders—and even some scholars—have sought to justify foreign

---

[3] A preliminary approach to such an analysis is presented in Theodore Geiger and Roger D. Hansen, "Decision Making on Foreign Aid," cited.
[4] For a realistic and balanced analysis of the U. S. national interests served by foreign aid, see Robert E. Asher, "Economic Assistance to Less Developed Countries: Does it Serve the National Interest?", *The Forensic Quarterly*, Vol. 40, No. 2, May 1966.

aid and to enlist support for big increases in it.[5] Because it is a way of expressing American values and expectations, this rhetoric has probably helped to motivate the American desire to provide foreign aid. But, over the longer term, it has had two kinds of adverse effects which by now outweigh its benefits—and will do so increasingly in the future. At home, the rhetoric of foreign aid is becoming more and more counterproductive: neither its diagnosis nor its promise is being borne out by events in Asia, Africa and Latin America, and it is, therefore, a major immediate cause of the growing American disillusionment with foreign aid. Abroad, the rhetoric of foreign aid has also stimulated unrealistic expectations in the recipient countries regarding the volume of aid they would receive and the ease and rapidity with which it would enable them to achieve higher living standards. By obscuring the nature of their own problems and tasks, and by fostering the notion that the West would soon provide the decisive means for overcoming their difficulties, the rhetoric of foreign aid has reinforced the adverse effects on their own efforts of the sociocultural characteristics of Asian, African and Latin American countries.

Within the U.S. foreign-aid agency, the rhetoric of foreign aid has been largely deflated in the course of the 1960s although it is still occasionally used in public pronouncements and in relations with the Congress. What remains is a tendency—natural perhaps in the circumstances—to exaggerate the importance of aid and the extent of the influence it gives the United States over the inter-

---

[5] Two examples of the continued use of the rhetoric of foreign aid by opinion leaders may be cited. A *New York Times* editorial of August 22, 1965, referred to the need to fill the gap so that the "developing countries . . . [could] achieve a 2.5 per cent annual increase in real per-capita income" but conceded that the United States could not do so alone. With the enthusiasm of technocratic positivism, it pointed out that "the systems engineers of the space age . . . could undoubtedly train their computers with good effect on the problems of the developing countries" and cited "some students of the problem [as insisting that] a breakthrough in development could be made through a sharp increase in aid." In his *Washington Post* column of October 5, 1965, Walter Lippmann concluded that the "disparity" between the rich and the poor countries "cannot be overcome by preaching and exhorting the developing countries to pull themselves up by their bootstraps. They cannot and will not do that. . . . The only solution is that the rich countries make available to the poor countries the foreign exchange which they can usefully employ to make themselves self-sufficient. . . . Unless the richer countries can rouse themselves to such an indispensable action, they should cease to pretend that they really care about peace among men."

nal and external actions of the recipient countries. This tendency also reflects inadequate American ways of thinking about Asia and Africa and the phenomena which foreign aid aims to influence. The most serious manifestation of this inadequacy is the failure to recognize that the transitional process in Asia and Africa and the modernization process in Latin America are far more complex, much slower, and more erratic and uncertain than they are assumed to be by most of those involved in the foreign-aid effort. Owing to their complexity, to the intricate interrelationships among their different aspects or dimensions, and to the continued power of their past histories to limit present capabilities and future prospects, these processes are much less susceptible to influence by deliberate policy measures than is generally imagined either by the ruling elites of these countries or by Americans intent upon "solving" their "development" problems. Nonetheless, there is significant scope for policy—for rational choices of ends and means and systematically planned and implemented action programs. But, policy measures can be effective in influencing these processes only to the extent that action is explicitly based upon adequate understanding of their complex and contradictory nature.

The main immediate cause of inadequate understanding of the transitional and modernization processes is the almost complete lack of knowledge about the pervasive and powerful roles played in them by cultural, political, psychological and social factors. Only the economic dimension of these processes is today reasonably well understood. This large discrepancy in knowledge, combined with the positivistic activism of American attitudes, has fostered the practice of regarding the economic dimension as though it were autonomous or were determinative of the others. In consequence of this nearly exclusive economic focus, the effect of foreign aid has been much more limited than it otherwise would have been and, even where it has produced perceptible changes, they have in too many cases been superficial or transient.

The remedy for this major deficiency of the foreign-aid program is a systematic and continuing effort to incorporate into it the relevant concepts, data and analytical methods of other social sciences in addition to economics. This is not, however, an easy task. The fact that economists so readily provided an intellectual framework for the foreign-aid program does not mean that other kinds of social scientists could also quickly contribute relevant analytical concepts and operationally useful insights or that the necessary working relationships between them and the aid agency could be developed with equal facility. By its nature, the relevance of economics to policy making has generally been clear, and economists and policy makers have had long experience of working together with increasing effectiveness. To the extent permitted by the intrinsic difficulties of communication between scholars and practitioners, many theoretical economic insights have been translated into useful operational guidelines. In turn, the theoretical work of many academic economists has benefited from opportunities to serve in the aid agency, and particularly from study trips and operating assignments under its auspices in Asia, Africa and Latin America. The increasing literature on the theory and problems of economic growth in these regions attests to the high quality and continuous improvement of the economic analysis made possible by this mutually beneficial relationship.

A comparably extensive and direct relationship has not existed between policy makers and other social scientists in coping with domestic policy problems—except in social-welfare programs—in the United States, and the disparity has been even greater in dealing with international problems, including foreign aid. Very little effort has been made by foreign-aid officials to utilize the services of political scientists, sociologists, anthropologists, social psychologists and cultural historians. For their part, scholars in these fields have tended to neglect—indeed, sometimes to denigrate—the translation of their concepts and insights into operational guidelines. Thus, both aid agency officials and social scientists are confronted with the formidable but necessary task of making the noneconomic dimensions of the social process better understood so that they could be taken into account with reasonable effectiveness in the conduct of the foreign-aid program.

In the last few years, the foreign-aid agency has begun to recognize this major need and to take some first tentative steps toward remedying it, particularly through the use of specialists other than economists in the research and technical assistance programs conducted for it by universities. This is a promising beginning, but the attitudes and practices blocking further progress are still formidable. One major attitudinal obstacle is evidenced by the fact that a

systematic and continuing research program into the economic and
other aspects of "development" was not begun until 1962 and,
despite its growing size in recent years, neither its content nor its
results is as yet effectively related to actual program activities in
Asia, Africa and Latin America.

The inadequate recognition of the crucial importance of relevant
knowledge may also be seen in the virtual absence even today of
retrospective assessments of the successes and failures of individual aid-financed investment projects and technical assistance programs. The practice of only very rarely attempting to evaluate the
results of specific programs and projects has meant that the foreign-
aid agency has generally been able to profit from its experiences
only to the extent that individual officials have been interested in
ascertaining—and remembering—the reasons for the success or
failure of particular efforts in which they were personally engaged.
Moreover, the lack of systematic continuing evaluations of completed projects and programs is largely responsible for the fact that
there is still no empirical basis for determining how effective foreign aid has actually been.[6] Until far more data have been collected
and analyzed, opinions—including those in this book—on the effec-

<hr>

[6] This is true not only of the foreign-aid agency but also of the universities
and independent research organizations. In contrast to the large volume of
hortatory and prescriptive publications on foreign aid, there have been virtually
no full-length studies by scholars assessing the results of aid-financed projects
and programs in particular countries. A recent exception is Eugene Bramer
Mihaly, *Foreign Aid and Politics in Nepal: A Case Study* (London and New
York: Oxford University Press for the Royal Institute of International Affairs,
1965) which concludes "that the nations and agencies which extended economic
aid to Nepal, with few though significant exceptions, failed to accomplish what
they set out to accomplish" (p. 175). An earlier study by Charles Wolf, Jr., *Foreign Aid: Theory and Practice in Southern Asia* (Princeton: Princeton University
Press for The Rand Corporation, 1960) is, insofar as economic aid is concerned,
focused almost exclusively on measuring the relationships between total amounts
of aid and the aggregative economic indicators for the countries concerned, and it
does not examine specific aid-financed programs and projects, as does Mihaly. One
other study based upon empirical research, John D. Montgomery, *The Politics of
Foreign Aid: American Experience in Southeast Asia* (New York and London:
Frederick A. Praeger for the Council on Foreign Relations, 1962) is concerned
with the political problems in the aid relationship, and with the politics of foreign
aid in the United States. However, there are many articles in scholarly jour-
nals by sociologists, anthropologists and economists evaluating their experiences
in specific aid projects sponsored by private agencies, governments and international organizations. But, these have not yet been collected and systematically

tiveness of foreign aid are at best impressionistic, derived from necessarily small and random samples.

Thus, the major current need of the U.S. foreign-aid program is a more adequate research effort directed toward improved understanding of the sociocultural factors operating in Asia, Africa and Latin America, and designed to be of practical use to the United States and the recipient countries in the planning and execution of programs and projects. One of the most effective ways of ensuring that research will be empirical and useful is to tie it specifically to the planning of individual projects and programs and to the evaluation of their results at appropriate intervals after their completion. The aim would be to discover how social change occurs and how it could be influenced in *micro* situations—that is, in the specific sets of norms and relationships with which particular programs and projects are concerned.

While the problem today is the gross inadequacy of the existing knowledge, particularly as it relates to the role of sociocultural factors, effective efforts to remedy this deficiency could in the future generate exaggerated notions about what the social sciences could accomplish. Like other problem areas of American life, the foreign-aid program has not been exempt from the utopian expectations of technocratic positivism. Beginning in the early 1950s, a succession of simplistic prescriptions has been fashionable among opinion leaders and, to a lesser extent, within the aid agency itself. These prescriptions were confidently expected to overcome easily and rapidly the obstacles impeding economic growth and social change. Such development panaceas have included capital investment, technical assistance, community development, comprehensive national development planning and, most recently, educational development. All of these aspects and activities are necessary parts of an effort to accelerate economic growth and social change, but even together—much less individually—they do not encompass the many interrelated cultural, political, economic and social institutional factors involved in the social process. Hence, when research into the sociocultural aspects of "development" is substantially expanded and begins to yield useful results,

---

studied for the lessons that could be learned from them by development theorists and foreign-aid practitioners.

the danger could arise that it, too, may be regarded as a panacea —an expectation that in turn could lead to grandiose efforts at social engineering. Such an attempt would in effect—though probably not in intent—mean that the United States either would be endeavoring itself to follow or would be encouraging the recipient countries to adopt a totalitarian development strategy as defined in Chapter 5. Assuming that an effort of this kind were possible, the first alternative would be futile—because the United States could not implement such a strategy without direct rule—and the second would be adverse to the longer-term interests of the United States.

While an attempt at social engineering is only a potential danger, American technocratic positivism and sense of vocational mission have already had a marked effect in other ways on the organization and operating procedures of the U.S. foreign-aid agency. These elements of U.S. motivation have predisposed Americans to play a very active role in initiating, programming and implementing aid-financed activities within the recipient countries. This practice has been encouraged by the latter's lack of technical skills, insufficient capacity to innovate and to make clear and firm decisions regarding priorities among national goals, and inadequate administrative and managerial experience. In consequence, in all recipient countries in which U.S. assistance has been substantial, the American aid missions have been large and staffed to cover all major program areas. They customarily operate by drawing up their own country programs, by endeavoring to persuade or pressure the responsible ministries of the recipient governments into adopting their prescriptions, and often by actively engaging in the planning and execution of projects, with only half-hearted or even merely nominal participation by the officials of the recipient country.

This activistic and directive approach has been unconsciously expressed in the terms used by U.S. foreign-aid personnel—as well as by opinion leaders generally in the United States—to refer to themselves and their work and to the recipient countries and their responsibilities. The pronoun "they" is very rarely used. In virtually all cases, Americans refer to "our" program for the recipient country and what "we" are or should be doing to "solve" its problems. Thus, the responsible and active agents in devising and implementing the development strategies of the recipient countries are thougght to be the Americans, and the responsible officials of the governments concerned are not always included even by implication in American use of first-person plural pronouns.

Earlier chapters have explained the essential role played in the transitional process by the development of a sense of self-confidence and self-accomplishment. As yet, there is no evidence that an Asian or African country can successfully transform itself while the representatives of a foreign government play as active and directive a role in the process as the personnel of the U.S. foreign-aid agency has been doing. Japan, the only Asian or African country that has so far successfully completed the transitional process, did so with the help of capital and technical skills obtained from the West but at its own initiative, under its own direction, and through programs and projects planned and executed by its own people. In the past year or two, U.S. officials involved in the foreign-aid effort have been stressing the need for greater "self-help" on the part of the recipient countries. However, this salutary trend is being—and will continue to be—in part negated by the well-intentioned paternalistic behavior of U.S. aid officials.

The implications of the "self-help" criterion need to be applied as much to restraining the vocational activism of Americans as to stimulating greater initiative and effort by the recipient countries. If "self-help" is to have significant and continuing operational effectiveness, Americans must learn to think and act in terms of third-person pronouns. It is the elite groups of Asia, Africa and Latin America who should have not pro forma but actual responsibility. They—and they alone—need to initiate, plan and implement their own development programs and projects. The responsibilities of the Americans should be limited to deciding whether or not to help finance *their* programs and to specify the terms and conditions of such aid; and to providing the advice and technical assistance which *they* request regarding projects in which the extent of *their* efforts demonstrates the strength of *their* interest. Regardless of how important Americans may consider a particular program or technical assistance project to be, little—if any —permanent benefit will be derived from undertaking it unless the country concerned is willing and able to give it adequate support and to play the active and directive role in planning and executing it. Americans have to think of their own role as reactive and advisory—and to behave accordingly.

Unfortunately, there can be no completely satisfactory solution to this problem because the aid relationship is inherently ambivalent. On the one hand, Asian, African and Latin American countries would have little ground for obtaining aid if they were capable of the degree of innovation, clear-cut decision making and effective administration necessary for increasing the volume and improving the use of available resources. Hence, one of their main needs is for assistance in planning and executing programs and projects. On the other hand, the more innovation, decision making and administration that are done for them by foreign-aid personnel, however well intentioned, the slower and more difficult will be their achievement of the requisite capabilities. The only way to deal constructively with a problem of this kind is to be fully conscious of the danger involved and to seek conscientiously in every particular situation for the specific ways by which the capabilities of the recipient countries can be enhanced and the role of the Americans can be minimized while the job gets done.

To stress the need for Americans to become aware of and to try to avoid the harmful effects of their positivistic activism and sense of vocational mission does not mean that U.S. aid should be given without conditions or that no effort should be made through the aid relationship to influence the behavior of the recipient countries. However, a distinction needs to be made between the *macro* level of development strategy and general economic policies and the *micro* level of specific aid-financed programs and projects. At each level, there are different possibilities and limitations with respect to the conditions that can effectively be placed upon the granting of U.S. aid, as well as differences in the nature and extent of the "leverage" it can provide on the behavior of the recipient countries. At the *macro* level, the influence of foreign aid is generalized; that is, the actual or potential reduction or termination of U.S. aid—if used with sufficient tactical skill—may induce recipient countries to make significant changes in the scope and emphasis of their development strategies (e.g., giving higher priorities to agriculture and to the development of export-promoting activities, providing more adequate incentives and assistance to stimulate initiative and investment outside the public sector, instituting more effective restraints on inflation). At the *micro* level, the influence of foreign aid is naturally specific, but its effective use is much more problematical due to the fundamental ambivalence explained above. The conflicted character of the aid relationship expresses itself in other ways related to the problem of U.S. "leverage" on the recipient countries. Two of them may also be briefly discussed. The first is the discrepancy between long- and short-term interests and objectives. In the short term, the granting or withholding of aid may serve the U.S. interest by sometimes enabling the United States to influence the international behavior of the recipient countries so that they will support—or at least not oppose—the foreign-policy objectives of the Western nations and not disrupt the world political and economic systems. Over the long term, the purpose of foreign aid in terms of Western interests is to influence the character of the societies that will eventually emerge in Asia, Africa and Latin America so as to increase the likelihood that they will be compatible with the future security and welfare of the donor countries of North America and Western Europe. Not only are the short- and long-term objectives difficult to reconcile but U.S. expectations regarding them have also been to a significant degree incongruent with reality. To the extent that aid is withheld or abruptly reduced or terminated for short-term foreign-policy purposes, it tends to be less effective for the achievement of long-term socioeconomic purposes owing to the lack of continuity in programming and to the interruption or non-completion of projects. Partly for this reason—and despite the fact that a justification for U.S. aid has been its presumed short-term "leverage" benefits —few attempts have been made over the past fifteen years to use the withdrawal or threat of withdrawal of aid as a means of putting pressure on recipient countries to support U.S. foreign policies. Moreover, the most publicized of such attempts—the refusal to finance the Aswan dam—proved to be counterproductive and, therefore, discouraged similar efforts. The United States has recently begun again to use the withdrawal or threat of withdrawal of aid for short-term foreign-policy purposes and, in consequence, the conflict between long- and short-term objectives may become more pronounced in the future.

The second expression of ambivalence relates to the U.S. interest in the character of the societies likely to evolve in the recipient countries over the long term. The aid relationship is by nature intergovernmental; and aid is very largely used by the recipient governments to finance investments and programs in the public sector for reasons explained in earlier chapters. Thus, in the short term, foreign aid is generally used by most recipient countries to support the authoritarian role of governments and directly or indirectly to promote the centralization of political and economic decision making, the spread of state enterprises, and the expansion of the public sector. However, over the long term, the societies that will develop in the recipient countries are likely to be compatible with those of the West to the extent to which they become increasingly pluralistic. As a result, there is an important incongruity in using aid in the short term to support the authoritarian strategies of recipient governments while expecting that, over the long term, it will be a means of fostering pluralistic societies.

This difficulty is not usually recognized as a problem with short-term operational implications. U.S. government officials and opinion leaders generally are convinced of the U.S. interest in fostering the development of pluralistic societies, but they are chary of trying to influence recipient countries along what they regard as "ideological" lines. Moreover, many development technicians—both inside and outside the U.S. government—tend to believe that very little can usefully be done in the shorter term to foster private decentralized forms of initiative and activity, and that it really makes no difference over the longer term whether, for example, new investments are in state or private enterprises so long as they contribute to increasing national productivity.

In consequence of these attitudes, far too little effort has as yet been made to find specific practicable ways of using U.S. aid to foster the development of pluralistic societies, even though a major theme of the rhetoric of foreign aid has been its alleged capacity to stimulate greater democracy and individual freedom in the recipient countries. Instead of seeking by such means to influence the nature of the societies gradually evolving in Asia, Africa and Latin

America, U.S. attention and effort have tended to be focused upon trying to bring about basic social and economic reforms in the short term. However desirable they may be, most reforms of this kind cannot usually be accomplished by the government officials and civil servants of the recipient countries in the face of the traditional elites who still dominate, or retain a major influence over, their political systems. Thus, U.S. energies and resources have sometimes been wasted in trying to instigate frontal assaults on powerful vested interests instead of being used to discover and to help effectuate the many subtle, roundabout and ingenious ways by which authoritarian oligarchical institutions can gradually be transformed and voluntary, diversified and decentralized initiative and activity fostered in political and economic life.

This does not mean that the United States should be indifferent to the need for basic social and economic reforms or that private enterprise per se is the panacea for the development of Asia, Africa and Latin America. With respect to the first, the long-term interest of the United States in the evolution of pluralistic societies in these regions requires it to support such reforms and to seek practicable ways of fostering them through aid-financed programs and projects. But, such specific and effective ways are not likely to be found in the absence of an adequate understanding of the wide range of factors comprised in the processes of change occurring in the recipient countries. Not only has the lack of such understanding limited the effectiveness of the foreign-aid program in fostering reforms, but it has also been responsible for the disillusionment on both sides of the aid relationship resulting from unrealistic expectations of imminent and easy reform—such as, for example, were generated both in the United States and in Latin America during the early years of the Alliance for Progress.

With respect to the role of nongovernmental decentralized decision making and initiative, the difficulty is equally great. The analysis in previous chapters has endeavored to show that neither the governmental sector nor the private sector in Asian and African—and even in many Latin American—countries is capable of the kind and extent of innovation, decision making and efficient management required for a major acceleration of the processes of economic growth and social change. In the realities of Asia, Africa and Latin America, the choice is not between one or the other; both sectors have to be utilized. However, because the institutions and relationships, external and internal, of these societies tend to be weighted in favor of perpetuating—and even expanding—the centralized authoritarian role of government, it is necessary to make deliberate efforts to strengthen and increase the capabilities for generating initiative and activity outside the central bureaucracy. This means not only private enterprise of the conventional Western types but also other kinds of economic organizations outside the direct and detailed control of the central government—e.g., cooperatives, trade-unions, and perhaps even government corporations if they are autonomously managed with efficient standards—as well as local governments, educational institutions with sufficient academic freedom, professional societies, and many other varieties of association that foster and express the diffusion of innovation and initiative throughout the society.

Again, such efforts to redress the balance between centralized authority and dispersed initiative are likely to be effective to the extent that they embody an understanding of the nature of the specific factors involved in each particular program and project. There are few, if any, program areas and investment and technical assistance projects that could not be organized in ways that would make some significant contribution to stimulating responsible initiatives by individuals and institutions outside the central government. To do so, however, requires much greater knowledge than we now have about the complex nature and intricate interrelationships of the different dimensions comprising the social process.

These and other perplexities of foreign aid are inherent in the nature of the relationship, granted the societies and cultures involved on both sides. Although most of them cannot be eliminated, they can be mitigated. However, the foregoing discussion has refrained from making specific suggestions for doing so in the conviction that the primary need is to explain and illustrate the more basic changes in attitudes and ways of thinking that must necessarily precede organizational and methodological improvements. One of the most urgent is a more realistic conception of what foreign aid can and cannot accomplish. It is neither the "missing catalyst" essential for speeding up the process of economic growth and social change, nor the "marginal increment of resources" that makes the difference between success and failure in these efforts, nor—except in a few countries—the "crucial element" which, if drastically reduced or withdrawn, would lead to economic collapse and Communist take-over. It does not provide powerful "leverage" for pressuring government officials and civil servants in recipient countries into instituting basic reforms, nor can such changes in the distribution of political power, economic wealth and social privilege be induced as the *quid pro quo* for U.S. altruism. Financial aid and technical assistance are at most only supplements to the willingness and ability of the recipient countries to grant economic growth and social reform a higher priority than other competing goals and to implement such choices effectively by appropriate administrative measures. Without such willingness and ability, foreign aid of double or triple the present magnitude would have little multiplying or lasting effect within the recipient countries.

In sum, the most fundamental change required in American ways of thinking is recognition of the complexities and uncertainties of the social processes now occurring in Asian, African and Latin American countries and of the ambivalences inherent in the nature of their relationships with the United States. These are all much greater and much more difficult to deal with conceptually and operationally than most Americans realize. To convey some notion of what is involved in trying to understand them better has been the major purpose of this book and its own shortcomings at least in part reflect how little we yet know about the nature of social change in these regions and about how it could be influenced. The limited and transient effectiveness of much American aid over the past decade and a half is largely owed to our very inadequate comprehension of the processes we have been trying to accelerate and guide. Nor can a valid case for substantially increased aid be made in the absence of more profound and extensive knowledge of the phenomena we expect to influence.

The problem is not that the U.S. foreign-aid program is unnecessary, as its opponents allege. It is the need substantially to improve its effectiveness by greatly improving our own understanding of the realities with which it deals. Ardent advocates of foreign aid, with the best of intentions, will impatiently dismiss this conclusion, urging the "critical" nature of the situation in Asia, Africa and Latin America and the magnitude of these countries' "needs." More action is required, they will insist, not more research. Certainly, where the situation is in fact critical and ordinary common sense tells us what has to be done—as when India faces famine— action must be taken fast and on a large scale. Careful studies at such a time would be cruelly absurd. But, such situations are exceptional. As preceding chapters have explained, the transitional process in Asia and Africa will extend over generations, and even the modernization of Latin America will take decades. Freed from the self-intoxication of our own rhetoric, we can see that speed is not of the essence in helping them to deal with their problems; knowledge is. Time well spent in relevant empirical research as an integral part of an ongoing foreign-aid program will yield greater substantive benefits to the recipient countries than rhetorical attempts to justify increased aid appropriations or enthusiastic efforts to implement the latest fashion in development panaceas. Such research would, indeed, provide the only kinds of information by which the size and content of an effective foreign-aid program could rationally be determined and justified. If the expression of America's positivistic activism and sense of vocational mission is to be morally valid and operationally useful, it must flow from more profound and realistic understanding of the possibilities and the limitations of action.

Index

COUNCIL ON FOREIGN RELATIONS

PUBLICATIONS

FOREIGN AFFAIRS (quarterly), edited by Hamilton Fish Armstrong.
THE UNITED STATES IN WORLD AFFAIRS (annual). Volumes for 1931, 1932 and 1933, by Walter Lippmann and William O. Scroggs; for 1934–1935, 1936, 1937, 1938, 1939 and 1940, by Whitney H. Shepardson and William O. Scroggs; for 1945–1947, 1947–1948 and 1948–1949, by John C. Campbell; for 1949, 1950, 1951, 1952, 1953 and 1954, by Richard P. Stebbins; for 1955, by Hollis W. Barber; for 1956, 1957, 1958, 1959, 1960, 1961, 1962 and 1963, by Richard P. Stebbins; for 1964, by Jules Davids; for 1965 by Richard P. Stebbins.

DOCUMENTS ON AMERICAN FOREIGN RELATIONS (annual). Volume for 1952 edited by Clarence W. Baier and Richard P. Stebbins; for 1953 and 1954 edited by Peter V. Curl; for 1955, 1956, 1957, 1958 and 1959 edited by Paul E. Zinner; for 1960, 1961, 1962 and 1963 edited by Richard P. Stebbins; for 1964 by Jules Davids; for 1965 by Richard P. Stebbins.

POLITICAL HANDBOOK AND ATLAS OF THE WORLD (annual), edited by Walter H. Mallory.

THE CONSCIENCE OF THE RICH NATIONS: The Development Assistance and the Common Aid Effort, by Seymour J. Rubin (1966).

ATLANTIC AGRICULTURAL UNITY: Is It Possible?, by John O. Coppock (1966).

TEST BAN AND DISARMAMENT: The Path of Negotiation, by Arthur H. Dean (1966).

COMMUNIST CHINA'S ECONOMIC GROWTH AND FOREIGN TRADE, by Alexander Eckstein (1966).

POLICIES TOWARD CHINA: Views from Six Continents, edited by A. M. Halpern (1966).

THE AMERICAN PEOPLE AND CHINA, by A. T. Steele (1966).

INTERNATIONAL POLITICAL COMMUNICATION, by W. Phillips Davison (1965).

MONETARY REFORM FOR THE WORLD ECONOMY, by Robert V. Roosa (1965).

AFRICAN BATTLELINE: American Policy Choices in Southern Africa, by Waldemar A. Nielsen (1965).

NATO IN TRANSITION: The Future of the Atlantic Alliance, by Timothy W. Stanley (1965).

ALTERNATIVE TO PARTITION: For a Broader Conception of America's Role in Europe, by Zbigniew Brzezinski (1965).

THE TROUBLED PARTNERSHIP: A Re-Appraisal of the Atlantic Alliance, by Henry A. Kissinger (1965).

REMNANTS OF EMPIRE: The United Nations and the End of Colonialism, by David W. Wainhouse (1965).

THE EUROPEAN COMMUNITY AND AMERICAN TRADE: A Study in Atlantic Economics and Policy, by Randall Hinshaw (1964).

THE FOURTH DIMENSION OF FOREIGN POLICY: Educational and Cultural Affairs, by Phillip H. Coombs (1964).

AMERICAN AGENCIES INTERESTED IN INTERNATIONAL AFFAIRS (Fifth Edition), compiled by Donald Wasson (1964).

JAPAN AND THE UNITED STATES IN WORLD TRADE, by Warren S. Hunsberger (1964).

FOREIGN AFFAIRS BIBLIOGRAPHY, 1952–1962, by Henry L. Roberts (1964).

THE DOLLAR IN WORLD AFFAIRS: An Essay in International Financial Policy, by Henry G. Aubrey (1964).

ON DEALING WITH THE COMMUNIST WORLD, by George F. Kennan (1964).

FOREIGN AID AND FOREIGN POLICY, by Edward S. Mason (1964).

THE SCIENTIFIC REVOLUTION AND WORLD POLITICS, by Caryl P. Haskins (1964).

AFRICA: A Foreign Affairs Reader, edited by Philip W. Quigg (1964).

THE PHILIPPINES AND THE UNITED STATES: Problems of Partnership, by George E. Taylor (1964).

SOUTHEAST ASIA IN UNITED STATES POLICY, by Russell H. Fifield (1963).

UNESCO: ASSESSMENT AND PROMISE, by George N. Shuster (1963).

THE PEACEFUL ATOM IN FOREIGN POLICY, by Arnold Kramish
(1963).

THE ARABS AND THE WORLD: Nasser's Arab Nationalist Policy, by
Charles D. Cremeans (1963).

TOWARD AN ATLANTIC COMMUNITY, by Christian A. Herter (1963).

THE SOVIET UNION, 1922–1962: A Foreign Affairs Reader, edited
by Philip E. Mosley (1963).

THE POLITICS OF FOREIGN AID: American Experience in Southeast
Asia, by John D. Montgomery (1962).

SPEARHEADS OF DEMOCRACY: Labor in the Developing Countries,
by George C. Lodge (1962).

LATIN AMERICA: Diplomacy and Reality, by Adolf A. Berle (1962).

THE ORGANIZATION OF AMERICAN STATES AND THE HEMISPHERE
CRISIS, by John C. Dreier (1962).

THE UNITED NATIONS: Structure for Peace, by Ernest A. Gross
(1962).

THE LONG POLAR WATCH: Canada and the Defense of North America, by Melvin Conant (1962).

ARMS AND POLITICS IN LATIN AMERICA (Revised Edition), by
Edwin Lieuwen (1961).

THE FUTURE OF UNDERDEVELOPED COUNTRIES: Political Implications of Economic Development (Revised Edition), by Eugene
Staley (1961).

SPAIN AND DEFENSE OF THE WEST: Ally and Liability, by Arthur P.
Whitaker (1961).

SOCIAL CHANGE IN LATIN AMERICA TODAY: Its Implications for
United States Policy, by Richard N. Adams, John P. Gillin,
Allan R. Holmberg, Oscar Lewis, Richard W. Patch, and
Charles W. Wagley (1961).

FOREIGN POLICY: THE NEXT PHASE: The 1960s (Revised Edition),
by Thomas K. Finletter (1960).

DEFENSE OF THE MIDDLE EAST: Problems of American Policy
(Revised Edition), by John C. Campbell (1960).

COMMUNIST CHINA AND ASIA: Challenge to American Policy, by
A. Doak Barnett (1960).

FRANCE, TROUBLED ALLY: De Gaulle's Heritage and Prospects, by
Edgar S. Furniss, Jr. (1960).

THE SCHUMAN PLAN: A Study in Economic Cooperation, 1950–
1959, by William Diebold, Jr. (1959).

SOVIET ECONOMIC AID: The New Aid and Trade Policy in Under-developed Countries, by Joseph S. Berliner (1958).

NATO AND THE FUTURE OF EUROPE, by Ben T. Moore (1958).

INDIA AND AMERICA: A Study of Their Relations, by Phillips Talbot and S. L. Poplai (1958).

NUCLEAR WEAPONS AND FOREIGN POLICY, by Henry A. Kissinger (1957).

MOSCOW-PEKING AXIS: Strength and Strains, by Howard L. Boorman, Alexander Eckstein, Philip E. Mosley, and Benjamin Schwartz (1957).

RUSSIA AND AMERICA: Dangers and Prospects, by Henry L. Roberts (1956).

About the Author

Theodore Geiger is Chief of International Studies, National Planning Association, in Washington, D.C. His previously published books include *The Development of African Enterprise.* He was also co-author of *The Political Economy of American Foreign Policy* and *The Economy of the American People.*